HORACE

SELECTED ODES
AND SATIRE 1.9

EXEGI MONUMENTUM AERE PERENNIUS *I have built a monument more lasting than bronze* CARPE DIEM *Seize the day* IBAM FORTE VIA SACRA *By chance I was going along the Sacred Way* TIGRIS UT ASPERA GAETULUSVE LEO *Like a fierce tiger or a Gaetulian lion* DULCE RIDENTEM ... DULCE LOQUENTEM *Sweetly laughing ... sweetly talking* POST EQUITEM SEDET ATRA CURA *Black care sits behind the horseman* NON HUMILIS MULIER *A not humble woman* BRUTO MILITIAE DUCE *when Brutus was leader of our army* EXEGI MONUMENTUM AERE PERENNIUS *I have built a monument more lasting than bronze* CARPE DIEM

HORACE

SELECTED ODES
AND SATIRE 1.9

Ronnie Ancona

LATIN TEXT
NOTES
VOCABULARY

Bolchazy-Carducci Publishers, Inc.
Wauconda, Illinois

General Editor
Laurie Haight Keenan

Contributing Editor
Allan Kershaw

Cover Design and Typesetting
Charlene M. Hernandez

Lyre Graphic
Adapted from
Costumes of the Greeks and Romans
by Thomas Hope

Printed in the United States of America

2000
by United Graphics

Bolchazy-Carducci Publishers, Inc.
1000 Brown Street
Wauconda, Illinois 60084 USA

http://www.bolchazy.com

ISBN 0-86516-416-9

Library of Congress Cataloging-in-Publication Data

Horace
    [Selections. 1999]
    Horace : selected odes and satire 1.9 / [edited and annotated by]
Ronnie Ancona.
        p.   cm.
    Includes bibliographical references (p.).
    ISBN 0-86516-416-9 (alk. paper)
    1. Latin language—Readers. 2. Verse satire, Latin—Problems,
exercises, etc. 3. Rome—In literature—Problems, exercises, etc.
4. Odes—Problems, exercises, etc. I. Ancona, Ronnie, 1951-
PA6393.A3A53 1999
874'.01--dc21
                                       99-13412
                                        CIP

IN MEMORIAM

Victor Ancona
1912-1998

Contents

Preface

Writing this book has been a joy and a challenge because it has given me the opportunity to attempt to make Horace, the Latin author about whom I have thought and written the most, accessible and exciting for students of Latin. I would like to thank Bolchazy-Carducci Publishers for providing me with the chance to look at Horace anew in order to articulate the ways in which I think the study of Horace can be enhanced.

The book is intended for use by students at the intermediate college level or the advanced high school level. The selections from Horace (twenty odes and one satire) are the required readings in Horace for the new Advanced Placement Latin Literature Examination given by the Educational Testing Service. I have limited the scope of the book to the poems on the AP syllabus in order to create a sense of coherence out of that particular curriculum. Of course, teachers at either the college or secondary level are encouraged to bring more poems into their courses, if appropriate.

The book includes an introduction to Horace's life and writings, a select bibliography, the Latin text of the poems, a short introduction to each poem (meant to be suggestive rather than constricting), and a line-by-line commentary located on the same pages with the Latin text, including vocabulary and notes of a grammatical, historical, metrical, or literary nature. Appendices include maps, discussion of the meters of the poems, definitions of metrical terms, explanations of particular tropes or figures of thought and rhetorical figures or figures of speech with examples from the poems of the book, and the Latin text of the poems without notes and vocabulary (for seeing and reading the poems without interruption). Although it does not include every single Latin word in the poems, the line-by-line vocabulary given with the text of each poem is quite extensive. I have provided such extensive vocabulary help in order to give the student extra time for his or her thinking about the material that otherwise might be spent looking up words. The vocabulary at the end of the book includes all of the words in the poems, so that the student who forgets even a basic Latin word may quickly look it up in the back of the book.

Both in the general vocabulary and in the line-by-line vocabulary I typically give the major meanings of a Latin word rather than one particular meaning that might work best for purposes of translation in a particular context. The reason for this is to preserve for the student the multiplicity of meanings many Latin words have in Horace and to allow him or her to see how Horace repeats vocabulary from poem to poem with the result that individual words resonate with their multiple meanings in different contexts. If I had chosen one English word to define a particular Latin word in a given context, I think I would have deprived the student of access to a central feature of Horace's style. In addition, the approach followed here helps students to increase their real Latin vocabulary, rather than merely to memorize a particular meaning of a word for translation of a particular poem. I also avoid translating difficult passages in the notes. I prefer to give help and then to let the student figure things out independently. When giving grammatical explanations I use standard grammatical terminology, rather than terminology geared to a specific Latin grammar. *OLD* refers to the *Oxford Latin Dictionary*. Other abbreviations should not cause difficulty.

The Latin text is used with permission, from *Horatius, Opera* ed. Borzsák © 1984 B. G. Teubner, Leipzig. The only place I have deviated from Borzsák is at Ode 1.25.11, where I add a hyphen. This text was chosen because it is considered one of the best currently available for Horace. Since many students using this book will be taking the Advanced Placement Examination, which does not supply long marks or macrons over vowels, I, too, have not included them in the text of the poems and in the line-by-line vocabulary and commentary. However, since many students at this stage will not know all of the long marks, I have marked the length of vowels in the Vocabulary at the back of the book. Therefore, the student will be able to find all necessary long marks within the book, except those contained in inflectional endings. These may be found in a Latin grammar or in the student's elementary Latin text. It is my hope that the student who looks at the text without long marks will start trying to scan the poem to determine, for example, whether a final "a" is ablative singular or nominative singular of the first declension. In this way he or she will learn quickly that knowledge of the meter can be a source of necessary grammatical information.

In writing this text I have consulted a wide range of material on Horace. The bibliography on Horace is vast and there is no way I could have consulted everything relevant. However I have tried to create a text for students that is informed by some of the latest research in Horatian scholarship. I think it is important for students to know that classics scholars are still discussing and arguing about Horace's poems. Therefore, I have included a bibliography that is quite extensive for a student text in order to familiarize the student with some of the sources for this scholarship. Just browsing through the titles of articles can be interesting, for it shows what kinds of issues scholars have chosen to address. The student using the bibliography may find it most helpful to consult recent sources first, for these will include references to relevant earlier works that are still being cited. The student should not feel that it is necessary to use the bibliography, unless required to do so by his or her teacher. However, regardless of particular class requirements, I think I owe students embarking upon serious study of Horace at any level access to information about the research that has been done. I would like to mention here, by author, the commentaries that I consulted most frequently as I wrote the line-by-line notes for each of the poems: Aronson, Aronson and Boughner, Bennett, Garrison, Morris, Nisbet and Hubbard, Palmer, and Quinn (full citations available in the Bibliography). These gave me a continuing sense of what others thought or did not think worthy of comment as well as a scholarly context in which to situate my own remarks.

This book has been in the thinking stage for many years, although the writing of it took place primarily over the last year and a half. I have many people to thank for giving me the professional opportunities that have allowed me to think about the teaching of Horace. For inviting me to be a Faculty Consultant for the Advanced Placement Latin Examination over several years: Sheila Dickison, Judith de Luce, and Peter Howard; for sharing their collective Horatian wisdom: the AP Latin Faculty Consultants of summer 1997, and again, Peter Howard for creating a time for me to talk with them. Sheila Dickison, for suggesting me as a speaker for a joint American Classical League–American Philological Association panel in 1995 devoted to New Approaches to Teaching the Odes of Horace, and my Horace students at The Bush School, Carleton College, and Hunter College and The Graduate School of the City University of New York, for asking tough questions.

Finally, there are several people I want to acknowledge for special assistance. For willingness to help in any way she could, my student and research assistant at Hunter, Georgia Tsouvala Yoranidis. For believing in this project, Lou Bolchazy, Publisher, and Laurie Haight, Editor, Bolchazy-Carducci

Publishers. In particular, Laurie's encouragement, wit, intelligence, gentle prodding, and availability helped this book to its completion more than she can know. For helpful suggestions and careful reading, the two anonymous readers for Bolchazy-Carducci. For feedback on an issue I was pondering, William Anderson. For computer help, Steve Cole. And for patiently stepping over the piles of Horace books that adorned the floor of our home for many months, Steve, again, and David Ancona-Cole.

December, 1998

Introduction

Historical Context

Horace's lifetime spanned a great period of turbulence for the Romans that ended with the establishment of peace under Augustus. Internal and external disturbances had been creating conflict in Rome and Italy for many years. By the time Horace was in his teens Pompey and Caesar were engaged in a civil war. In 48 B.C.E. Caesar defeated Pompey at the battle of Pharsalus and went on to rule Rome alone until his assassination in 44 B.C.E. After Caesar's death, fighting continued, with the liberators or tyrannicides, led by Brutus and Cassius, opposing Antony and Octavian (later Augustus), the heirs to Caesar's power. The republican forces, which included Horace, were defeated at the battle of Philippi in 42 B.C.E., which signalled the defeat of the republican cause and the victory of Antony and Octavian. For a time Antony and Octavian held power together, but soon hostilities between them escalated into another civil war. Antony allied himself with Cleopatra, queen of Egypt. Their forces were defeated by those of Octavian at the battle of Actium in 31 B.C.E. (see Ode 1.37 below). After the suicides of Antony and Cleopatra Octavian's power was secure.

Horace wrote at a time that included great political upheaval and great literary achievement. In the work of both Horace and his contemporary and friend, Vergil, one can see a struggle with how to write in turbulent times as well as how to write when absolute rule emerges as the solution to the problems of the Roman republic. How the work of both of these authors "comments" on Augustan rule has been the subject of ongoing literary-critical debate.

Horace's Life

The main sources of information about Horace's life are his own writings and a short biography, transmitted along with some of the manuscripts of Horace's work, that is likely a version of the life of Horace written by Suetonius (born c. 69 C.E.) for the *de poetis* section of his collection of biographies of Roman literary figures, *de viris illustribus*. Quintus Horatius

Flaccus was born on December 8, 65 B.C.E. in the town of Venusia, on the border between Apulia and Lucania in southern Italy.

His name is attested in his own writings as well as in the extant inscription that mentions Horace's composition of the **carmen saeculare**, or centennial hymn, which was commissioned for the Secular Games (a periodic celebration) of 17 B.C.E., held by Augustus. Horace was the son of a freedman, or ex-slave, who worked as an auction agent or **coactor argentarius**. His father may have become enslaved during the Social Wars in which the town of Venusia (which had a lesser version of citizenship called Latin rights) was taken by the Romans. At the conclusion of hostilities Venusia was granted full Roman citizenship. Nothing is known of Horace's mother.

His father provided him with the kind of education that was typical for those from families of the equestrian or senatorial class. He brought him to Rome for his early education. There Horace studied, among other things, the poetry of Livius Andronicus, an early Latin writer, and Homer. He continued his education in philosophy at the university in Athens. Among the other students there at the time was the son of Cicero, the orator and politician. Political turmoil broke out during Horace's stay in Athens when Julius Caesar was assassinated in 44 B.C.E. About six months later Marcus Brutus, the liberator and tyrannicide, appeared in Athens looking for men to recruit for his side. Horace, like Cicero's son, joined the cause of reestablishing the Roman republic.

Serving in Brutus' army, Horace was appointed **tribunus militum**, or military tribune. This was a post typically given to those headed for the Senate and it conferred upon the individual equestrian status. Being a military tribune was uncommon for the son of a freedman and Horace reports being taunted about it. However it is likely that Horace had already met the financial qualifications for being an equestrian even before he received the appointment.

He fought on the losing side at the battle of Philippi in 42 B.C.E., which secured the defeat of the republican cause and the victory of Antony and Octavian (later Augustus), the heirs to Caesar's power (see Ode 2.7 below).

When Horace returned to Italy, pardoned by the victors, he found himself without his paternal home and estate, which were probably, like those of many others, confiscated for Octavian's victorious soldiers. Horace writes that at this point poverty drove him to write. What is probably meant by this statement is that his changed political fortune and his loss of property helped to pave the way for his becoming a "professional" poet. It is very unlikely that the statement meant he expected to be supported by his writings. Despite his altered circumstances, Horace was still able to purchase for himself the job of **scriba quaestorius**, clerk to the quaestors who were in charge of the public treasury. This was an important position, held for life, with duties involving public finances and the public records. The job only intermittently required a great deal of work, yet always brought in a salary, providing an excellent situation for the poet.

By the early thirties B.C.E. Horace must have started sharing his writing with others. He became friends with the poets Vergil and Varius (see Satire 1.9 below), who in turn introduced him to Gaius Cilnius Maecenas. Nine months after the introduction, Maecenas invited Horace to become part of his group of friends, which included several famous poets. Maecenas was a very wealthy equestrian, originally from Etruria, who served as an important adviser to Octavian (later Augustus) until the late twenties B.C.E. Thus, through Maecenas Horace became connected with the ultimate leader of the Roman state. That connection was to last for the rest of his life. While Horace's relationship with Maecenas has often been characterized as that between "client" and "patron," the terms "friend" and "supporter" may describe more accurately Maecenas' role with respect to Horace, for their relationship seems to have been based not on financial dependence, but rather on mutual respect and friendship in addition to artistic support. While Maecenas did give Horace gifts, as friends often do, there is no specific evidence, for example, that Horace needed Maecenas for his livelihood or that Horace's Sabine farm, the country home that he valued greatly, was necessarily a gift from Maecenas. Maecenas' significance to Horace, however, is indisputable, and one sign of this is the fact that the first poem of Horace's initial lyric collection (*Odes*, Books 1–3) is addressed to Maecenas as are the beginning poems of the *Epodes*, *Satires* Book 1, and *Epistles* Book 1.

Little is known of Horace's later life. While he accepted Augustus' commission to write the **carmen saeculare**, mentioned above, he graciously turned down a request by Augustus to serve as his personal secretary. Horace died on November 27, 8 B.C.E., shortly after the death of Maecenas.

Horace's Writings

Horace wrote poetry over a period of about thirty years. His first publication in 35 B.C.E., at the age of thirty, was Book 1 of the *Satires* or *Sermones* ("conversations"), followed five years later by Book 2. Horace's *Satires* (eighteen poems) follow in the tradition of Lucilius (second century B.C.E.), whom Horace calls the founder of Latin satire, or *satura*, a genre considered original to the Romans. Latin satire is verse in a conversational style on a variety of topics written from an individual point of view. Latin satirists who followed Horace are Persius (first century C.E.) and Juvenal (first to second centuries C.E.). While showing admiration for Lucilius, Horace attempted to write verse that was more polished. Horace's satires, composed in dactylic hexameter, touch on a variety of literary, social, and ethical topics and include attacks on various human faults. Satire 1.9, selected for this book, is a witty narrative that deftly combines a critique of a pushy social climber with discourse on literary values. While its fast-paced, colloquial style is quite different from that of the *Odes*, its literary sensibility and its carefully polished Latin show a continuity with Horace's later writing in the *Odes*.

The *Epodes*, or *Iambi* as they are sometimes called, written early in Horace's career like the *Satires*, consist of seventeen dactylic or iambic poems that primarily utilize epodic couplets, that is, one line of a particular metrical structure and length, followed by a line of a different length and sometimes a different metrical structure. These poems are written in the tradition of the early Greek poet, Archilochus of Paros, who wrote poems of attack and blame. According to Horace, his meters and spirit come from Archilochus, but the subject matter and words do not. The *Epodes* include several poems with political themes as well as a number on erotic topics. Stylistically, they stand, in a sense, midway between the "talk"of the *Satires* and the "song" of lyric. While technically the *Epodes* can be called "lyric," this term is typically used to refer exclusively to Horace's *Odes*.

In 23 B.C.E. Horace published Books 1 through 3 of his collection of lyric poetry, the *Odes* or *Carmina*. (These terms come from the Greek for "song" and the Latin for "song" or "poem.") He returned to lyric ten years later and published Book 4 of the *Odes*, which includes much that is in praise of Augustus. Scholars differ as to how this later book of lyrics does or does not allow Horace to retain some kind of independence from the Augustan regime.

Lyric poetry originally signified poetry written to the accompaniment of the lyre. While Horace makes allusion to the musical quality of his lyrics, scholars generally agree that his lyric poems were spoken and not sung. More specifically, lyric poetry meant poetry written in the meters used by the Greek lyric poets: Alcaeus, Sappho, Anacreon, Alcman, Stesichorus, Ibycus, Simonides, Pindar, and Bacchylides. While Catullus, writing a generation earlier than Horace, wrote some poems in the lyric meters used by the Greek lyric poets (for example, Poem 51, his translation and adaptation of a poem by Sappho), Horace took great pride in being the first to do so on a large scale. The Greek lyric poets to whom Horace especially looked for inspiration were Sappho and Alcaeus, who lived and wrote on the island of Lesbos, in Aeolia, the Greek area of Asia Minor, at the close of the seventh century B.C.E. When expressing both his hopes for his lyric collection in Ode 1.1 and his pride in his lyric achievement in Ode 3.30 Horace alludes to Sappho and Alcaeus through the phrases **Lesboum...barbiton** ("Lesbian lyre") and **Aeolium carmen** ("Aeolic song"). Horace, like his predecessor Catullus, was also influenced by the Alexandrian aesthetics of Callimachus (third century B.C.E.), the Hellenistic Greek poet who described his Muse as "slender," a term that Horace uses for his own Muse as well. These literary aesthetics placed a high value on the small, learned, carefully wrought poem.

The odes range widely in subject matter—from politics to love to literature and beyond. The personal is often mixed with the public. What Horace says is beyond the scope of lyric is frequently incorporated into his poems under the guise of refusal. That is, in the very refusal to write a certain kind of poem Horace addresses topics supposedly at odds with lyric. While Horace was self-consciously writing in a long literary tradition that included much Greek influence, his poems are very contemporary. In addition to the Roman political world that pervades the *Odes*, the social environment Horace inhabited is also evident. For example, while moral and legal codes made illegal and theoretically unacceptable sexual relations between a Roman citizen woman and a man not her husband, Horace's world included many non-citizens, freedwomen, and slaves with whom such relations would have been tolerated. Therefore, the social relations of such poems as Odes 1.23 and 1.25 should not be seen as alien to Horace's Roman world.

The 103 poems of the *Odes* (88 in Books 1–3 and 15 in Book 4) are pieces that form a collection. They can be read selectively, as they will be by users of this text. However, even in the reading of just twenty odes I think it will become clear that the individual pieces relate to each other in countless ways, at the level of vocabulary, theme, and meter. Part of getting to know Horace as a lyric poet involves recognition of these many connections.

In some ways Horace's lyrics may seem to the student quite different from Latin read before, for Horace's exploitation of the possibilities of the Latin language is extraordinary. Word order, which in Latin is already quite flexible, is with Horace even more so. Words that agree with each other may be separated widely, creating a kind of framing or phrasing effect, while words right next to each may not agree with each other grammatically, but may affect each other in terms of sense. The best readers of Horace will be open to the aural and visual effects of his language. At times the lyrics are brief and elliptical. Often they end up at a different place from where they began. The German philosopher and classicist, Friedrich Nietzsche, described the effectiveness of Horace's lyrics as a "... mosaic of words, in which every unit spreads its power to the left and to the right over the whole, by its sound, by its place in the sentence, and by its meaning..." (*The Complete Works of Friedrich Nietzsche*, vol. 16, *The Twilight of the Idols*, Oscar Levy, ed., Anthony Ludovici, trans., London and New York, 1927: 113). While students may want to and may be asked to "translate" Horace's lyrics (a requirement of the AP Examination), they should be aware of the extent to which translation will shut down possibilities of meaning in this author. For example, it is usually impossible to "translate" into English Horace's careful placement of words. In addition, while translating requires picking the best English meaning for a particular Latin word in a given context, that very process of "selection" limits to one the multiple senses which that word may have in Latin and which may be operating in a particular poem. The student will quickly find out that "translating" and "understanding" Horace's lyrics may overlap but are not identical, for "understanding" involves grasping the concept that turning Horace into English necessarily entails the loss of so much that is essentially Horatian.

While Horace utilized lyric meter in the **carmen saeculare**, or centennial hymn of 17 B.C.E., he returned to the meter used in the *Satires*, dactylic hexameter, for the writing of the *Epistles*. These verse essays (Book 1 contains twenty, Book 2 contains three), written in the form of letters, address a variety of topics, many of a literary or philosophical nature. Epistle 2.3, also called the Ars Poetica, includes comments on the problems of literary composition.

Bibliography

This is a select bibliography of works in English. An attempt has been made to include much that has been written on Horace recently. While articles on individual poems have been listed at the end of the bibliography, the student will find it valuable to consult any pages relevant to a given poem in the book-length works as well.

Commentaries:

Aronson, A. and Robert Boughner. *Catullus and Horace: Selections from Their Lyric Poetry*. White Plains, N.Y., 1988.

Aronson, Andrew. *Catullus and Horace: A Selection with Facing Vocabularies and Notes*. Amherst. Mass., 1989–90.

Bennett, Charles E. *Horace: Odes and Epodes*. 1901. Reprinted, New Rochelle, N.Y., 1981.

Brown, P. Michael. *Horace Satires I*. With Introduction, Text, Translation and Commentary. Warminster, England, 1993. Reprinted 1995.

Garrison, Daniel H. *Horace: Epodes and Odes*. Norman, Okla. and London, 1991.

Holder, Alfred, ed. *Pomponi Porfyrionis Commentum in Horatium Flaccum*. 1894. Reprinted, New York, 1979. (ancient commentary on Horace, in Latin)

Hornsby, Roger A. *Reading Latin Poetry*. Norman, Okla., 1967.

McKay, A. G. and D. M. Shepherd. *Roman Lyric Poetry*. London, 1969.

Morris, Edward P. *Horace: Satires and Epistles*. 1939. Reprinted, Norman, Okla., 1968.

Nisbet, R. G. M., and Margaret Hubbard. *A Commentary on Horace: Odes Book 1*. Oxford, 1970.

Nisbet, R. G. M., and Margaret Hubbard. *A Commentary on Horace: Odes Book 2*. Oxford, 1978.

Page, T. E. *Q. Horati Flacci: Opera*. London, 1896.

Quinn, Kenneth. *Horace: The Odes*. London, 1980. Reprinted, Bristol, 1997.

Shorey, Paul, and Gordon J. Laing. *Horace: Odes and Epodes*. 1910. Reprinted, Pittsburgh, 1960.

Smith, Clement L. *The Odes and Epodes of Horace*. New York, 1894, 1903.

West, David. *Horace Odes 1: Carpe Diem: Text, Translation, and Commentary*. Oxford, 1995.

Wickham, Edward C. *Q. Horati Flacci Opera*. Oxford, 1912.

Williams, Gordon. *The Third Book of Horace's Odes*. Oxford, 1969.

General Works:

Ancona, Ronnie. *Time and the Erotic in Horace's Odes*. Durham, N. C., 1994.

Anderson, William S., ed. *Why Horace? A Collection of Interpretations*. Wauconda, Ill., 1999.

Anderson, William S. *Essays on Roman Satire*. Princeton, 1982.

Armstrong, David. *Horace*. New Haven and London, 1989.

Armstrong, David, ed. *Arion: Horace Issue* 9, 2 and 3. Austin, 1970.

Babcock, Charles. "*Carmina operosa*: Critical Approaches to the 'Odes' of Horace, 1945–75." *Aufstieg und Niedergang der Römischen Welt* 2.31.3. Berlin, 1981: 1560–1611.

Boyle, A. J. "The Edict of Venus: An Interpretive Essay on Horace's Amatory Odes." *Ramus* 2 (1973): 163–88.

Campbell, A. Y. *Horace: A New Interpretation.* London, 1924.

Coffey, Michael. *Roman Satire.* London and New York, 1976.

Collinge, N. E. *The Structure of Horace's Odes.* London, 1961.

Commager, Steele. *The Odes of Horace: A Critical Study.* New Haven and London, 1962. Reprinted, with forward by D. Armstrong, Norman, Okla. 1995.

Connor, Peter. *Horace's Lyric Poetry: The Force of Humour.* Berwick, Victoria, Australia, 1987.

Davis, Gregson. *Polyhymnia: The Rhetoric of Horatian Lyric Discourse.* Berkeley, 1991.

Dettmer, Helena. *Horace: A Study in Structure.* Hildesheim, 1983.

Fraenkel, Eduard. *Horace.* Oxford, 1957.

Freudenburg, Kirk. *The Walking Muse: Horace on the Theory of Satire.* Princeton, 1993.

Gold, Barbara, ed. *Literary and Artistic Patronage in Ancient Rome.* Austin, Tex., 1982.

Griffin, Jasper. *Latin Poets and Roman Life.* Chapel Hill, N.C., 1986.

Habinek, Thomas N. *The Politics of Latin Literature: Writing, Identity, and Empire in Ancient Rome.* Princeton, 1998.

Harrison, S. J., ed. *Homage to Horace: A Bimillenary Celebration.* Oxford, 1995.

Johnson, W. Ralph. *The Idea of Lyric: Lyric Modes in Ancient and Modern Poetry.* Berkeley, 1982.

Konstan, David. *Horace: 2000 Years. Arethusa* 28.2 and 3, Baltimore, 1995.

Kresic, Stephanus, ed. *Contemporary Literary Hermeneutics and Interpretation of Classical Texts*. Ottawa, 1981. (includes articles on Ode 1.9 by Michael Murray, Richard Palmer, Charles Segal)

Leach, Eleanor Winsor. "Horace's Sabine Topography in Lyric and Hexameter Verse." *American Journal of Philology* 114 (1993): 271–302.

Lee, M. Owen. *Word, Sound, and Image in the Odes of Horace*. Ann Arbor, 1969.

Lowrie, Michèle. *Horace's Narrative Odes*. Oxford, 1997.

Lyne, R. O. A. M. *Horace: Behind the Public Poetry*. New Haven and London, 1995.

Lyne, R. O. A. M. *The Latin Love Poets: From Catullus to Horace*. Oxford, 1980.

Martindale, Charles, and David Hopkins, eds. *Horace Made New: Horatian Influences on British Writing from the Renaissance to the Twentieth Century*. Cambridge, 1993.

Miller, Paul Allen. *Lyric Texts and Lyric Consciousness: The birth of a genre from archaic Greece to Augustan Rome*. London and New York, 1994.

Minadeo, Richard. *The Golden Plectrum: Sexual Symbolism in Horace's Odes*. Amsterdam, 1982.

Oliensis, Ellen. *Horace and the Rhetoric of Authority*. Cambridge, 1998.

Palmer, Arthur. *The Satires of Horace*. London and New York, 1964.

Porter, David H. *Horace's Poetic Journey: A Reading of Odes 1–3*. Princeton, 1987.

Putnam, Michael C. J. *Artifices of Eternity: Horace's Fourth Book of Odes*. Ithaca and London, 1986.

Putnam, Michael C. J. *Essays on Latin Lyric, Elegy, and Epic*. Princeton, 1982.

Raaflaub, Kurt A., and Mark Toher, eds. *Between Republic and Empire: Interpretations of Augustus and His Principate*. Berkeley, 1990.

Reckford, Kenneth. *Horace*. New York, 1969.

Reckford, Kenneth. "Some Studies in Horace's Odes on Love." *Classical Journal* 55 (1959): 25–33.

Rudd, Niall, ed. *Horace 2000: A Celebration*. Ann Arbor, 1993.

Rudd, Niall. *The Satires of Horace*. Berkeley and Los Angeles, 1966.

Santirocco, Matthew, ed. *Recovering Horace. Classical World* 87.5. Pittsburgh, Penn., 1994.

Santirocco, Matthew. *Unity and Design in Horace's Odes*. Chapel Hill, N.C. and London, 1986.

Shackleton Bailey, D. R. *Profile of Horace*. Cambridge, Mass., 1982.

West, David. *Reading Horace*. Edinburgh, 1967.

Wilkinson, L. P. *Horace and His Lyric Poetry*. Cambridge, 1945. Second edition, 1951.

Williams, Gordon. *The Nature of Roman Poetry*. Oxford, 1983.

Witke, Charles. *Horace's Roman Odes*. Leiden, 1983.

Translations:

Alexander, Sidney. *The Complete Odes and Satires of Horace*. Princeton, 1999.

Carne-Ross, D. S., and Kenneth Haynes, eds. *Horace in English*. London, 1996.

Clancy, Joseph P. *The Odes and Epodes of Horace*. Chicago, 1960.

Ferry, David. *The Odes of Horace*. New York, 1997.

Passage, Charles. *The Complete Works of Horace*. New York, 1983.

Raffel, Burton. *The Essential Horace*. San Francisco, 1983.

Rudd, Niall. *Horace: Satires and Epistles, Persius: Satires*. London, 1979. Reprinted, London, 1981.

Storrs, Ronald, ed. *Ad Pyrrham: A Polyglot Collection of Translations of Horace's Ode to Pyrrha (Book 1, Ode 5)*. London, 1959.

West, David. *The Complete Odes and Epodes*. Oxford, 1997.

Recordings:

Sonkowsky, Robert P. *The Living Voice of Latin Literature: Selections from Catullus and Horace*. Booklet and two cassettes. Guilford, Conn., 1984. Distributed by Bolchazy-Carducci Publishers, Wauconda, Ill.

References Works:

Bo, Domenicus. *Lexicon Horatianum*. (2 volumes) Hildesheim, 1965.

Halporn, James W., Martin Ostwald, and Thomas G. Rosenmeyer. *The Meters of Greek and Latin Poetry*. Revised edition, Indianapolis, 1994.

Works on Individual Poems or Groups of Poems:

Satire 1.9

Anderson, William S. "Horace, The Unwilling Warrior: *Satire* I,9." *American Journal of Philology* 77 (1956): 148–66. Reprinted in Anderson, William. *Essays on Roman Satire*. Princeton, 1982.

Brucia, Margaret A., and Madeleine Henry. *Satire 1.9: The Boor*. Wauconda, Ill., 1998.

Courtney, E. "Horace and the Pest." *Classical Journal* 90 (1994): 1–8.

Feldman, Louis. "The Enigma of Horace's Thirtieth Sabbath." *Scripta Classica Israelica* 10 (1989–90): 87–112.

Harrison, S. J. "Fuscus the Stoic: Horace Odes 1.22 and Epistles 1.10." *Classical Quarterly* 42 (1992) 543–47.

Henderson, J. "Be Alert (Your Country Needs Lerts): Horace, *Satires* 1.9." *Proceedings of the Cambridge Philological Society* 39 (1993): 67–93.

Mazurek, Tadeusz, "Self-Parody and the Law in Horace's *Satires* 1.9," *Classical Journal* 93 (1997): 1–17.

Rudd, Niall. "Horace's Encounter with the Bore." *Phoenix* 15 (1961): 90–96.

Zetzel, J. E. G. "Horace's *Liber Sermonum*: The Structure of Ambiguity." *Arethusa* 13 (1980): 59–77.

Ode 1.1
Dunn, Francis. "Horace's Sacred Spring (Odes I,1)." *Latomus* 48 (1989): 97–109.

Gold, Barbara. "Openings in Horace's *Satires* and *Odes*: Poet, Patron, and Audience." *Yale Classical Studies* 29 (1992): 161–85.

Mader, G. "Poetry and Politics in Horace's First Roman Ode: a Reconstruction." *Acta Classica* 30 (1987): 11–30.

Musurillo, H. "The Poet's Apotheosis: Horace, *Odes* 1.1." *Transactions and Proceedings of the American Philological Association* 93 (1962): 230–39.

Pomeroy, Arthur J. "A Man at a Spring: Horace, Odes 1.1." *Ramus* 9 (1980): 34–50.

Shey, H. J. "The Poet's Progress: Horace Odes I.1." *Arethusa* 4 (1971): 185–96.

Ode 1.5
Brown, J. C. "The Verbal Art of Horace's *Ode to Pyrrha*." *Transactions and Proceedings of the American Philological Association* 111 (1981): 17–22.

Fredricksmeyer, Ernst A. "Horace's Ode to Pyrrha (*Carm.* 1.5)." *Classical Philology* 60 (1965): 180–5.

Gold, Barbara. "Mitte sectari, rosa quo locorum sera moretur: Time and Nature in Horace's Odes." *Classical Philology* 88 (1993): 16–31.

Hoppin, Meredith Clarke. "New Perspectives on Horace, *Odes* 1.5." *American Journal of Philology* 105 (1984): 54–68.

Nielsen, Rosemary, and Robert Solomon. "Rescuing Horace, Pyrrha and Aphra Behn: a Directive." *Ramus* 22 (1993): 60–77.

Putnam, Michael C. J. "Horace *Carm.* 1.5: Love and Death." *Classical Philology* 65 (1970): 251–54. Reprinted in Michael C. J. Putnam, *Essays on Latin Lyric, Elegy, and Epic* (Princeton, 1982).

Quinn, Kenneth. "Horace as a Love Poet: A reading of *Odes* 1.5." *Arion* 2.3 (1963): 59–77.

Sutherland, Elizabeth. "Audience Manipulation and Emotional Experience in Horace's 'Pyrrha Ode'." *American Journal of Philology* 116 (1995): 441–52.

Vessey, D. W. T. "Pyrrha's Grotto and the Farewell to Love: A Study of Horace Odes 1.5." *American Journal of Philology* 105 (1984): 457–69.

Ode 1.9

Anderson, William S. "Horace's Different Recommenders of Carpe Diem in C. 1.4, 7, 9, 11." *Classical Journal* 88 (1993): 115–22.

Cameron, H. D. "Horace's Soracte Ode: (*Carm.* 1.9)." *Arethusa* 22 (1989): 147–59.

Clay, Jenny Strauss. "Ode 1.9: Horace's September Song." *Classical World* 83 (1989): 102–05.

Connor, W. R. "Soracte Encore." *Ramus* 1 (1972): 102–12.

Edmunds, Lowell. *From a Sabine Jar: Reading Horace Odes 1.9*. Chapel Hill, N.C., 1992.

Moritz, L. A. "Snow and Spring: Horace's Soracte Ode Again." *Greece and Rome* n.s. 23.2 (1976): 169–76.

Nielsen, R. M. and R. H. Solomon. "Soracte and Sacred Space: Centuries of *carpe diem*." *Latomus* 47 (1988): 821–29.

Springer, Carl P. E. "Horace's Soracte Ode: Location, Dislocation, and the Reader." *Classical World* 82 (1988): 1–9.

Striar, Brian. "Soracte Reconsidered: The Burden of Youth and the Relief of Age in Horace *Odes* I.9." In *Collection Latomus: Studies in Latin Literature and Roman History* 5, edited by C. Deroux, 203–15. Brussels, 1989.

Vessey, D. W. T. "From Mountain to Lovers' Tryst: Horace's Soracte Ode." *Journal of Roman Studies* 75 (1985): 26–38.

Ode 1.11

Anderson, William S. (see under Ode 1.9).

Arkins, Brian. "Horace, *Odes* 1.11." *Collection Latomus: Studies in Latin Literature and Roman History* 1, edited by C. Deroux, Brussels, 1979: 257–65.

Ode 1.13

Keyser, Paul. "Horace Odes 1.13, 3–8, 14–16: Humoural and Aetherial Love." *Philologus* 133 (1989): 75–81.

Owens, William. "Double Jealousy: an Interpretation of Horace, Odes 1.13." *Collection Latomus: Studies in Latin Literature and Roman History* 6, edited by C. Deroux, Brussels, 1992: 237–44.

Segal, Charles. "*Felices Ter et Amplius*: Horace, *Odes*, I.13." *Latomus* 32 (1973): 39–46.

Ode 1.22

Davis, Gregson. "*Carmina/Iambi*: The Literary-Generic Dimension of Horace's *Integer Vitae* (*C.* I,22)." *Quaderni Urbinati di Cultura Classica*, n.s., 27, no. 3 (1987): 67–78.

Harrison, S. J. (see under Satire 1.9).

Hendrickson, G. L. "'Integer Vitae'." *Classical Journal* 5 (1910): 250–58.

McCormick, Jane. "Horace's *Integer Vitae.*" *Classical World* 67 (1973): 28–33.

Olstein, Katherine. "Horace's Integrity and the Geography of Carm. I.22." *Grazer Beiträge* 11 (1984): 113–20.

Ullman, B. L. "Horace and the Philologians." *Classical Journal* 31 (1935–36): 403–17.

Zumwalt, N. K. "Horace, *C.* 1.22: Poetic and Political Integrity." *Transactions and Proceedings of the American Philological Association* 105 (1975): 417–431.

Ode 1.23

Ancona, Ronnie. "The Subterfuge of Reason: Horace, *Odes* 1.23 and the Construction of Male Desire." *Helios* 16 (1989): 49–57.

Bannon, Cynthia. "Erotic Brambles and the Text of Horace Carmen 1.23.5–6." *Classical Philology* 88 (1993): 220–22.

Estevez, Victor. "Chloe and the Fawn: The Structure of *Odes* 1.23." *Helios* 7.1 (1979–80): 35–44.

Fredricksmeyer, Ernst, "Horace's Chloe (*Odes* 1.23): Inamorata or Victim?" *Classical Journal* 89 (1994): 251–59.

Lee, M. Owen. "Horace *Carm.* 1.23: Simile and Metaphor." *Classical Philology* 60 (1965): 185–86.

Nielsen, Rosemary. "Horace Odes 1.23: Innocence." *Arion* 9 (1970): 373–78.

Ronnick, Michele. "Green Lizards in Horace: *lacertae virides* in Odes 1.23." *Phoenix* 47 (1993): 155–57.

Ode 1.24

Akbar Khan, H. "Horace's Ode to Virgil on the Death of Quintilius: 1.24." *Latomus* 26 (1967): 107–17.

Pascal, C. B. "Horatian Chiaroscuro (*Carm*. I,24)." *Hommages à M. Renard 1. Collection Latomus* 101, edited by J. Bibauw. Brussels, 1969: 622–33.

Putnam, Michael C. J. "The Languages of Horace Odes 1.24," *Classical Journal* 88 (1992-93): 123–35.

Ode 1.25
Ancona, Ronnie. "Horace *Odes* 1.25: Temporality, Gender, and Desire." in *Collection Latomus: Studies in Latin Literature and Roman History* 6, edited by C. Deroux, 245–59. Brussels, 1992.

Arkins, Brian. "A Reading of Horace, *Carm*. 1.25." *Classica et Mediaevalia* 34 (1983): 161–75.

Armstrong, Michael. "Hebro/Euro: Two Notes on Horace Carm. 1.25.20." *Philologus* 136 (1992): 313–15.

Catlow, L. W. "Horace, *Odes* I,25 and IV, 13: a Reinterpretation." *Latomus* 35 (1976): 813–21.

Esler, Carol Clemeau. "Horace's Old Girls: Evolution of a Topos." in *Old Age in Greek and Latin Literature*, edited by T. Falkner and J. de Luce, Albany, N.Y., 1989, 172–82.

Lee, M. Owen. "Horace, Odes 1.25: The Wind and the River." *The Augustan Age* 4 (1985): 39–44.

Odes 1.23–25
Fuqua, Charles. "Horace *Carm*. 1.23–25." *Classical Philology* 63 (1968): 44–46.

Ode 1.37
Commager, Steele. "Horace, *Carmina* 1.37." *Phoenix* 12 (1958): 47–58.

De Forest, Mary Margolies. "The Central Simile of Horace's Cleopatra Ode." *Classical World* 82 (1989): 167–73.

Hendry, Michael. "Three Problems in the Cleopatra Ode." *Classical Journal* 88 (1992–93): 137–47.

Johnson, W. R. "A Quean, a Great Queen? Cleopatra and the Politics of Misrepresentation." *Arion* 6 (1967): 388–402.

Mader, G. "Heroism and Hallucination: Cleopatra in Horace C. 1.37 and Propertius 3.11." *Grazer Beiträge* 16 (1989): 183–201.

Nussbaum, G. B. "A Study of Odes I, 37 and 38: The Psychology of Conflict and Horace's *Humanitas*." *Arethusa* 4 (1971): 91–97.

Ode 1.38

Fitzgerald, William. "Horace, Pleasure and the Text." *Arethusa* 22 (1989): 81–103.

Gold, Barbara (see under Ode 1.5).

Nussbaum, G. B. (see under Ode 1.37).

Sklenář, Robert. "Multiple Structural Divisions in Horace, Odes 1.38." *La Parola del Passato* 46 (1991): 444–47.

Toohey, P. G. "A Note on Horace, Odes I.38." *Maia* 32 (1980): 171–74.

Ode 2.3

Gold, Barbara (see under Ode 1.5).

Witke, Charles. "Questions and Answers in Horace *Odes* 2.3." *Classical Philology* 61 (1966): 250–52.

Woodman, A. J. "Horace, *Odes*, II,3." *American Journal of Philology* (1970): 165–80.

Ode 2.7

Moles, John L. "Politics, Philosophy, and Friendship in Horace Odes 2,7." *Quaderni Urbinati di Cultura Classica* 25 (1987): 59–72.

Ode 2.10

Levin, D. N. "Horace, Carm. 2.10: Stylistic Observations." *Classical Journal* 54 (1958-59): 169-71.

Reagan, Christopher. "Horace, Carmen 2.10: The Use of Oxymoron as a Thematic Statement." *Rivista di Studi Classici* 18 (1970): 177-85.

Ode 2.14

Anderson, William. "Two Odes of Horace's Book Two." *California Studies in Classical Antiquity* 1 (1968): 35-61.

Roberts, Michael. "Reading Horace's Ode to Postumus (2.14)." *Latomus* 50 (1991): 371-75.

Ode 3.1

Schenker, David. "Poetic Voices in Horace's Roman Odes." *Classical Journal* 88 (1992-93): 147-66.

Silk, E. T. "Towards a Fresh Interpretation of Horace *Carm.* III.1." *Yale Classical Studies* 23 (1973): 131-45.

Solmsen, F. "Horace's First Roman Ode." *American Journal of Philology* 68 (1947): 337-52.

Witke, Charles (chapter on Ode 3.1; see General Works, above).

Ode 3.9

Nielsen, Rosemary. "Catullus 45 and Horace *Odes* 3.9: The Glass House." *Ramus* 6 (1977): 132-38.

Putnam, Michael C. J. "Horace Odes 3.9: The Dialectics of Desire." *Ancient and Modern: Essays in Honor of Gerald F. Else*, edited by John D'Arms and John Eadie. Ann Arbor, 1977, 139-57. Reprinted in Michael C. J. Putnam, *Essays on Latin Lyric, Elegy, and Epic* (Princeton, 1982).

Ode 3.13

Brown, Jerrold C. "Poetic Grammar in Horace's Ode to the Fountain at Bandusia." *Helios* 18 (1991): 137–46.

Fitzgerald, William (see under Ode 1.38).

Hexter, Ralph. "O Fons Bandusiae: Blood and Water in Horace, Odes 3.13." in *Homo Viator: Classical Essays for J. Bramble*, edited by M. Whitby, P. Hardie, M. Whitby, 131–39. Bristol, 1987.

Ode 3.30

Putnam, Michael, C. J. "Horace C.3.30: The Lyricist as Hero." *Ramus* 2 (1973): 1–19. Reprinted in Michael C. J. Putnam, *Essays on Latin Lyric, Elegy, and Epic* (Princeton, 1982).

Woodman, Tony."Exegi Monumentum: Horace, Odes 3.30." in *Quality and Pleasure in Latin Poetry*, edited by Tony Woodman and David West, 115–28. Cambridge, 1975.

Ode 4.7

Woodman, A. J. "Horace's Odes *Diffugere niues* and *Soluitur acris hiems*." *Latomus* 31 (1972): 752–78.

HORACE

SELECTED ODES
AND SATIRE 1.9

Satire 1.9

In Satire 1.9 Horace explores both literary and social values. Horace (or, more precisely, the character he takes on in this poem) encounters a man who aggressively keeps after him in an effort to gain access to Horace's literary friend and supporter, Maecenas. The poem is filled with irony and humor as this unwanted companion pursues Horace and Horace tries to escape. The intentional failure of Horace's friend, Aristius Fuscus, to save him adds to the poem's wit. On one level, the person Horace encounters is his opposite: they have completely different literary values. However, while Horace wants to distance himself from the aggressive, ambitious position the man represents, it should be noted that elsewhere (Satire 1.6) Horace shares his own social anxiety when he feels the need to defend himself, as the son of a freedman, against the charge of being an overly ambitious social climber because of his relationship to Maecenas.

Meter: dactylic hexameter

❀ ❀ ❀

Ibam\forte via sacra, sicut meus est mos,
nescio quid meditans nugarum, totus in illis.

---

1   **forte, adv.,** *by chance, as luck would have it, as it so happened*
   Ibam forte…: a fragment of Lucilius (died 102/101 B.C.E.), the inventor of the
      Latin genre of satire according to the satirists, Horace, Persius, and Juvenal,
      begins: **Ibat forte aries.** Horace is echoing his predecessor here.
   via sacra: The Via Sacra, or Sacred Way, was the main street in Rome. It went
      through the Forum and on to the Capitolium.
   mos, moris, m., *custom, tradition;* (plural) *character, habits*

2   **nescio, nescire, nescivi, nescitum,** *not know, be ignorant of, not to know
      how to, not to be able to*
   nescio: the "o" is regularly short in poetry
   nescio quid: *something or other,* literally, "I do not know what"

(notes contd. next page)

nescio quid: *something or other,* literally, "I do not know what"

meditor, meditari, meditatus sum, *think over, contemplate, practice*

nugae, -arum, f. pl., *trifles, nonsense, things of no importance;* cf. Catullus' use of the word to refer to his own literary work in lines 3–4 of the first poem of his collection: **Corneli, tibi: namque tu solebas/meas esse aliquid putare nugas. Nugae** can refer to a literary work of light character.

totus in illis: elliptical; *totally* (involved) *in it*

3   **accurro, accurrere, accurri/accucurri, accursum,** *run or hurry up to*

     tantum, adv., *so much, only*

     notus mihi nomine tantum: notice that he is never named

4   **arripio, arripere, arripui, arreptum,** *seize, take hold of, arrest, bring before a court*

     quid agis: idiomatic, "how are you?"

     dulcissime rerum: cf. Horace's characterization of Maecenas as **dulce decus meum** in Ode 1.1.2

     rerum: partitive genitive with superlative adjective, "in the world"

5   **suaviter,** adv., *pleasantly, delightfully, nicely*

     inquam, inquit, defective verb, only a few forms occur, most often used parenthetically or before or after a quotation, *say*

     inquam: present indicative active, first person singular

     cupio omnia quae vis: common polite phrase

6   **adsector, adsectari, adsectatus sum,** *follow closely, attend, escort*

     numquid, interrogative particle, introduces question where a negative answer is expected, *surely...not; you don't, do you?*

     occupo, occupare, occupavi, occupatum, *seize, forestall, take the lead over*

     occupo: here, *take the lead over,* in sense of breaking into the conversation

7   **nosco, noscere, novi, notum,** *get to know, learn; know* (in perfect tense)

     noris: noris is the syncopated form of **no(ve)ris,** perfect subjunctive; **noris nos** is the answer to **numquid vis?;** normally the answer contains a statement of what the person wants in the subjunctive with **ut** understood.

     nos, docti, sumus: all plural for singular, as often in Latin

     inquit: see **inquam** above; present indicative active, third person singular

     doctus, -a, -um, adj., *learned, taught*

     docti: *learned,* especially as it applies to poetry; cf. Ode 1.1.29–30: **me doctarum hederae praemia frontium/dis miscent superis;** and Ode 3.9.10: **dulcis docta modos et citharae sciens.**

     hic: the "i" is long

     pluris: genitive of indefinite value

8   **hoc:** ablative of cause

     inquam: see line 5

accurrit quidam notus mihi nomine tantum,
arreptaque manu: 'quid agis, dulcissime rerum?'
'suaviter, ut nunc est' inquam, 'et cupio omnia, quae vis.' 5
cum adsectaretur: 'numquid vis?' occupo, at ille
'noris nos' inquit, 'docti sumus.' hic ego: 'pluris
hoc' inquam 'mihi eris.' misere discedere quaerens
ire modo ocius, interdum consistere, in aurem
dicere nescio quid puero, cum sudor ad imos   10
manaret talos. 'o te, Bolane, cerebri
felicem' aiebam tacitus, cum quidlibet ille
garriret, vicos, urbem laudaret. ut illi

---

9   **ire**: historical infinitive, as are **consistere** (9) and **dicere** (10)
    modo, adv., *only, just now*
    ocius, adv., *sooner, quicker*
    interdum, adv., *at times*
    consisto, consistere, constiti, *stop, pause, stand still, take a position*

10 **nescio quid**: see line 2 for meaning and meter
    puero: Horace is being accompanied by a slave to whom he whispers.
    sudor, sudoris, m., *sweat*
    imus, -a, -um, adj., *lowest, bottom of*

11 **mano, manare, manavi, manatum**, *flow, spread*
    talus, -i, m., *ankle bone, ankle, knuckle bone* used in games
    te: accusative of exclamation, as is **felicem** (12)
    Bolanus, -i, m., *Bolanus*, Roman cognomen; identity unknown
    cerebrum, -i, n., *brain, seat of intelligence, seat of anger, anger*
    cerebri: genitive of reference, stating respect with which the adjective, **felicem**,
        is applicable; in Classical Latin an ablative of respect would be used more
        typically

12 **aio**, defective verb, *say yes, say*
    aiebam: imperfect tense, first person singular
    tacitus, -a, -um, adj., *silent*
    quilibet, quaelibet, quidlibet, pron., *whoever or whatever you please, any-
        one or anything whatever*

13 **garrio, garrire, garrivi**, *talk rapidly, chatter,* (do this in writing)
    vicus, -i, m., *group of dwellings, village; block of houses, street, group of
        streets*, often forming a social or administrative unit (used of specific
        districts in Rome)

14 **nil: nil** = **nihil**
  inquit: see line 7

15 **dudum**, adv., *some time ago, previously, just now; for a long time* (with **iam**)
  video: present tense with **iam dudum**; translate into English present perfect
  nil: see line 14
  nil agis: colloquial, *it's no use*
  usque, adv., *continuously, continually, all the way*
  tenebo: **teneo** has the sense "persist" here

16 **persequor, persequi, persecutus sum,** *pursue, chase*
  iter, itineris, n., *journey*
  nil: see line 14
  nil: used adverbially here
  opus, operis, n., *work, business, task, genre;* with **esse**, *be necessary, be
    needed;* here, with accusative and infinitive (**te circumagi**)

17 **circumago, circumagere, circumegi, circumactum,** *drive or lead around,
    lead around in circles*
  volo: the second "o" is short here, perhaps in imitation of early Latin comedy,
    which employed the metrical law of **brevis brevians**, or iambic shorten-
    ing. (An iamb is a short syllable followed by a long syllable.) According
    to this law, a long syllable, if preceded by a short syllable, may be counted
    as short if the word's natural accent falls on the syllable directly preced-
    ing or following it. Here, **volo** (∪ —) can become (∪ ∪) because the word
    is accented on the first syllable, i.e., the syllable preceding the change.
  viso, visere, visi, *look at, go and see*

18 **Tiberis, Tiberis,** m., *the river Tiber*
  longe, adv., *far, far off, far away in time*
  cubo, cubare, cubui, cubitum, *lie down or be lying down, recline, be in bed
    or on one's couch, be confined to bed by illness, recline at table*
  Caesar, Caesaris, m., *Caesar;* here, Julius Caesar, (100–44 B.C.E.), Roman
    general who defeated Pompey at the battle of Pharsalus in 48 B.C.E. and
    was made dictator for life in 44 B.C.E., shortly before his assassination in
    the conspiracy led by Brutus and Cassius. Cf. notes to Ode 2.7 for Horace's
    association with Brutus.
  hortus, -i, m., *garden;* usually in plural, *pleasure grounds or gardens*
  Caesaris hortos: an estate on the Janiculum left by Julius Caesar in his will as
    a public park for the people.

19 **nil**: see line 14
  agam: subjunctive in relative clause of characteristic
  piger, pigra, pigrum, adj., *inactive, lazy*
  usque: see line 15

20 **demitto, demittere, demisi, demissum,** *let fall, lower*

nil respondebam: 'misere cupis' inquit 'abire;
iam dudum video. sed nil agis; usque tenebo.   15
persequar hinc, quo nunc iter est tibi.' 'nil opus est te
circumagi: quendam volo visere non tibi notum;
trans Tiberim longe cubat is prope Caesaris hortos.'
'nil habeo, quod agam, et non sum piger: usque sequar te.'
demitto auriculas, ut iniquae mentis asellus,   20
cum gravius dorso subiit onus. incipit ille:
'si bene me novi, non Viscum pluris amicum,
non Varium facies: nam quis me scribere pluris

---

demitto auriculas: the sense of **demittere aures ad**, *deign to listen to*, (*OLD*
under **demitto**, 10. c) may be relevant here. He shows his feeling of defeat.
The elision between the two words calls attention to the gesture.
auricula, -ae, f., *ear*
iniquus, -a, -um, adj., *uneven, unfavorable, treacherous, discontented*
asellus, -i, m., *young ass, young donkey*

21   **dorsum, -i**, n., *back*
subeo, subire, subii, subitum, *go under, undergo*
subiit: the second "i" is long, as is typical with compounds of **eo** in the
perfect tense
onus, oneris, n., *burden*
onus: accusative

22   **novi**: see line 7
si bene me novi: idiomatic, *as certainly as I know myself*
Viscus, -i, m., *Viscus;* there were two brothers with this name; both were
literary figures and friends of Horace and Maecenas. In Satire 1.10.83
they are mentioned along with several others, including Varius (cf. line
23 below), Vergil, Maecenas (cf. line 43 below), and Aristius Fuscus (cf.
line 61 below) as people whose approval of his writing mattered greatly
to Horace. One of them is also mentioned as a guest, along with Varius, at
a dinner in honor of Maecenas described in Satire 2.8.
pluris: genitive of indefinite value

22–23   Note the anaphora with asyndeton, **non Viscum...non Varium**, which
emphasizes the names.
non Viscum...facies: **facies** (*regard*) plus accusative (**amicum**) plus genitive
of indefinite value (**pluris**), *you will not regard Viscus, Varius, as a friend
of more value*

(notes contd. next page)

23 **Varius, Varii**, m., *L. Varius Rufus,* epic and tragic poet, a very significant
figure to Horace. He, along with Vergil, introduced Horace to his future
friend and supporter, Maecenas (cf. Satire 1.6.55). In Satire 1.6.52–55
Horace emphasizes the fact that his relationship with Maecenas was not a
product of chance, but rather of his friends' introduction and Maecenas' care-
ful choice. Contrast that process with the chance encounter (**Ibam** *forte*
via sacra) of this satire and the desire of Horace's unwanted companion
to become part of Horace's literary circle. In addition, compare his lack of
literary credentials (cf. note below on lines 23–24). In Satire 1.5.39–42
Horace says that no one is more attached to Varius, Vergil, and Plotius
Tucca than he is and that there are no people better than they are. (Varius
and Plotius Tucca served as Vergil's literary executors.) In Ode 1.6 Horace
begs off from writing epic (while he simultaneously appropriates epic for
lyric) and Varius is the epic writer whom he suggests in his place for sing-
ing the praises of Agrippa, who commanded the fleet of Augustus at the
battle of Actium in 31 B.C.E. in which the forces of Antony and Cleopatra
were defeated. Cf. the notes to Ode 1.37.

 pluris: **-is** ending, alternate accusative plural ending for **-es**; modifies **versus**
(24); since the final syllable in the line can be considered either long or
short, there may be a sense of the genitive of indefinite value as well (see
line 22).

23–24 **nam...versus**: Cf. Satire 1.4.11 ff. for Horace's dislike of writing that is
done too quickly or at too great length. He criticizes Lucilius (cf. note on
line 1) for these very qualities. What Horace's unwanted companion sees
as his literary credentials are the very literary qualities Horace abhors.

24 **citius**, adv., *quicker, sooner*
 possit: potential subjunctive
 versus, -us, m., *line of verse*
 membrum, -i, n., *limb or member of the body, limb, member, part of anything*
 movere: understand **possit** again

25 **mollis, -e**, adj., *soft, gentle, flexible, voluptuous*
 invideo, invidere, invidi, invisum, *envy, begrudge, refuse*
 invideat: potential subjunctive
 quod: relative pronoun, direct object of **canto**, antecedent understood
 et: *even*
 Hermogenes, Hermogenis, m., *Hermogenes.* In Satire 1.10.80 Horace places
a Hermogenes Tegellius in a group of people whose opinions do not mat-
ter to him as opposed to those of his literary friends (cf. note on **Viscus**,
line 22).
 canto, cantare, cantavi, cantatum, *sing, sing about, recite*
 canto: cf. line 10 of Ode 1.22
 mollius...canto: this line is completely dactylic except for the obligatory last
foot that has a long syllable followed by a syllable that can be either long

aut citius possit versus? quis membra movere
mollius? invideat quod et Hermogenes ego canto.' 25
interpellandi locus hic erat: 'est tibi mater,
cognati, quis te salvo est opus?' 'haud mihi quisquam;
omnis composui.' 'felices! nunc ego resto.
confice! namque instat fatum mihi triste, Sabella

---

or short. Line 31 is the only other equally dactylic line in the poem. The
heavily dactylic meter of line 25 echoes the value the speaker places on
quick writing.

26 **interpello, interpellare, interpellavi, interpellatum**, *interrupt, break in on,
impede*
interpellandi: notice how this word's five long syllables in a row put a halt to
the chattering of the heavily dactylic previous line
hic: the "i" is long

27 **cognatus, -a, -um**, adj., *related;* here, as noun, *relative*
cognati: understand the verb "to be" again from **est** (26)
quis: alternate form for **quibus** (dative and ablative plural of relative pro-
noun); here, dative of person who has the need, with **est opus**
te: ablative with **est opus** (see line 16)
salvus, -a, -um, adj., *safe, alive, well*
salvo: ablative modifying **te**
haud, adv., *not*
mihi: dative of possession, understand **est**

28 **omnis**: -**is** ending, alternate accusative plural ending for -**es**
compono, componere, composui, compositum, *put together, arrange, com-
pose, calm, bury*
resto, restare, restiti, *remain, remain to be dealt with*

29–34 These lines are a parody of epic passages in which the hero's death is
foretold. Of course, the fate proclaimed for Horace is not a heroic one: he
will be killed by an excessive talker!

29 **conficio, conficere, confeci, confectum**, *complete, destroy, finish off, kill*
confice: understand a **me** as the direct object
insto, instare, institi, *be pressing, loom, threaten*
fatum, -i, n., *fate;* plural, *the Fates*
mihi: dative with **insto**
tristis, -e, adj., *sad*
Sabellus, -a, -um, adj., *Sabine;* the Sabines were a people of central Italy.

30 **puero**: understand **mihi**, *for me when I was a boy*
 divina mota...urna: ablative absolute
 anus, -us, f., *old woman*
 urna, -ae, f., *urn*

31 **dirus, -a, -um**, adj., *terrible, awful, dire*
 venenum, -i, n., *poison, magical or medicinal potion*
 hosticus, -a, -um, adj., *belonging to an enemy*
 aufero, auferre, abstuli, ablatum, *take away, carry off, kill*
 ensis, ensis, m., *sword*

32 **latus, lateris**, n., *side, extreme part or region, flank, lungs, body*
 dolor, doloris, m., *pain, anguish, grief*
 tussis, tussis, f., *cough*
 tardus, -a, -um, adj., *slow, late, moving slowly, dull*
 podagra, -ae, f., *gout*

33 **garrulus, -a, -um**, adj., *talkative, loquacious*
 quandocumque, adv., *at some time or other*
 quando...cumque: tmesis, **quandocumque**
 consumo, consumere, consumpsi, consumptum, *consume, destroy, kill*
 loquax, loquacis, adj., *talkative, loquacious, talking*

34 **sapio, sapere, sapivi**, *have taste, be wise*
 vito, vitare, vitavi, vitatum, *avoid, shun*
 simul, conj., *as soon as* (also with **atque**); adv., *at the same time, together*
 adolesco, adolescere, adolevi, adultum, *grow up*, (of a season or time)
  reach its peak
 aetas, aetatis, f., *time, age*

35 **ventum erat**: intransitive verb used impersonally in the passive, literally, *it
  had been come*, i.e., *we had come;* person and number for translation
  supplied from context; this impersonal construction allows the speaker
  to avoid joining himself "grammatically" in the first person plural with
  this person he finds so distasteful.
 Vesta, -ae, f., *Vesta*, Roman goddess of the domestic hearth; *temple or shrine
  of Vesta;* she was served by the Vestal Virgins, who were chosen by the
  pontifex maximus (cf. Ode 3.30 for the image of Vestal Virgin and pontifex
  ascending the Capitolium)
 Vestae: genitive; the accusative **templum** is the understood object of **ad**;
  temple of Vesta
 quartus, -a, -um, adj., *fourth*

35–36 **quarta...praeterita**: ablative absolute; about 9 a.m., when business went
  on in the law courts

quod puero cecinit divina mota anus urna: 30
hunc neque dira venena, nec hosticus auferet ensis,
nec laterum dolor aut tussis, nec tarda podagra:
garrulus hunc quando consumet cumque. loquaces,
si sapiat, vitet, simul atque adoleverit aetas.'
ventum erat ad Vestae, quarta iam parte diei   35
praeterita, et casu tum respondere vadato
debebat, quod ni fecisset, perdere litem.
'si me amas' inquit, 'paulum hic ades.' 'interream, si

---

36 **praetereo, praeterire, praeterii, praeteritum**, *go by, go past, pass by, go beyond, omit*
casus, -us, m., *fall, event, misfortune, chance*
respondeo, respondere, respondi, responsum, *answer, reply;* technical sense, *appear in court*
vador, vadari, vadatus sum, (of a plaintiff) *to accept a guarantee from the other party that the party will appear or reappear in court at an appointed date*
vadato: impersonal ablative absolute, or dative of perfect participle as noun, *the plaintiff*

37 **ni**: **ni** = **nisi**
nisi, conj., *if not, unless*
perdo, perdere, perdidi, perditum, *destroy, lose*
perdere: understand **debebat**
lis, litis, f., *quarrel, lawsuit*

38 **si me amas**: colloquial expression for "please" found, e.g., in Roman comedy and Cicero's letters
me: monosyllabic hiatus (no elision with **amas**) with shortening of the long vowel; **me amas** scans, ∪ ∪ —
inquit: see line 7
paulum, adv., *for a short while*
adsum, adesse, adfui, *be present;* in technical sense, *be present in court as a friend or adviser*
ades: present imperative singular of **adsum**
intereo, interire, interii, interitum, *perish, die*
interream: *may I perish...* (hyperbolic)

39 **valeo, valere, valui, valitum,** *be powerful, be strong enough to, be well*
   stare: literally, *stand,* or can have technical sense of **adsum** given above
      (Plautus, the Roman comic playwright, uses the word in this sense)
   novi: see line 7; the long "o" makes this form the verb, not the adjective,
      novus, -a, -um
   civilis, -e, adj., *civil*
   ius, iuris, n., *law, right, court*

40 **propero, properare, properavi, properatum,** *hurry, hasten*
   dubius, -a, -um, adj., *uncertain, indecisive*
   faciam: subjunctive in indirect question
   inquit: see line 7

41 **ne,** interrogative enclitic particle, in direct questions; in indirect questions
      with alternatives, often used with **an,** *whether...or*
   rem: here, in the technical sense of a legal matter; it would go by default if he
      did not appear
   sodes: **sodes = si audes,** *please;* **audeo** typically means "wish" in Plautus

42 **praecedo, praecedere, praecessi, praecessum,** *go in front, go on ahead*
   coepi, coepisse, coeptum, typically appears in perfect system; *begin*
   contendo, contendere, contendi, contentum, *stretch, hasten, compete, con-*
      tend
   durum: understand **est**

43 **victor, victoris**, m., *victor, winner, conqueror*
   Maecenas, Maecenatis, m. *Gaius Cilnius Maecenas,* friend and supporter of
      Horace and of other contemporary poets, including Vergil
   quomodo, interr., rel. adv., *how, in the manner in which*
   Maecenas...tecum: elliptical because a verb is lacking; the sense is, "how
      are things with you and Maecenas?" This kind of ellipsis is common in
      colloquial Latin.

44 **repeto, repetere, repetivi, repetitum,** *seek again, recall, resume*
   sanus, -a, -um, adj., *healthy, sane*
   paucorum hominum...mentis...sanae: genitives of description
   paucorum...sanae: commentators differ about who is speaking here, but agree
      that Maecenas is the one to whom the speaker refers. Cf. Satire 1.6.51 ff.
      for Maecenas' selectivity in choosing those with whom he would associ-
      ate.

45 **fortuna**: ablative with **usus est (utor)**
   fortuna: cf. the note on Varius, line 23, for the lack of chance involved in his
      becoming part of Maecenas' circle of friends
   nemo...usus: some attribute these lines to Horace and take him to be speak-
      ing about Maecenas, while others (including the editor of the text printed

aut valeo stare aut novi civilia iura,
et propero, quo scis.' 'dubius sum, quid faciam' inquit,   40
'tene relinquam, an rem.' 'me, sodes.' 'non faciam' ille
et praecedere coepit. ego, ut contendere durum
cum victore, sequor. 'Maecenas quomodo tecum?'
hinc repetit, 'paucorum hominum et mentis bene sanae;
nemo dexterius fortuna est usus. haberes   45
magnum adiutorem, posset qui ferre secundas,
hunc hominem velles si tradere. dispeream, ni
summosses omnis.' 'non isto vivimus illic,
quo tu rere, modo. domus hac nec purior ulla est,

---

here) attribute the lines to Horace's follower; these latter disagree as to
whether the follower is referring to Maecenas or to Horace.
haberes: apodosis of a present contrary to fact condition; cf. **velles** (47) below

46 **adiutor, adiutoris**, m., *helper*
posset qui: postposition; the relative pronoun **qui**, the subject of the clause,
   is placed after **posset**
ferre: here, has the sense of "play" a part
secundus, -a, -um, adj., *following, second, favorable*
secundas: understand **partes**; the second actor supports the primary actor
pars, partis, f., *part, party; stage role* (usually in plural)

47 **hunc hominem**: colloquial for **me**
velles: protasis of present contrary to fact condition
si: postposition; note how late in its clause this word appears
trado, tradere, tradidi, traditum, *hand over, deliver, introduce*
dispereo, disperire, disperii, *perish, be destroyed* (frequently hyperbolic)
dispeream: *may I perish…* (hyperbolic)
ni: see line 37

48 **summoveo, summovere, summovi, summotum**, *move away, remove, ward
   off, banish*
summosses: syncopated form of **summo(vi)sses**; the pluperfect, rather than
   the imperfect, may emphasize the idea of completion
omnis: **-is** ending, alternate accusative plural ending for **-es**
omnis: all those competing for Maecenas' attention

49 **reor, reri, ratus sum**, *think*
rere: alternate form of second person singular, **reris**
quo…modo: see line 43
purior: cf. the beginning of Ode 1.22, **Integer vitae scelerisque** *purus*

50 **alienus, -a, -um**, adj., *of another, alien, strange* (with ablative or dative)
nil: see line 14; used adverbial here; *not at all*
mi: mi = mihi
officio, officere, offeci, offectum, *impede, interfere with* (with dative)
inquam: see line 5

51 **dis, ditis**, adj., *rich, wealthy;* comparative, **ditior**
hic: long "i" here for the nominative singular masculine of **hic, haec, hoc**
quia: postposition; note the postponement of this conjunction
doctus, -a, -um, *learned, taught*

52 **credibilis, -e**, adj., *believable*
atqui, conj., *but, nevertheless*

53 **sic habet: habeo**, used impersonally with adv. of manner, *be in (such and
    such) a way; it is so;* a similar expression is **sic se res habet**
accendo, accendere, accendi, accensum, *kindle, arouse, ignite*

54 **proxumus, -a, -um**, adj., *nearest, next*
tantummodo, adv., *only*
velis tantummodo: ironic; literally, *you would wish it only;* the sense is, *you
    only need to wish for it*
quae tua virtus: an example of the antecedent incorporated into the relative
    clause, *such is your valor* (literally, *which is your valor*)

55 **expugno, expugnare, expugnavi, expugnatum**, *storm, conquer, overcome*
possit: subjunctive in relative clause of characteristic
eo, adv., ablative of **is**, *therefore*

56 **difficilis**: **-is** ending, alternate accusative plural ending for **-es**
aditus, -us, m., *approach, access*
haud: see line 27
desum, deesse, defui, *be missing, fail* (with dative of person)
dero: dero = deero, from **desum**; the **dee-** usually contracted to **de-** in
    poetry

57 **munus, muneris**, n., *service, duty, gift, entertainment*
corrumpo, corrumpere, corrupi, corruptum, *damage, spoil, bribe, seduce*

58 **excludo, excludere, exclusi, exclusum**, *shut out, exclude*
exclusus fuero: exclusus fuero = exclusus ero; alternate form for the fu-
    ture perfect passive
exclusus fuero: the language here is similar to that of the "shut-out" lover
    who cannot gain access to the house of the one he desires
desisto, desistere, destiti, *cease, desist*

59 **occurro, occurrere, occurri/occucurri, occursum**, *meet, hurry to meet,
    arrive, turn up*

nec magis his aliena malis. nil mi officit, inquam,   50
ditior hic aut est quia doctior: est locus uni
cuique suus.' 'magnum narras, vix credibile.' 'atqui
sic habet.' 'accendis, quare cupiam magis illi
proxumus esse.' 'velis tantummodo: quae tua virtus,
expugnabis, et est, qui vinci possit, eoque   55
difficilis aditus primos habet.' 'haud mihi dero:
muneribus servos corrumpam; non, hodie si
exclusus fuero, desistam; tempora quaeram,
occurram in triviis, deducam. nil sine magno
vita labore dedit mortalibus.' haec dum agit, ecce   60
Fuscus Aristius occurrit, mihi carus et illum

---

trivium, trivii, n., *meeting place of three roads, crossroads*
deduco, deducere, deduxi, deductum, *lead away, lead down, escort, bring a person or army back with one to Rome, bring home in procession as a bride, spin, compose, adapt*
deducam: understand Maecenas as the direct object
nil: see line 14

60 **ecce**, interj., *look, behold*

61 **Fuscus, -i**, m., *Aristius Fuscus*, Horace's literary friend in Satire 1.10.83, the person to whom Epistle 1.10 is addressed—and there he and Horace are linked as "twins," but separated by their love for the city and the country, respectively—as well as the character who refuses to save Horace from his unwanted companion, here, in Satire 1.9. Porphyrio, the ancient commentator on Horace (third and fourth centuries c.e.), calls Aristius Fuscus a very outstanding **grammaticus** (philologist or grammarian) and a writer of comedies. His appearance in Ode 1.22 (see later in this text), a poem about the poet's invulnerability, can be seen as an "answer" to his refusal to help the poet in Satire 1.9. In the city the poet needs help and does not receive it from Fuscus; later, in the ode, he claims his invulnerability in the country and in remote lands. **Fuscus, -a, -um** is an adjective meaning "dark." For punning on Fuscus' name, cf. the note on Apollo, line 78 below. For further punning on Fuscus, cf. the note on **Hydaspes**, Ode 1.22.8. Putting **Fuscus** before **Aristius** and at the beginning of the line calls attention to the word.
Aristius, Aristii, m., see **Fuscus**, line 61
occurrit: see line 59
carus, -a, -um, adj., *dear, beloved*

62   **qui**: postposition; **qui** placed after **illum,** which belongs to the same clause
    pulchre: colloquial for **bene**; common in the comedies of Plautus and Terence
    nosset: syncopated form of **no(vi)sset**; subjunctive in relative clause of char-
        acteristic with an accessory notion of cause
    consistimus: see line 9

63   **quo**, adv., *where, for what purpose*
    tendo, tendere, tetendi, tentum/tensum, *stretch out, extend, proceed, direct*
        one's course
    rogat et respondet: they each ask and answer each other
    respondet: see line 36
    vello, vellere, velli, vulsum, *pull, tug at*
    coepi: see line 42

64   **presso, pressare, pressavi, pressatum,** *press*
    lentus, -a, -um, adj., *slow, lingering, unresponsive*
    brachium, brachii, n., *arm*
    nuto, nutare, nutavi, nutatum, *nod with the head, nod, hesitate*

65   **distorqueo, distorquere, distorsi, distortum,** *twist this way and that, distort,*
        torment
    eripio, eripere, eripui, ereptum, *snatch away, rescue*
    male, adv., *badly, insufficiently, wickedly, scarcely*
    salsus, -a, -um, adj., *salted, witty, funny*

66   **dissimulo, dissimulare, dissimulavi, dissimulatum,** *pretend that something*
        is not what it is, pretend not to notice, ignore
    dissimulare: historical infinitive
    iecur, iecoris, n., *liver, the seat of the feelings*
    uro, urere, ussi, ustum, *burn;* in pass., *be on fire*
    urere: historical infinitive
    bilis, bilis, f., *gall, bile, anger*
    meum...bilis: cf. the language of Ode 1.13

67   **certus, -a, -um,** adj., *certain, definite*
    nescio quid: see line 2 for meaning and meter
    secreto: adv., *secretly*

68   **aiebas**: see line 12; imperfect tense, second person singular
    memini, meminisse, perfect with present meaning; *remember, recollect*
    melior, melius, adj., *better*

69   **tricesimus, -a, -um,** adj., *thirtieth*
    sabbata, sabbatorum, n. pl., *the Jewish sabbath*
    tricesima sabbata: this refers to no known Jewish celebration and is likely an
        invention on Fuscus' part. Just as Horace creates obstacles for his un-
        wanted companion, so Fuscus does the same for Horace.

qui pulchre nosset. consistimus. 'unde venis?' et
'quo tendis?' rogat et respondet. vellere coepi
et pressare manu lentissima brachia, nutans,
distorquens oculos, ut me eriperet. male salsus   65
ridens dissimulare, meum iecur urere bilis:
'certe nescio quid secreto velle loqui te
aiebas mecum.' 'memini bene, sed meliore
tempore dicam: hodie tricesima sabbata. vin tu
curtis Iudaeis oppedere?' 'nulla mihi' inquam   70
'religio est.' 'at mi! sum paulo infirmior, unus

---

vin: vin = visne

70 **curtus, -a, -um,** adj., *having a part missing, mutilated, circumcized*
    curtis: male circumcision is a Jewish practice
    Iudaeus, -i, m., *Jew*
    oppedo, oppedere, *fart in the face of* (with dative)
    inquam: see line 5

71 **religio, religionis,** f., *religious awe or conscience, religious practice, particu-
    lar set of religious observances, cult, religious feeling, superstition*
    mi: see line 50
    at mi: elliptical; understand with **religio est**
    paulum, -i, n., *a little*
    infirmus, -a, -um, adj., *weak, lacking strength of purpose, not resolute*

72 **multorum**: cf. **paucorum hominum**, line 44. Horace, the writer (as opposed to the persona in the satire) has Fuscus humorously identify himself as one of the "many" in contrast to Maecenas who is a person of "few" people.
    ignosco, ignoscere, ignovi, ignotum, *forgive, pardon*
    alias, adv., *at another time*
    huncine: **huncine** = **huncne**
    -ne, here, affirmative particle with infinitive in exclamation; see **surrexe** below

72–73 **huncine solem...nigrum**: accusatives of exclamation with infinitive in exclamation
    solem: **sol** can have the meaning of "a day," as determined by the rising of the sun

73 **niger, nigra, nigrum**, *black, dark, gloomy, black as a color of ill omen, evil*
    nigrum: pun in connection with the meaning of Fuscus' name; Aristius Fuscus is the "dark sun," or unlucky day.
    surgo, surgere, surrexi, surrectum, *get up, rise* (of heavenly bodies)
    surrexe: syncopated form of **surrex(iss)e**; infinitive in exclamation
    fugit: present tense, short "u"
    inprobus, -a, -um, adj., *unprincipled, immoderate, unruly, relentless, shameless*

74 **culter, cultri**, m., *knife*
    sub cultro: *under the knife*, i.e., like a sacrificial victim with the knife ready to fall, or like a warrior with the opponent's weapon about to fall
    linquo, linquere, liqui, *go away from, abandon, leave behind*
    casu: see line 36
    venit: present tense, short "e"
    obvius, -a, -um, adj. (with dative), *in the way, placed so as to meet, situated so as to confront*

75 **adversarius, adversarii**, m., *adversary, opponent*
    adversarius: the plaintiff; see line 36
    quo: see line 63
    quo tu turpissime: elliptical; understand a verb of going
    turpissime: cf. **dulcissime**, line 4
    turpis, -e, adj., *ugly, shameful, disgraceful*

76 **inclamo, inclamare, inclamavi, inclamatum**, *call out, cry out*
    licet, licere, licuit/licitum est, impersonal verb, *it is permitted*
    antestor, antestari, antestatus sum, *call as a witness*
    licet antestari: elliptical; *is it permitted* (to me) *to call* (you) *as a witness?* The context makes it clear that this is a question even though there is no question word or enclitic; standard legal phrase; this is the question asked

multorum. ignosces; alias loquar.' huncine solem
tam nigrum surrexe mihi! fugit inprobus ac me
sub cultro linquit. casu venit obvius illi
adversarius et 'quo tu, turpissime?' magna   75
inclamat voce, et 'licet antestari?' ego vero
oppono auriculam. rapit in ius: clamor utrimque,
undique concursus. sic me servavit Apollo.

---

by a plaintiff who wants a witness to the legal seizure of a defendant who
fails to appear in court.
vero, adv., *in fact, indeed, certainly, truly*
vero: possibly with ironic force here

77 **oppono, opponere, opposui, oppositum,** *place against, place in front, espe-
cially put before someone for acceptance, proffer*
auricula: see line 20
oppono auriculam: letting the plaintiff touch one's ear was the sign that one
agreed to serve as a witness
oppono auriculam: cf. what is signified by the ears in line 20
ius: see line 39
clamor, clamoris, m., *shout, shouting, clamor*
utrimque, adv., *on both sides*
clamor utrimque: elliptical; understand **est**

78 **undique,** adv., *on all sides, everywhere*
concursus, -us, m., *running to and fro*
undique concursus: elliptical; understand **est**
Apollo, Apollinis, m., *Apollo,* son of Jupiter and Latona, brother of Diana,
god of archery, music, poetry, etc.
Apollo: the mention of Apollo, who is associated with the sun, continues the
pun on Fuscus' name. Fuscus (the dark one) abandons him, while Apollo
(the bright one) seems to save him. Apollo's connections with poetry and
justice are important as well. Horace, the poet, appears to be saved by the
intervention of a legal case. It has been argued, though, that the ending of
the poem is ironic and that by agreeing to serve as a witness Horace is not
saved, but rather, is caught up in the affairs of his unwanted companion
since he will have to accompany the litigants to the magistrate.
sic me servavit Apollo: a translation of the Greek of Homer, *Iliad* 20.443,
where Apollo rescues Hector, quoted in Greek by Lucilius in his sixth
satire. Horace criticizes Lucilius in Satire 1.10.20 ff. for his use of Greek
words in his Latin satires.

Ode 1.1

Horace begins his lyric collection with this ode addressed to his friend
and supporter, Maecenas. In the course of the poem he gives an ex-
tended description of the pursuits other people choose to follow. He ends
with his own choice, the writing of lyric poetry.

Meter: first or lesser Asclepiadean

Maecenas atavis edite regibus,
o et praesidium et dulce decus meum:

---

1   **Maecenas, Maecenatis,** m., *Gaius Cilnius Maecenas,* friend and supporter of
    Horace and of other contemporary poets, including Vergil; friend and
    adviser to Augustus (Octavian); vocative. Note the emphatic position of
    Maecenas' name here. It begins the first poem of Horace's initial lyric
    collection (*Odes,* Books 1–3). Horace's *Epodes, Satires* Book 1, and *Epistles*
    Book 1 also begin with an address to Maecenas.

2   **atavus, -i,** m., *a great-great-great grandfather,* or (here) *a remote ancestor*
    editus, -a, -um, adj., "descended from," perfect passive participle of **edo,
      edere, edidi, editum,** *put forth, give out, give birth to*
    rex, regis, m., *king,* here used adjectivally, meaning "royal." Cf. Vergil *Aeneid*
      1.273, **regina sacerdos,** for another example of two nouns in apposition
      where one (**regina**) is used adjectivally, "royal priestess."
    atavis edite regibus: Maecenas traced his family background to Etruscan
      kings.
    o, interj., *O* (with vocative)
    o et: hiatus (lack of elision) between **o** and **et.**
    praesidium, praesidii, n., *protection, defense*
    dulcis, -e, adj., *sweet,* (of persons) *dear, beloved;* vocative
    decus, decoris, n., *that which adorns or beautifies, honor, glory*

3 **sunt quos**: **Illi** is the understood antecedent of the relative pronoun **quos**. "There are those whom..." Such a relative clause of characteristic normally takes the subjunctive in prose, but here takes the indicative (**iuvat**). Cf. lines 19, 21 below, **est qui...spernit**. **Sunt quos** begins a catalog of various occupations (racing, politics, trade, farming, relaxation, war, hunting), which continues through line 28. Understand **iuvat** with **hunc** (7) and **illum** (9) below, which are its direct objects along with **quos**. **Me**, the first word of line 29 signals the shift from others' occupations to that of the speaker of the poem.
curriculum, -i, n., *a running, course, race, racing chariot*
pulvis, pulveris, m., *dust*
Olympicus, -a, -um, adj., *Olympic, Olympian;* Olympia, in Elis, Greece, was the site of the ancient Olympic games, held every four years in honor of Olympian Zeus. The games, founded in 776 B.C.E., were still held in Horace's lifetime. Olympus was the name of several mountains in Greece, including one in Thessaly considered the home of the gods and another in the region of Elis.

4 **colligo, colligere, collegi, collectum**, *to gather or bring together, collect;* with **pulverem** (3) the idea is the raising of dust in the track through high speed racing.
iuvat: from **iuvo**; used here impersonally; the infinitive **collegisse** is the subject of **iuvat**, **quos** is the direct object.
meta, -ae, f., *turning point, end.* This is the turning post at either end of the race track. Take **meta...evitata** either as a second subject of **iuvat** (4) or as a subject of **evehit** (6) along with **palma** (5).
fervidus, -a, -um, adj., *boiling, burning, hot, impetuous*

5 **evitata**: The chariot must go around the **meta** without hitting it.
rota, -ae, f., *wheel*
palma, -ae, f., *palm tree, palm branch, palm wreath, token of victory;* subject of **evehit** (6); metonymy for "victory."
nobilis: transferred epithet; the adjective grammatically modifies **palma** rather than the victor.

6 **terrarum**: in plural, "the world."
dominus, -i, m., *master, lord, ruler*
eveho, evehere, evexi, evectum, *carry out, lift up, raise*
terrarum dominos: **Dominos** looks to both the victors in the chariot race and to the gods and can be seen as in apposition to another **quos** understood from line 3 or as in apposition to **deos** (6). While the former may be more appealing in terms of the general sense of the poem—the victors become masters of the world—it is important when reading Latin, and Horace's poetry in particular, to preserve such ambiguities. This kind of ambiguity concerning what modifies what is very typical of Horace and

sunt, quos curriculo pulverem Olympicum
collegisse iuvat metaque fervidis

evitata rotis palmaque nobilis   5
terrarum dominos evehit ad deos;

hunc, si mobilium turba Quiritium
certat tergeminis tollere honoribus,

---

should be understood not as lack of clarity but rather as the poet's attempt to say more than he could if he narrowed his possibilities to just one option. Notice the position of **terrarum dominos** between **quos** (3) and **deos** (6). Remember that Latin word order is flexible because of the inflected nature of Latin. Horace exploits this flexibility perhaps more than any other Latin poet.

3–6 The shifts in construction in lines 3–6, from **collegisse**, an infinitive, as an impersonal subject of **iuvat**, to **meta**, a noun, as a second subject of **iuvat** or as a possible subject of **evehit**, to **palma** as definite subject of **evehit**, are typical of Horace's style. Where parallelism of construction might be expected, Horace often avoids it. This may present some initial difficulties, but the reader who remains open to these shifts will quickly be on the road to understanding a basic feature of the poet's style.

7 **mobilis, -e**, adj., *moveable, changeable, inconstant, pliant*
turba, -ae. f., *crowd*
Quiris, Quiritis, m., *Roman citizen*

8 **certo, certare, certavi, certatum**, *contend, strive*
tergeminus, -a, -um, *triple*
tollo, tollere, sustuli, sublatum, *lift, raise, extol, take away, destroy;* understand an **eum** as direct object of **tollere**.
honor (honos), honoris, m., *honor, office*
tergeminis...honoribus: "triple offices" (aedile, praetor, consul) or possibly "reiterated applause," the suggestion of Porphyrio, the ancient commentator on Horace.

9   **proprius, -a, -um**, adj., *one's own, personal*
    condo, condere, condidi, conditum, *found, establish, store up*
    horreum, -i, n., *storehouse, granary*

10 **Libycus, -a, -um**, adj., *Libyan*, sometimes *African*, in general
    verro, verrere, versum, *sweep together, collect*
    area, -ae, f., *open space, threshing floor*

11 **gaudeo, gaudere, gavisus sum**, *delight in, rejoice*
    patrius, -a, -um, adj., *of a father, ancestral, native, inherited, belonging to*
       one's country
    findo, findere, fidi, fissum, *split, separate, divide*
    sarculum, -i, n., *hoe*

12 **Attalicus, -a, -um**, adj., *of King Attalus or his dynasty, rich, splendid;* King
    Attalus III of Pergamum, in Asia Minor, known as the other Attalids be-
    fore him for his wealth, left his territory to the Romans in 133 B.C.E. The
    wealth of the Attalids was proverbial for the Romans, like that of Croesus
    for the Greeks.
    condicio, condicionis, f., *condition, term, agreement*
    Attalicis condicionibus: suggests a huge amount of money

13 **ut**: with subjunctive, **secet** (see below, line 14)
    trabs, trabis, f., *beam of wood, trunk of tree, ship*
    Cyprius, -a, -um, adj., *Cyprian, of the island of Cyprus;* Cyprus was famous
    for its trees and its shipbuilding.

14 **Myrtous, -a, -um**, adj., *Myrtoan;* **Myrtoum...mare**, Myrtoan Sea; southwestern
    part of the Aegean Sea between the Peloponnese and the Cyclades; note
    how **Myrtoum...mare** surrounds **pavidus nauta**, the frightened sailor.
    Horace often uses word order as a vehicle for meaning. While the idea is
    that no one could get the one who is enjoying working his ancestral fields
    to go to sea, the Latin "shows" the reader through word order a "picture"
    of a sailor enveloped by the sea. Horace often images what he is negating.
    Cf. the note on line 34 below, as well as notes on Ode 1.23.
    pavidus, -a, -um, adj., *frightened, terrified, trembling, fearful*
    seco, secare, secui, sectum, *cut, divide, traverse;* subjunctive because of
    indirect command introduced by **demoveas**, which functions here as a
    verb of persuading

15 **luctor, luctari, luctatus sum**, *wrestle, struggle, contend*
    Icarius, -a, -um, adj., *of Icarus, Icarian;* Icarus, the son of Daedalus, drowned
    in the Aegean Sea while flying from Crete with wings his father had
    made. He gives his name to the area where he landed, the Icarian Sea,

illum, si proprio condidit horreo,
quicquid de Libycis verritur areis.   10

gaudentem patrios findere sarculo
agros Attalicis condicionibus

numquam demoveas, ut trabe Cypria
Myrtoum pavidus nauta secet mare;

luctantem Icariis fluctibus Africum   15
mercator metuens otium et oppidi

laudat rura sui, mox reficit rates
quassas indocilis pauperiem pati.

est, qui nec veteris pocula Massici
nec partem solido demere de die   20

which is part of the Aegean. Cf. Horace Ode 2.20.13 for Horace's comparison of himself to Icarus.
Icariis fluctibus: dative case, with **luctor**
Africus (ventus) or **Africus**, *southwestern, stormy wind*

16 **mercator, mercatoris**, m. *merchant*
otium, otii, n., *free time, leisure, peace*
oppidum, -i, n., *town*

17 **reficio, reficere, refeci, refectum**, *make again, repair*
ratis, ratis, f., *raft, boat, ship*

18 **quatio, quatere, quassum**, *shake, beat upon*
indocilis, -e, adj., *untrained, hard to instruct*
pauperies, pauperiei, f., *poverty*
pati: epexegetical infinitive explaining the adjective **indocilis**

19 **vetus, veteris**, adj., *old*
poculum, -i, n., *cup, drink*
Massicus, -a, -um, adj., *Massic;* **Massicum (vinum)**, *wine from the area of* **Mons Massicus**, in the Campanian region of Italy

20 **demo, demere, dempsi, demptum**, *take away, subtract*

21 **sperno, spernere, sprevi, spretum**, *remove, reject, spurn*
   viridis, -e, adj., *green, fresh, young*
   membrum, -i, n., *limb or member of the body, limb, member, part of anything*
   arbutus, -i, f., *the wild strawberry or arbutus tree*

22 **sterno, sternere, stravi, stratum**, *stretch out, spread out, level, overthrow*
   lenis, -e, adj., *smooth, gentle, mild*
   caput, capitis, n., *head, person, person's life;* (here) *source*

23 **multos castra iuvant**: Notice how simply stated this is: direct object, subject, verb. It contrasts with the much more extended phrases found with **iuvat** (4) earlier in the poem. This kind of stylistic variation is typical of Horace.
   lituus, litui, m., *curved cavalry trumpet*
   lituo: dative or ablative case with **permixtus**
   tuba, -ae, f., *straight war trumpet*

24 **permisceo, permiscere, permiscui, permixtum**, *mix together, confuse*
   sonitus, -us, m., *sound*
   matribus: dative of agent with perfect passive participle

25 **detestor, detestari, detestatus sum**, *pray against, curse;* **detestata,** although deponent, is passive in sense here
   Iuppiter, Iovis, m., *Jupiter,* supreme god of the Romans, god of sky and weather; here, by metonymy, *air, sky*
   sub Iove: under the open air

26 **venator, venatoris**, m., *hunter*
   tener, tenera, tenerum, adj., *tender, delicate, soft, young*
   coniunx, coniugis, c., *spouse, wife, husband*
   inmemor, inmemoris, adj., *forgetful, unmindful*

27 **catulus, -i**, m., *a young animal,* especially *a young dog*
   cerva, -ae, f., *deer, female deer*
   fidelis, -e, adj., *faithful*

28 **rumpo, rumpere, rupi, ruptum**, *break, shatter, destroy*
   teres, teretis, adj., *rounded, smooth, polished*
   Marsus, -a, -um, adj., *Marsian, of the Marsi,* a people of central Italy
   aper, apri, m., *wild boar*
   plaga, -ae, f., *hunting net, trap*

29 **doctus, -a, -um**, *learned, taught*
   hedera, -ae, f., *ivy*
   hederae: poetic plural

spernit, nunc viridi membra sub arbuto
stratus, nunc ad aquae lene caput sacrae;

multos castra iuvant et lituo tubae
permixtus sonitus bellaque matribus

detestata; manet sub Iove frigido   25
venator tenerae coniugis inmemor,

seu visa est catulis cerva fidelibus,
seu rupit teretes Marsus aper plagas.

me doctarum hederae praemia frontium
dis miscent superis, me gelidum nemus   30

Nympharumque leves cum Satyris chori
secernunt populo, si neque tibias

---

praemium, praemii, n., *prize, reward*
frons, frontis, f., *forehead, brow, front*

30 **dis**: dative plural; alternate form for **deis**
  misceo, miscere, miscui, mixtum, *mix, mingle*
  superus, -a, -um, adj., *upper, higher*
  gelidus, -a, -um, adj., *cold, icy*
  nemus, nemoris, n., *grove, forest*

31 **nympha, -ae**, f., *nymph*, semi-divine female spirit of nature
  levis, -e, adj., *light, swift, gentle, unimportant, fickle*
  Satyrus, -i, m., *satyr;* demi-god of wild places, especially forests, having the
    form of a man with some animal characteristics
  chorus, -i, m., *choral dance, people singing and dancing, crowd, troop*

32 **secerno, secernere, secrevi, secretum**, *separate, distinguish*
  tibia, -ae, f., *shin bone, tibia, pipe, flute*

Euterpe cohibet, nec Polyhymnia
Lesboum refugit tendere barbiton.

quodsi me lyricis vatibus inseres,   35
sublimi feriam sidera vertice.

---

33 **Euterpe, Euterpes** f., *Euterpe,* one of the Muses. The Muses, daughters of
Zeus and Mnemosyne, were goddesses who presided over the arts.
cohibeo, cohibere, cohibui, cohibitum, *hold together, hold back, confine*
Polyhymnia, -ae, f., *Polyhymnia,* one of the Muses

34 **Lesbous, -a, -um,** adj., *Lesbian,* of the Greek island of Lesbos, birthplace of
the poets Sappho and Alcaeus
refugio, refugere, refugi, *run away, avoid*
tendo, tendere, tetendi, tentum/tensum, *stretch out, extend, proceed*
barbitos, barbiti, m., *lyre*
barbiton: Greek accusative singular
Lesboum...barbiton: Notice how this phrase, which encompasses the whole
line, imitates the idea of "stretching." The word order here, as in line 14
above, is bound up with the meaning of the line. The words themselves
enact the stretching that the speaker needs from Polyhymnia.

35 **quodsi,** conj., *but if*
lyricus, -a, -um, adj., *of the lyre, lyric*
vates, vatis, c., *prophet, singer, poet*
insero, inserere, inserui, insertum, *introduce, insert, put in or among*
inseres: the subject is "you, Maecenas," the poem's addressee, but, perhaps,
"you, the reader" as well

36 **sublimis, -e,** adj., *high, raised, elevated, sublime, lofty*
ferio, ferire, *strike, hit*
sidus, sideris, n., *star, sky* (plural)
vertex, verticis, m., *head, summit*

Ode 1.5

In this ode sea, fire, and storm combine as images for erotic engage-
ment. Pyrrha, the youth, and the speaker become entangled in a vision
of love present, past, and future. While the more specific involvement of
the speaker revealed in the final stanza is something of a surprise, his
presence is felt from the beginning of the poem where he interrogates
the present relationship between Pyrrha and her young man.

Meter: fourth Asclepiadean

Quis multa gracilis te puer in rosa
perfusus liquidis urget odoribus
   grato, Pyrrha, sub antro?
    cui flavam religas comam

---

1   **quis**: used here as interrogative adjective modifying **puer**
    gracilis, -e, adj., *slender, thin*
    rosa, -ae, f., *rose*
    rosa: singular as collective
    multa...rosa: chiastic arrangement of words with **te** in the middle; the young
       man and the roses surround or embrace the direct object

2   **perfundo, perfundere, perfudi, perfusum**, *pour over, fill with*
    urgeo, urgere, ursi, *push, press upon*

3   **gratus, -a, -um**, adj., *pleasing*
    Pyrrha, -ae, f., *Pyrrha*, woman's name; the Greek word for fire (**pyr**) con-
       tained in this name may suggest a fiery nature or flame-colored hair.
    sub: possible meaning here, *down in* (Cf. *OLD* A.2.)
    antrum, i, n., *cave, hollow space*

1–3 Note the word order in these lines. In line 1, **te** is surrounded by the
    gracilis...puer, which in turn is surrounded by **multa...rosa**. Mystery

(notes contd. next page)

begins the line, with an interrogative word (**quis**), and then two adjectives (**multa** and **gracilis**). The rest of the line, which follows the diaeresis, completes the meaning of these initial words. The addressee's name is not revealed until line 3, and once again, as in line 1, she is enclosed within a frame (**grato...antro**).

4   **flavus, -a, -um**, adj., *yellow, golden, blonde, auburn*
     religo, religare, religavi, religatum: *tie, fasten behind; untie* (occasionally), cf. Catullus 63, line 84

5   **simplex, simplicis**, adj., *simple, artless, plain*
     munditia, -ae, f., *neatness, elegance*
     quotiens, adv., *how often*
     fides, fidei, f., *trust, belief, faith, honesty, honor*
     fidem: understand **mutatos** (changed) with **fidem** as well as **deos**

6   **fleo, flere, flevi, fletum**, *weep for, lament*
     asper, aspera, asperum, adj., *rough, violent*

6–7 **aspera / nigris aequora ventis**: an example of synchysis, or interlocked word order

7   **niger, nigra, nigrum**, *black, dark, gloomy*
     aequor, aequoris, n., *a flat level surface, the flat surface of the sea,* (often used in plural)

8   **emiror, emirari**, *wonder at exceedingly, be astonished at*
     insolens, insolentis, adj., *unaccustomed, excessive*

9   **fruor, frui, fructus sum**, *enjoy* (with ablative)
     credulus, -a, -um, adj., *credulous, trustful*
     aureus, -a, -um, adj., *golden, splendid*

10   **vacuus, -a, -um**, adj., *empty, free, available*

11   **nescius, -a, -um**, adj., *ignorant, unaware*
     aura, -ae, f., *breeze*

12   **fallax, fallacis**, adj., *deceitful, deceptive*
     miseri: understand **sunt** (*unhappy are they...*)

13   **me**: Note the emphatic position of this word which shifts attention from the young man and Pyrrha to the speaker of the poem. It begins a sentence and appears right after the diaeresis in the line.
     intemptatus, -a, -um, adj., *untried, unattempted*

simplex munditiis? heu quotiens fidem   5
mutatosque deos flebit et aspera
   nigris aequora ventis
     emirabitur insolens,

qui nunc te fruitur credulus aurea,
qui semper vacuam, semper amabilem   10
   sperat, nescius aurae
     fallacis. miseri, quibus

intemptata nites. me tabula sacer
votiva paries indicat uvida
   suspendisse potenti   15
     vestimenta maris deo.

---

niteo, nitere, nitui, *shine, be radiant with beauty*
tabula, -ae, f., *board, plank, writing tablet*, (votive) *tablet*

13–16 **me...deo**: These final lines add a complication to the poem, namely, the involvement of the speaker. Their almost convoluted word order reflects this complication.

14 **votiva, -a, -um**, *votive, relating to a vow*
    tabula...votiva: meter shows both are ablative
    paries, parietis, m., *wall*
    indico, indicare, indicavi, indicatum, *point out, show, declare*
    uvidus, -a, -um, *wet*
    suspendo, suspendere, suspendi, suspensum, *hang up*
    suspendisse: those who escaped from being shipwrecked often made a votive offering to Neptune, god of the sea. Here the wet garments, themselves, are hung up.
    potens, potentis, *able, powerful, potent*

16 **vestimentum, -i**, n., *clothes, garments*

Ode 1.9

This poem travels from a wide, opening vista of Mount Soracte to a final focus on the specificity of a finger—or is it the arms? Contrasts abound: youth and age, green and white, warm and cold. While the advice given to Thaliarchus (and the reader), and the speaker himself (?) may at first seem clear, the final "spin-off" of the poem does not provide closure.

Meter: Alcaic

Vides, ut alta stet nive candidum
Soracte, nec iam sustineant onus
    silvae laborantes, geluque
        flumina constiterint acuto?

---

1   **vides**: questions sometimes do occur in Latin without the enclitic, **-ne,** or another question indicator; some texts punctuate this sentence with a period instead of a question mark.
       ut: (here) interrogative adverb, *how*
       ut: introducing dependent exclamatory clauses in the subjunctive, **stet, sustineant, constiterint** (*OLD*, under **ut**, A.2.b)
       nix, nivis, f., *snow*
       candidus, -a, -um, adj., *bright, radiant, white*

2   **Soracte, Soractis,** n., *Soracte,* mountain in the south of Etruria
       sustineo, sustinere, sustinui, sustentum, *hold up, support, withstand*
       onus, oneris, n., *burden*

3   **gelu, -us,** n., *frost, cold, chill*

4   **flumen, fluminis,** n., *river, waters of a river*
       consto, constare, constiti, *stand together, stand still*
       acutus, -a, -um, *sharp, severe*

5 **dissolvo, dissolvere, dissolvi, dissolutum**, *dissolve, free*
X **frigus, frigoris**, n., *cold*
X **lignum, -i**, n., *wood* (often in plural)
super, preposition with ablative, *above*
X **focus, -i**, m., *hearth, fireplace*

6 **large**, adv., *generously, plentifully*
repono, reponere, reposui, repositum, *put down, place*
X **benigne**, adv., *lavishly, liberally*
benignius: comparative adverb

7 **depromo, depromere, deprompsi, depromptum**, *bring out, produce*
quadrimus, -a, -um, *four-year-old*
Sabinus, -a, -um, adj., *Sabine;* the Sabines were a people of central Italy.

8 **Thaliarchus, -i**, m., *Thaliarchus,* man's name, whose Greek roots mean "festivity" (**thalia**) and "ruler" (**arch**).
X **merus, -a, -um**, *pure, unmixed;* with **vinum**, or with **vinum** understood, *wine not mixed with water*
X **diota, -ae**, f., *two-handled wine jar*

9 **divus, -a, -um**, adj., *divine;* as noun, **divus, -i**, m., *god*

X 10 **sterno, sternere, stravi, stratum**, *stretch out, spread out, level, overthrow*
aequore = (in) aequore
fervidus, -a, -um, adj., *boiling, burning, hot, impetuous*

11 **deproelior, deproeliari**, *fight fiercely, struggle violently;* verb appears only here in Latin literature
cupressus, -i, f., *cypress;* the cypress had funereal associations

12 **agito, agitare, agitavi, agitatum**, *drive, agitate, excite*
ornus, -i, f., *flowering ash tree*

13 **quid...cras**: indirect question dependent on **quaerere**; **futurum** is a predicate adjective agreeing with **quid**
fuge quaerere: functionally equivalent to negative imperative, **noli** + infinitive, however considering the importance of time and its flight in this poem and others of Horace, it is best to retain the sense of "fleeing" in **fuge**.

14 **quem...cumque**: tmesis, **quemcumque**
fors, fortis, f., *chance, luck*
dierum: partitive genitive with **quemcumque**
X **lucrum, -i**, n., *profit, gain*

dissolve frigus ligna super foco   5
large reponens atque benignius
    deprome quadrimum Sabina,
        o Thaliarche, merum diota.

permitte divis cetera, qui simul
stravere ventos aequore fervido   10
    deproeliantis, nec cupressi
        nec veteres agitantur orni.

quid sit futurum cras, fuge quaerere, et
quem Fors dierum cumque dabit, lucro
    adpone, nec dulcis amores   15
        sperne puer neque tu choreas,

✕ 15 **adpono, adponere, adposui, adpositum,** *add; treat as, count as* (with **lu-crum**); **lucro**: dative; **lucro adpone,** *add to gain, count as gain*
    amores: literally "loves," can mean "love affairs"

16 **sperno, spernere, sprevi, spretum,** *remove, reject, scorn*
    puer: vocative; likely refers to Thaliarchus, but lines 13 ff. seem to offer
      more generalizing advice as well as advice to the specific addressee.
    chorea, -ae, f., *dance*
    choreas: direct object of **sperne**, along with **amores**

✗ 17 **vireo, virere, virui**, *be green, fresh, youthful*
canities, canitiei, f., *white or grey coloring, grey or white hair;* by metonymy, *old age*
virenti canities: example of **callida iunctura**, or clever arrangement, a device used often by Horace. The term comes from Horace's Ars Poetica: Epistle 2.3.47–48. The juxtaposition of these two words captures the contrasts in the poem between green and white, young and old, etc.

18 **morosus, -a, -um**, adj., *difficult*
nunc: note the emphatic position of this monosyllabic word as it begins a sentence mid-line, a sentence that extends until the end of the poem (line 24). The two **nunc**s, along with the connective words, structure these lines (18–24). The outline is: **nunc et...et...-que; nunc et...-que**.
campus, -i, m., *plain, level surface; plain, field;* often refers specifically to the Campus Martius in Rome
area, -ae, f., *open space, threshing floor*

18–19 **campus, areae, susurri**: all subjects of **repetantur**

19 **lenis, -e**, adj., *smooth, gentle, mild, soft*
sub noctem: just before night
✗ **susurrus, -i**, m., *whispering*

20 **compono, componere, composui, compositum**, *put together, arrange, compose, calm, bury*
repeto, repetere, repetivi, repetitum, *seek again, recall, resume*

21 **lateo, latere, latui**, *lie hidden;* **latentis** modifies **puellae**
✗ **proditor, proditoris**, m., *betrayer, traitor;* in apposition to **risus**
✗ **intumus, -a, -um**, adj., *innermost, most secret*

21–22 **intumo...angulo**: hyperbaton; wide separation between adjective and modifier. Note also how the adjective precedes the noun, a common practice in Horace that differs from typical Latin prose word order. The hyperbaton, here, creates a framing effect.

22 **gratus**: modifies **risus**
risus, -us, m., *laughter*
angulus, -i, m., *angle, corner*

22–23 **risus, pignus**: additional subjects of **repetantur**

23 **pignus, pigneris/pignoris**, n., *pledge, token, symbol*
deripio, deripere, deripui, dereptum, *tear down, snatch away;* **dereptum** modifies **pignus**

donec virenti canities abest
morosa. nunc et campus et areae
   lenesque sub noctem susurri
      composita repetantur hora,   20

nunc et latentis proditor intumo
gratus puellae risus ab angulo
   pignusque dereptum lacertis
      aut digito male pertinaci.

---

      lacertus, -i, m., *upper arm;* **lacertis** and **digito**, datives of separation with
      dereptum

24 **digitus, -i**, m., *finger*
    male, adv., *badly, insufficiently, wickedly, scarcely*
    pertinax, pertinacis, adj., *very tenacious, holding fast, persisting*
    male pertinaci: literally, *badly holding fast.* Some take **male** here as a quasi-
    negative almost equivalent to **non**. While such a use of **male** is not un-
    common, the adverb's literal meaning, "badly," is significant, for it would
    suggest not that the girl puts up hardly any resistance, but rather that her
    resistance is not very successful.

18–24 Lines 18–24 contain a kind of "spin-off" ending for the poem. There is a
    furtive, elusive, and indeterminate quality to these final lines. **Repetantur**
    suggests both "things to be sought" and "things to be recalled or remem-
    bered." The speaker simultaneously gives injunctions about behavior as
    well as topics for recollection. **Composita...hora** suggests both a quiet
    time (which could occur in the solitude of recollection) as well as an ar-
    ranged "date." The possible suggestion of a game between boy and girl is
    countered by the violence of the language of their interaction (**dereptum**).
    The poem ends with the ambiguous **male pertinaci**.

Ode 1.11

This ode to Leuconoe has elements of a serious, philosophical statement of Epicurean values (e.g., it is better not to foresee the future, it is better to endure whatever will be) as well as elements of an attempted seduction of Leuconoe. How one reads this poem will depend in part on how one interprets the role and interests of the speaker. Is he attempting to impart wisdom for its own sake? Or is he developing a rhetorical strategy whose purpose is winning over Leuconoe for himself? The long, yet rapidly moving, greater Asclepiadean line emphasizes the theme of the speed with which time proceeds.

Meter: fifth or greater Asclepiadean

Tu ne quaesieris (scire nefas), quem mihi, quem tibi
finem di dederint, Leuconoe, nec Babylonios

1   **ne**: with perfect subjunctives, **quaesieris** and **temptaris** in prohibition, or negative command; this construction is equivalent to **noli(te)** plus infinitive
     nefas, n., indeclinable, *crime, offense against divine law, sacrilege*
     nefas: understand **est**
     quem mihi, quem tibi: note the word order, which joins and makes parallel the speaker and his addressee

2   **finem**: take with each **quem**
     di: alternate form of **dei**, nominative plural
     dederint: perfect subjunctive in indirect question dependent on **quem finem**
     Leuconoe, Leuconoes, f., *Leuconoe*, woman's name, vocative. The name, from Greek **leukos** (clear, bright, white) and **nous** (mind) may suggest equally, "clear-minded" or "empty-minded."

2–3 **Babylonios...numeros**: Babylonian numbers; astrological tables predicting the future

3   **temptaris**: syncopated form of **tempta(ve)ris**
       ut, interrogative adverb, *how* (exclamatory use, cf. *OLD*, under **ut**, A.2.)
       melior, melius, comparative adjective, *better*
       ut melius: understand **cst**
       quidquid erit: direct object of **pati**

4   **pluris**: -is = -es (accusative plural)
       hiems, hiemis, f., *winter, storm;* metonymy for "year," but the sense of
          "winter" as a way of reckoning the years is significant for the theme of
          death that pervades the poem. Cf. Ode 1.9, where winter also leads to
          thoughts of what to enjoy in the moment.
       pluris hiemes: understand **tribuit** (present) or a future form of the verb
       tribuo, tribuere, tribui, tributum, *allot, assign;* **tribuit** (present or perfect)
       ultimam: understand **hiemem**

5   **oppositus, -a, -um**, adj., *placed against, hostile*
       debilito, debilitare, debilitavi, debilitatum, *weaken*
       pumex, pumicis, m., *pumice-stone*
       oppositis...pumicibus: note that the stones are what make the sea become
          weakened, not the reverse
6   **Tyrrhenus, -a, -um**, adj., *Tyrrhenian, Etruscan;* **mare Tyrrhenum**, *Tyrrhenian*
          Sea, the sea lying between the west coast of Italy, and Sardinia, and Sic-
          ily; direct object of **debilitat**
       sapio, sapere, sapivi, *have taste, be wise;* **sapias** operates on both a sensory
          and an intellectual level
       sapias, liques: jussive subjunctives
       vina: plural for singular
       liquo, liquare, liquavi, liquatum, *melt, strain;* the Romans strained their
          wine before drinking it to remove the sediment.
       spatium, spatii, n., *space, period of time*
       spatio brevi: probably best taken as a causal ablative (because of the brief
          time [of our lives]) or (because of the brief time [appropriate for our
          hopes])

7   **reseco, resecare, resecui, resectum**, *cut back, prune, restrain*
       reseces: jussive subjunctive, like **sapias, liques**
       fugerit: effective use of the future perfect tense; while the conversation takes
          place, time "will have fled."
       invidus, -a, -um, adj., *envious, jealous;* **invida** personifies time; **invida aetas**
          almost becomes a third party jealous of Leuconoe and the speaker

8   **aetas, aetatis**, f., *time, age*
       carpo, carpere, carpsi, carptum, *pluck, seize*
       carpe diem: this Horatian phrase has become very famous. For poems in
          English that utilize the **carpe diem** theme, see Marvell's "To his Coy
          Mistress," and Herrick's "To the Virgins, to make much of Time."

temptaris numeros. ut melius, quidquid erit, pati!
seu pluris hiemes, seu tribuit Iuppiter ultimam,

quae nunc oppositis debilitat pumicibus mare   5
Tyrrhenum: sapias, vina liques et spatio brevi

spem longam reseces. dum loquimur, fugerit invida
aetas: carpe diem, quam minimum credula postero.

---

quam minimum: **quam** with the superlative (*as...as possible*); *to the least
   extent possible*
credulus, -a, -um, adj., *credulous, trustful;* takes dative
posterus, -a, -um, adj., *next, following, future, later*
postero: this adjective does not modify a noun; understand **diei**, (because of
   diem earlier in the line) or, somewhat more humorously, **viro**

Ode 1.13

In this poem the speaker's desire for Lydia is mediated by the relationship Lydia has with Telephus. Her enthusiastic praise of Telephus' body and the evidence upon her body of their sexual activity are what drive the speaker's reactions. While he attempts to dissuade Lydia from her relationship with Telephus, the wildness of his own reactions makes him seem little different from his version of Telephus. The poem ends on a somewhat ambiguous note. Who are the happy ones? And how do they relate to the trio of Lydia, Telephus, and the speaker?

Meter: second Asclepiadean

Cum tu, Lydia, Telephi
    cervicem roseam, cerea Telephi
laudas brachia, vae meum
    fervens difficili bile tumet iecur.

---

1   **Lydia, -ae**, f., *Lydia*, woman's name
    Telephus, -i, m., *Telephus*, man's name; note the repetition of his name at the end of the next line

2   **cervix, cervicis**, f., *neck*
    roseus, -a, -um, adj., *rosy*
    cereus, -a, -um, adj., *waxen, supple*

3   **brachium, brachii**, n., *arm*
    vae, interjection, *alas, woe*

3–4 **meum...iecur**: hyperbaton; cf. note on Ode 1.9.21–22

4   **fervens, ferventis**, adj., *boiling, seething*
    bilis, bilis, f., *gall, bile, anger*

(notes contd. next page)

tumeo, tumere, tumui, *swell*

✕ **iecur, iecoris**, n., *liver, the seat of the feelings;* bile, secreted by the liver, was thought to produce anger

6 **certus, -a, -um**, adj., *certain, definite*
   sedes, sedis, f., *seat, site, home*
   umor, umoris, m., *moisture, liquid*
✕ **gena, -ae**, f., *cheek*

7 **furtim**, adv., *secretly*
   labor, labi, lapsus sum, *glide, slip, pass*
✕ **arguo, arguere, argui, argutum**, *prove, show*

8 **quam**: modifies **penitus**
   lentus, -a, -um, adj., *slow, lingering, unresponsive*
   penitus, adv., *deeply*
   macero, macerare, maceravi, maceratum, *soften, make weak, torment*

9 **uro, urere, ussi, ustum**, *burn;* in passive, *be on fire*
   seu: correlative with **sive** (11)
   candidus, -a, -um, adj., *bright, radiant, white*

10 **turpo, turpare, turpavi, turpatum**, *make ugly*
   turparunt: syncopated form of **turpa(ve)runt**
   umerus, -i, m., *shoulder*
   merus, -a, -um, adj., *pure, unmixed*

✕ 11 **rixa, -ae**, f., *fight*
   puer, pueri, m., *boy, non-adult male, male beloved,* (young) *male slave*
   furens, furentis adj., *mad, wild*

12 **inprimo, inprimere, inpressi, inpressum**, *press upon*
   memor, memoris, adj., *mindful, remembering*
   labrum, -i, n., *lip*
   nota, -ae, f., *mark, sign, wine of a specified quality or vintage*

14 **perpetuus, -a, -um**, adj., *continuing, permanent, connected*
   barbare, adv., *roughly, cruelly*

15 **laedo, laedere, laesi, laesum**, *harm, strike*
   osculum, -i, n., *kiss, mouth, lips* (as used in kissing)
   venus, veneris, f., *Venus,* Roman goddess of love; *love, charm, sexual activity; best throw at dice*

16 **quinta...parte**: fifth part = one-fifth

tunc nec mens mihi, nec color   5
    certa sede manet, umor et in genas
furtim labitur arguens,
    quam lentis penitus macerer ignibus.

uror, seu tibi candidos
    turparunt umeros inmodicae mero   10
rixae, sive puer furens
    inpressit memorem dente labris notam.

non, si me satis audias,
    speres perpetuum dulcia barbare
laedentem oscula, quae Venus   15
    quinta parte sui nectaris imbuit.

---

nectar, nectaris, n., *nectar,* drink of the gods
imbuo, imbuere, imbui, imbutum, *wet, fill, inspire*
imbuit: present or perfect

felices ter et amplius,
   quos inrupta tenet copula, nec malis
divolsus querimoniis
   suprema citius solvet amor die.   **20**

17–20   Commentators have traditionally taken **inrupta** to mean "unbroken" and have understood **nec** twice, once with **divolsus** and again with **solvet**. **Inrupta,** as "unbroken," is unprecedented in Latin and taking **nec** twice, while possible, is not necessary. A traditional reading of the last four lines yields the following: "Happy three times and more are those whom an *unbroken* bond holds, and whose love, torn apart by *no* serious complaints, will *not* loosen them sooner than the final day!" Another possible reading, which allows for the standard meaning of **inrupta,** would be: "Happy three times and more are those whom an *interrupted* bond holds and a love torn apart by serious complaints will *not* loosen sooner than the final day!" The former reading describes an idealized love with no difficulties that lasts until the "final day." The latter reading describes a love whose power is based not on its problem-free nature, but rather on its ability to endure despite difficulties. Cf. Ancona, *Time and the Erotic in Horace's Odes,* 121–28, for an argument in favor of the latter reading.

17 **ter**, adv., *three times*
     amplius, adv., *more*

18 **inruptus, -a, -um**, *broken into, interrupted; unbroken*
     copula, -ae, f., *bond, link*

19 **divello, divellere, divelli, divolsum**, *tear apart*
     querimonia, -ae, f., *complaint*

20 **citius**, adv., *quicker, sooner*
     solvo, solvere, solvi, solutum, *loosen, break up*
     suprema...die: *final day,* i.e., *death*

Ode 1.22

Catullus wrote only two poems in the Sapphic meter, Poems 11 and 51. Poem 51 is Catullus' translation or adaptation of Sappho's famous Poem 31, which details the experiencing of desire. Catullus adapts that poem for his own purposes, in part by making "Lesbia" its addressee. Poem 11, his only other poem in Sapphics, is a blunt farewell to his girlfriend. Horace clearly had Sappho 31 and Catullus Poems 11 and 51 in mind when composing this poem. As is mentioned below in the notes, there are specific echoes of their language. The poet/lover, though, in this poem is very different from those in Sappho and Catullus. This poet/lover is not overwhelmed by desire, but rather constructs a love that incorporates the notion of invulnerability.

Meter: Sapphic

Integer vitae scelerisque purus
non eget Mauris iaculis neque arcu,
nec venenatis gravida sagittis,
    Fusce, pharetra,

---

1   **integer, integra, integrum**, adj., *whole, untouched, upright*
    vitae: genitive of reference, stating respect with which the adjective, **integer**, is applicable; in classical Latin an ablative of respect would be used more typically
    scelus, sceleris, n., *wrongdoing, crime, affliction*
    sceleris: genitive of reference with **purus**; see definition of this genitive above (note on **vitae**)
    integer...purus: note the chiastic arrangement of the words,
        a   b   b   a
    integer vitae scelerisque purus.

(notes contd. next page)

2 **egeo, egere, egui**, *need, want* (with ablative)
Maurus, -a, -um, adj., *Moorish, African*
iaculum, -i, n., *javelin*
arcus, -us, m., *bow*

3 **venenatus, -a, -um**, adj., *poisonous*
gravidus, -a, -um, adj., *laden, weighed down*

4 **Fuscus, -i**, m., *Aristius Fuscus,* Horace's literary friend in Satire 1.10.83, the person to whom Epistle 1.10 is addressed—and there he and Horace are linked as "twins," but separated by their love for the city and the country, respectively—and the character who refuses to save Horace from his unwanted companion in Satire 1.9 (**Ibam forte via sacra**). His appearance here in a poem about the poet's invulnerability can be seen as an "answer" to his refusal to help the poet in Satire 1.9. In the city the poet needed help and did not receive it from Fuscus; here, in the country and in remote lands he claims he is invulnerable.
pharetra, -ae, f., *quiver*

5 **Syrtis, Syrtis**, f., *Syrtis* (especially plural), name of two areas of sandy flats on the coast between Carthage and Cyrene; whole desert region next to this coast. Cato the Younger, the anti-Caesarian Stoic who chose to commit suicide rather than give in to the opposition, made a famous march across the Syrtes in 47 B.C.E. The integrity for which Cato was known may be suggested by the first word of this poem, **integer.**
iter, itineris, n., *journey*
aestuosus, -a, -um, adj., *very hot, agitated*

5–6 **sive...sive**: The form in which the catalog of places is presented recalls Catullus Poem 11 whose geographical catalog also repeats the word **sive** in enumerating alternatives.

7 **Caucasus, -i**, m., *Caucasus Mountains.* The Caucasus may evoke Pompey the Great, the first Roman general to have reached the area, or perhaps Alexander the Great who, while not reaching the Caucasus, did reach the Hindu-Kush, which was later identified with the Caucasus.
quae loca: here, the antecedent (**loca**) is incorporated into the relative clause
fabulosus, -a, -um, adj., *legendary, storied*

8 **lambo, lambere, lambi**, *lick, wash*
Hydaspes, Hydaspis, m., *Hydaspes,* tributary of river Indus, the Jhelum; Horace calls this river **fuscus** in Satire 2.8.14. **Fuscus, -a, -um** is an adjective meaning "dark." Hydaspes, then, would recall Aristius Fuscus. For further punning on Fuscus' name, cf. note on Apollo, line 78 of Satire 1.9.

sive per Syrtis iter aestuosas   5
sive facturus per inhospitalem
Caucasum, vel quae loca fabulosus
     lambit Hydaspes.

namque me silva lupus in Sabina,
dum meam canto Lalagen et ultra   10
terminum curis vagor expeditis,
     fugit inermem,

[handwritten annotation: wolf fled me unarmed in a Sabine wood, while I was singing my Lalage]

That Horace calls the Hydaspes **fabulosus** is self-referential, for the river
is "storied" in part because Horace has *written* about it before, in Satire
2.8. The river Hydaspes is associated with Alexander the Great, who in
326 B.C.E. won a great military victory there and sailed down the river.

9   **lupus, -i**, m., *wolf*
     silva…in Sabina: Horace's country home, his Sabine farm, was located in
        Sabine territory.

10   **canto, cantare, cantavi, cantatum**, *sing, sing about, recite*
     Lalage, Lalages, f., *Lalage,* woman's name; Greek for "chatterer"
     Lalagen: Greek accusative
     ultra, preposition with accusative, *beyond*

11   **terminus, -i**, m., *boundary line, limit*
     cura, -ae, f., *care, concern, worry, a person or thing constituting an object of
        care*
     vagor, vagari, vagatus sum, *wander*
     expedio, expedire, expedivi, expeditum, *free, extricate, release*

12   **fugit**: perfect tense, not present, because the "u" is long
     inermis, -e, adj., *unarmed*

13 **portentum, -i**, n., *portent, abnormal phenomenon*
   quale portentum: accusative, direct object of **alit** (14)

14 **Daunias, Dauniadis**, f., *Apulia,* region of southeastern Italy; Daunus was a
      legendary king of Apulia; Horace comes from the town of Venusia on the
      border between Apulia and Lucania.
   alo, alere, alui, altum, *nourish*
   aesculetum, -i, n., *oak forest*

15 **Iuba, -ae**, m., *Juba,* Juba I, Numidian king who supported Pompey in the
      civil war; Juba II, son of Juba I, fought for Octavian (Augustus) at the
      battle of Actium, made king of Maurentania by Augustus, known for his learning
   tellus, telluris, f., *land, earth, country, ground*
   genero, generare, generavi, generatum, *produce, create*

16 **aridus, -a, -um**, adj., *dry*
   nutrix, nutricis, f., *nurse,* especially a *wet-nurse*
   arida nutrix: oxymoron

17 **pone**: repeated as the first word of line 21; the anaphora makes more em-
      phatic the bold commands
   piger, pigra, pigrum, adj., *inactive, lazy*
   campus, -i, m., *plain, level surface; plain, field*

18 **aestivus, -a, -um**, adj., *summer*
   recreo, recreare, recreavi, recreatum, *recreate, restore, revive*
   aura, -ae, f., *breeze*

19 **latus, lateris**, n., *side, extreme part or region, flank, lungs, body*
   quod latus mundi: parallel to **ubi...aura** (17–18); the antecedent, **latus
      (mundi)**, is incorporated into the relative clause; cf. **quae loca** (7) above
   mundus, -i, m., *world*
   nebula, -ae, f., *mist, fog*

20 **Iuppiter**: (with **malus**, line 19), *bad weather* (by metonymy)

21 **pone** (understand **me** again)
   currus, currus, m., *chariot.* The chariot of the sun is driven across the sky
      each day by the god of the sun; the Tropics would represent the area
      where his chariot gets too near the earth.
   nimium, adv., *too, too much, very*
   propinquus, -a, -um, adj., *near, neighboring*
   propinqui is genitive, modifying **solis** (22); understand the idea of **terra** (22)
      with **nimium propinqui** (too near the earth), as well as in its own phrase

[handwritten: in such a way a phenomena]

quale portentum neque militaris
Daunias latis alit aesculetis, *[handwritten: Apulia nourished in such a way]*
nec Iubae tellus generat, leonum *[handwritten: a phenomena the wide oak forest w/ military]*   15
    arida nutrix.
[handwritten: Land did not had not created, the dry nurse of a lions. of Nuba]

pone me, pigris ubi nulla campis *[handwritten: place me, where no tree]*
arbor aestiva recreatur aura, *[handwritten: is revived by the summer breeze]*
quod latus mundi nebulae malusque *[handwritten: in the lazy field,]*
    Iuppiter urget, *[handwritten: where god Jupiter urges]*   20
[handwritten: the which side of the world of fog]

pone sub curru nimium propinqui
solis in terra domibus negata:
dulce ridentem Lalagen amabo,
    dulce loquentem.

[handwritten: place under too much heat chariot of the sun in the lands denied by houses: I will love the sweet laughing Lalage, sweet talking]

---

22 **domibus**: dative because of **negata** (22)

23 **dulce**: adverb

23–24 These two lines echo both Catullus 51.5 (**dulce ridentem** "sweetly laughing") and Sappho 31.3–5 (**adu phoneisas...kai gelaisas imeroen** "sweetly speaking...and laughing in a lovely manner"). Note that Horace "reintroduces" Sappho's "sweetly speaking" which Catullus chooses not to follow in his adaptation of Sappho 31.

24 **dulce**: adverb

Ode 1.23

In this poem the speaker's rhetorical goal is to persuade Chloe that she has nothing to fear from him. He describes her fears as "empty." Yet the language he uses to persuade her is filled with violent and aggressive imagery, e.g., lions and tigers chasing her to break her. What is the effect of this clash between the literal meaning of his words and the emotions that his words evoke?

Meter: fourth Asclepiadean

Vitas inuleo me similis, Chloe,
quaerenti pavidam montibus aviis
   matrem non sine vano
     aurarum et siluae metu.

---

1   **vito, vitare, vitavi, vitatum,** *avoid, shun*
   in(n)uleus, -i, m., *fawn*
   inuleo: dative because of **similis**
   Chloe, Chloes, f., *Chloe,* woman's name; the **oe** is not a diphthong in the name; two syllable word. Chloe in Greek means "green bud" or "shoot." The name appears as an epithet of the Greek goddess of agriculture, Demeter, while there is inscriptional evidence of a festival of Demeter Chloe and Kore (which refers to her daughter, Persephone) at Eleusis in Greece. Thus through its association with Demeter, the name Chloe suggests simultaneously both female youth (Persephone) and female maturity (Demeter). Horace's use of this name in the poem evokes both the image of spring, and the life cycle of women.
   vitas...Chloe: Note the word order; **me** is in the center, surrounded immediately by **inuleo** and **similis** (words related to Chloe), and further surrounded by more Chloe words (**vitas** and **Chloe**).

(notes contd. next page)

2   **pavidus, -a, -um**, adj., *frightened, terrified, trembling, fearful*
     montibus: ablative of place where; **in** frequently omitted in poetry
     avius, -a, -um, adj., *pathless, remote*

3   **non sine**: litotes
     vanus, -a, -um, adj., *empty, groundless, imaginary*

4   **aura, -ae**, f., *breeze*
     siluae: three syllables here; the letter *v/u* is being treated as a vowel, not a
          consonant
     metus, -us, m., *fear*

5   **mobilis, -e**, adj., *moveable, changeable, inconstant, pliant*
     ver, veris, n., *spring*
     inhorresco, inhorrescere, inhorrui, *begin to tremble, bristle, become stiffly
          erect*

6   **adventus, -us**, m., *arrival, approach*
     folium, folii, n., *leaf*
     viridis, -e, adj., *green, fresh, young*
     rubus, -i, m., *bramble, prickly bush*

7   **dimoveo, dimovere, dimovi, dimotum**, *move apart, separate*
     dimovere: **-ere**, alternate form of the third person plural perfect tense ending,
          -erunt
     lacerta, -ae, f., *lizard*

6–7 **virides rubum/dimovere lacertae**: can be seen as sexual imagery

8   **cor, cordis**, n., *heart*
     genu, -us, n., *knee*
     tremo, tremere, tremui, *tremble, quiver*

9   **atqui**, conj., *but, nevertheless*
     tigris, tigris/tigridis, f., *tiger*
     asper, aspera, asperum, adj., *fierce, rough*

10   **Gaetulus, -a, -um**, adj., *Gaetulian, of Gaetulia*, region of northwest Africa
          known for its lions
     frango, frangere, fregi, fractum, *break, crush*
     frangere: infinitive expressing purpose
     persequor, persequi, persecutus sum, *pursue, chase*

9–10   **atqui...persequor**: Note how the literal sense of these two lines (I am not
          chasing you etc.) is countered by the fierceness of the imagery (lion and

nam seu mobilibus veris inhorruit   5
adventus foliis, seu virides rubum
    dimovere lacertae,
        et corde et genibus tremit.

atqui non ego te tigris ut aspera
Gaetulusve leo frangere persequor: 10
    tandem desine matrem
        tempestiva sequi viro.

       tiger) and the word order, which has "I" following/pursuing "you" (**ego te**) and **persequor** as the final word, with its negative (**non**) long forgotten.

11 **desino, desinere, desii, desitum**, *stop, cease*
    desine: takes infinitive, **sequi**
    matrem: direct object of **sequi**

11–12 Note how the word order allows for words to affect each other that do not depend on each other grammatically: **desine** at first seems to have **matrem** as its direct object (stop the mother); **sequi viro** suggests following a man, even though **viro** is not its grammatical object.

12 **tempestivus, -a, -um**, adj., *timely, seasonable, ripe*
    viro: dative, with **tempestiva**

Ode 1.24

This ode is a lament for Quintilius, addressed to Vergil. Here we see death, a frequent theme in Horace, personalized by the specificity of a friend's death as well as generalized about through the use of the mythic figures, Mercury and Orpheus. Here, the power of song creates a space for Horace and Vergil to mourn. Perhaps Vergil's "patience" in part entails being open to the "lightening" effect of Horace's song.

Meter: third Asclepiadean

Quis desiderio sit pudor aut modus
tam cari capitis? praecipe lugubris
cantus, Melpomene, cui liquidam pater
    vocem cum cithara dedit.

---

1   **quis**: for **qui**, the interrogative adjective; modifies **pudor** and **modus**
     desiderium, desiderii, n., *desire, longing* (for something or someone lost or
          absent)
     sit: deliberative subjunctive
     pudor, pudoris, m., *restraint, feeling of shame*
     modus, -i, m., *limit, way, rhythmic pattern;* in plural, *poetry*

2   **caput, capitis**, n., *head, person, person's life*
     cari capitis: objective genitive, with **desiderio**
     praecipio, praecipere, praecepi, praeceptum, *take beforehand, teach*
     lugubris, -e, adj., *mournful*
     lugubris: -is ending, alternate accusative plural ending for **-es**

3   **cantus, -us**, m., *singing, song, poetry*
     Melpomene, Melpomenes, f., *Melpomene*, one of the Muses (tragedy)
     liquidus, -a, -um, adj., *flowing, clear, melodious, liquid*
     pater: Jupiter; the Muses were daughters of Jupiter and Mnemosyne (Memory)

4   **cithara, -ae**, f., *lyre*

5 **ergo**, particle, *then, consequently*
    Quintilius, Quintilii, m., *Quintilius Varus*, friend of Horace and Vergil; he is
        the addressee of Ode 1.18 as well; Horace praises him in Epistle 2.3 (Ars
        Poetica) 438 ff. as an honest and frank critic of others' writing.
    perpetuus, -a, -um, adj., *continuing, permanent, connected*
    sopor, soporis, m., *sleep*

6 **urgeo, urgere, ursi**, *push, press upon*
    cui, connecting relative pronoun; dative because of **parem** (8)
    iustitia, -ae, f., *justice*

6–7 **Pudor, Fides, Veritas**: personified virtues

7 **fides, fidei**, f., *trust, belief, faith, honesty, honor*
    nudaque Veritas: cf. Quintilius' honest criticism mentioned above, line 5.

9 **multis...bonis**: datives, parallel with **nulli** and **tibi** (10)
    flebilis, -e, adj., *worthy of tears, lamentable*
    occido, occidere, occidi, occasum, *fall, die*
    occidit: present or perfect tense

9–10 **flebilis...flebilior**: the figura etymologica underscores the idea of lament

10 **Vergilius, Vergilii**, m., *Publius Vergilius Maro* (70–19 b.c.e.), Horace's friend
    and contemporary; author of the *Aeneid, Eclogues*, and *Georgics*; it was
    Vergil who introduced Horace to Maecenas, who became his friend and
    supporter.

11 **frustra**, adv., *in vain, to no purpose*
    pius, -a, -um, adj., *dutiful, devoted*
    pius: Note the use of this epithet of Aeneas' to describe Vergil, author of the
    Aeneid.
    heu, interjection expressing grief or pain, *oh, alas*
    credo, credere, credidi, creditum, *trust, believe, entrust*
    non ita creditum: i.e., not entrusted to you on the basis that the gods would
    return him if asked

12 **posco, poscere, poposci**, *demand*
    Quintilium, deos: both accusatives with **poscis**, which takes the accusative
    of the thing asked for and of the individual asked

13–18 Note the length and complexity of the long sentence that spans these six
    lines in contrast with the simple statement "**durum**" that follows it. The
    abruptness of **durum** and the brief words that follow underscores the
    theme of the finality of death.

ergo Quintilium perpetuus sopor   5
urget? cui Pudor et Iustitiae soror,
incorrupta Fides nudaque Veritas
    quando ullum inveniet parem?

multis ille bonis flebilis occidit,
nulli flebilior, quam tibi, Vergili.   10
tu, frustra pius, heu, non ita creditum
    poscis Quintilium deos.

quid, si Threicio blandius Orpheo
auditam moderere arboribus fidem,
num vanae redeat sanguis imagini,   15
    quam virga semel horrida

---

13 **Threicius, -a, -um**, adj., *Thracian*
  blandus, -a, -um, adj., *charming, persuasive, seductive*
  Orpheus, -i, m., *Orpheus;* he was able to charm animals and nature with his
      music; Vergil tells the story of Orpheus and Eurydice in his fourth Georgic.

14 **moderor, moderari, moderatus sum**, *handle, control;* (here) *play*
  moderere: alternate form of second person singular, **modereris**
  arboribus: dative of agent with perfect passive participle
  fides, fidis, f., *lyre*

15 **vanus, -a, -um**, adj., *empty, groundless, imaginary*
  imago, imaginis, f., *image, likeness, shape*

16 **virga, -ae**, f., *staff, wand*
  virga: Mercury's caduceus, with which he leads the dead to the underworld
  horridus, -a, -um, adj., *rough, harsh, dreadful*

non lenis precibus fata recludere
nigro compulerit Mercurius gregi?
durum, sed levius fit patientia,
    quicquid corrigere est nefas.   20

17 **non lenis**: litotes
    lenis, -e, adj., *smooth, gentle, mild, soft*
    prex, precis, f., *prayer*
    precibus: dative, with **recludere**
    fatum, -i, n., *fate;* plural, *the Fates*
    recludo, recludere, reclusi, reclusum, *open up, undo*
    recludere: epexegetical infinitive explaining the adjective **lenis**

18 **niger, nigra, nigrum**, adj., *black, dark, gloomy*
    compello, compellere, compuli, compulsum, *bring together, drive together,*
      round up
    Mercurius, Mercurii, m., *Mercury,* son of Jupiter and Maia
    grex, gregis, m., *flock, herd, company, crowd*

19 **durum**: understand **est**
    levis, -e, adj., *light, swift, gentle, unimportant, fickle*
    levius: predicate adjective modifying **quicquid**
    patientia: ablative of means

20 **corrigo, corrigere, correxi, correctum**, *make straight, correct, remedy*
    nefas, n., indeclinable, *crime, offense against divine law, sacrilege*

Ode 1.25

The comparative word **parcius**, the poem's first word, signals a major theme of the poem: change over time. This theme is picked up by **minus et minus iam** and then by **invicem**, which sends the poem careening off into a future imagined (hoped for?) by the speaker. It is worth thinking about the effect of comparing the "future" Lydia to a mare in heat and dry leaves, and associating her with winter and Bacchic revels. What does this suggest about cultural expectations regarding the decorousness of active desire in the older woman?

Meter: Sapphic

Parcius iunctas quatiunt fenestras
iactibus crebris iuvenes protervi,
nec tibi somnos adimunt, amatque
    ianua limen,

---

1   **parce**, adv., *sparingly*
    parcius: *more sparingly,* hence, *less often*
    iungo, iungere, iunxi, iunctum, *join, yoke, mate*
    iunctas...fenestras: windows with shutters, closed
    quatio, quatere, quassum, *shake, beat upon*

2   **iactus, -us**, m., *throwing, hurling*
    iactibus: the idea is that those interested in Lydia throw stones at her windows to get her attention
    creber, crebra, crebrum, adj., *crowded together, frequent*
    protervus, -am -um, adj., *bold, violent*

3   **tibi**: dative of separation
    somnus, -i, m., *sleep*
    adimo, adimere, ademi, ademptum, *take away*

(notes contd. next page)

nec tibi somnos adimunt: normally, not losing sleep might be thought of as positive; here, it is a sign of declining interest in Lydia

amatque: **amo** can mean "keep to," but maintaining the erotic sense of "loves" seems useful in this context of Lydia becoming a less sought-after object of others' desire; cf. the use of this same verb with an inanimate subject in Ode 2.3.9–10.

4   **ianua, -ae**, f., *door*
    limen, liminis, n., *threshold*

5   **multum**, adv., *much*
    multum: can modify **facilis** or **movebat**
    facilis: can be nominative singular modifying **quae**, which has as its antecedent, **ianua**, or can modify **cardines**, as an accusative plural (**-is** for **-es**)

6   **cardo, cardinis**, m., *hinge*

7   **tuo**: substantive use of the adjective
    pereo, perire, perii, peritum, *perish, die*
    longas…noctes: accusative of extent of time

7–8   These are the words of a shut-out lover who pines away for his beloved in front of her house door. This type of serenade is called a **paraclausithyron**, Greek for "at the closed door."

8   **Lydia, -ae**, f., *Lydia*, woman's name
    dormis: notice the repetition of the idea of sleep from line 3

9   **invicem**, adv., *in turn*
    invicem: this word switches the poem into a future imagined by the speaker
    moechus, -i, m., *adulterer*
    anus, -us, f., *old woman*
    adrogans, adrogantis, adj., *arrogant, insolent*

10   **fleo, flere, flevi, fletum**, *weep for, lament*
    levis, -e, adj., *light, swift, gentle, unimportant, fickle*
    angiportus, -us, m., *alley*
    in solo…angiportu: Horace's language recalls the abusive description of Lesbia in Catullus 58.4–5, where Lesbia engages in sexual activity in crossroads and alleys: **nunc in quadriviis et angiportis/glubit magnanimi Remi nepotes.**

11   **Thracius, -a, -um**, adj., *Thracian*
    bacchor, bacchari, bacchatus sum, *celebrate the festival of Bacchus, rave, rage*

quae prius multum facilis movebat 5
cardines. audis minus et minus iam:
'me tuo longas pereunte noctes,
　　Lydia, dormis?'

invicem moechos anus adrogantis
flebis in solo levis angiportu, 10
Thracio bacchante magis sub inter-
　　lunia vento,

---

bacchante: note the diaeresis delayed until after the sixth syllable; this un-
common metrical variation heightens the sense of things out of control

 11–12　**interlunium, interlunii**, n., *the period between the old moon and the new*
inter-lunia: I vary from the text here, adding a hyphen between **inter** and
lunia, as most other texts do, since **interlunia** is one word. For another
line end separating a word in Sapphic meter, cf. **uxorius**, Ode 1.2.19–20.
This is an example of synapheia, or the joining together of two lines as if
they were one.

13   **tibi**: dative of reference
     flagrans, flagrantis, adj., *hot, blazing, passionate*
     libido, libidinis, f., *desire, lust*

14   **matres...equorum**: the lust of mares in heat was a traditional theme
     soleo, solere, solitus sum, *be accustomed*
     furio, furiare, furiavi, furiatum, *madden*

15   **saevio, saevire, saevii, saevitum**, *rage, rave*
     circa, preposition with accusative, *around*
     iecur, iecoris, n., *liver, the seat of the feelings*
     ulcerosus, -a, -um, adj., *full of ulcers or sores*

16   **non sine**: litotes; ironic or sarcastic
     questus, -us, m., *complaint, lament*

17   **laetus, -a, -um**, *happy, glad, fertile*
     laeta: very strategic placing of the word **laeta**. Coming right after a lengthy description of Lydia, one expects it to describe *her*, however it belongs to the clause which the postpositive **quod** introduces and one discovers only after reaching the word **pubes**, which is feminine, that **laeta** modifies *it*. This placement of **laeta** *before* the word that would more typically introduce the clause to which **laeta** belongs is typical of Horace's style and can prove tricky for first-time readers of Horace.
     pubes, pubis, f., *adult population, age of puberty, the pubic region*
     hedera, -ae, f., *ivy*
     vireo, virere, virui, *be green, youthful, fresh*

17–19   There are three items listed here (with their modifiers): ivy, myrtle, and (dry) leaves. Depending on how one takes **atque** (below), ivy *and* myrtle are enjoyed more by the youth, or ivy is enjoyed more *than* myrtle. In either scenario, the dry leaves are an object for dismissal. The latter may be a better interpretation for it continues the comparative idea that is so central to the poem, starting with **parcius** and continuing with **minus et minus**. In any case, the ivy, myrtle, and dry leaves are metaphors for three stages of a woman's life: youth, maturity, and old age.

18   **gaudeo, gaudere, gavisus sum**, *rejoice, delight in* (with ablative)
     gaudeat: subjunctive in implied indirect statement introduced by **quod**; cf.
        dedicet below, line 20
     pullus, -a, -um, adj., *gray, somber*
     pulla: ablative with **myrto**, which is feminine
     atque, conj., *and;* after comparatives, *than* (*OLD* 15); some take **atque** as "and," others as "than."

cum tibi flagrans amor et libido,
quae solet matres furiare equorum,
saeviet circa iecur ulcerosum,   15
    non sine questu,

laeta quod pubes hedera virenti
gaudeat pulla magis atque myrto,
aridas frondes hiemis sodali
    dedicet Hebro.   20

---

myrtus, -i, f., *myrtle*

19 **aridus, -a, -um**, adj., *dry*
    frons, frondis, f., *leaf*
    hiems, hiemis, f., *winter, storm*
    sodalis, sodalis, m., *companion*

20 **dedico, dedicare, dedicavi, dedicatum**, *dedicate*
    dedicet: asyndeton; adds to the dismissive tone; cf. note on **gaudeat** above,
        line 18
    Hebrus, -i, m., *Hebrus*, river in Thrace
    Hebro: this is the manuscript reading; a conjecture that some texts adopt is
        Euro, from **Eurus, -i**, m., *Eurus, the east wind*

Ode 1.37

The historical context for this ode is the defeat of Octavian's enemy, Cleopatra VII of Egypt, at the battle of Actium off the west coast of Greece in 31 B.C.E. Cleopatra and Antony were the final obstacles standing in the way of Octavian's total power. After their defeat at Actium, Antony and Cleopatra returned to Alexandria, Egypt. When their land forces were defeated and Octavian entered Alexandria, both committed suicide. The fact that Horace does not mention Antony in the poem helps to portray the conflict not as a civil war, but rather as a foreign threat.

The endings of Horace's odes are frequently a source of interest (and sometimes of surprise). In this ode Horace follows five stanzas of celebration about the defeat of a **fatale monstrum** with an extended evocation in the last three stanzas of Cleopatra's nobility in the face of defeat. What are we to make of this? Does this express ambivalence on the part of Horace about Octavian's defeat of his final obstacle to complete rule? Or does it make Octavian's conquest all the more outstanding because of the notable dignity of the one he has conquered?

Meter: Alcaic

Nunc est bibendum, nunc pede libero
pulsanda tellus, nunc Saliaribus
   ornare pulvinar deorum
      tempus erat dapibus, sodales.

---

1   **bibo, bibere, bibi**, *drink*
    est bibendum: passive periphrastic construction
    pede libero: suggests the physical freedom to dance unrestrained as well as the political freedom to exist unenslaved; there also may be a sense here of "metrical" freedom (cf. notes on **nefas**, line 5, and **lymphatam**, line 14, below)

(notes contd. next page)

1-2 **Nunc...nunc...nunc**: note the anaphora, which heightens the importance of
the need for present celebration. The beginning of the poem echoes a
fragment of Alcaeus (Lobel-Page Z,8) in which the poet calls for drinking
to celebrate the death of the tyrant, Myrsilus, on Lesbos.

2 **pulso, pulsare, pulsavi, pulsatum**, *beat, strike repeatedly*
pulsanda: understand **est** from line 1; passive periphrastic construction
tellus, telluris, f., *land, earth, country, ground*
Saliaris, -e, adj., *of the Salii*, who were a group of priests (at Rome usually
associated with Mars) who performed ritual dances on certain occasions.
They were known for the sumptuousness of their banquets
(**Saliaribus...dapibus**, 2–4).

3 **orno, ornare, ornavi, ornatum**, *prepare, decorate, adorn, honor* (with ablative)
pulvinar, pulvinaris, n., *sacred couch on which the image of a god was placed;*
images of the gods were put on these couches for a ceremony the Romans
took over from the Greeks called the **lectisternium,** in which the gods
were treated as guests at a meal.

4 **erat**: the imperfect tense with **nunc** implies that the appropriate moment for
celebration has existed for some time
daps, dapis, f., *feast, banquet*
sodalis, sodalis, m., *companion*

5 **antehac**, adv., *previously*
antehac: two syllables, by synizesis
nefas, n., indeclinable, *crime, offense against divine law, sacrilege*
nefas: understand **erat**
nefas: Normally the first two lines of the Alcaic meter have a diaeresis after
the fifth syllable. That pattern, which is broken only here and in line 14 of
this poem, seems to have the effect here of speeding up the line and thus
hastening the bringing out of the wine.
depromo, depromere, deprompsi, depromptum, *bring out, produce*
Caecubum, -i, n., *choice wine from Caecubum*, a district in south Latium

6 **cella, -ae**, f., *storeroom, wine cellar*
avitus, -a, -um, adj., *of a grandfather, ancestral*
Capitolium, Capitolii, n., *Capitolium*, the Capitoline hill in Rome on which
the Capitoline gods, Jupiter, Juno, and Minerva, were worshipped

6-7 **Capitolio/regina**: the juxtaposition of these two words emphasizes Cleopatra's
threat to Roman rule

7 **demens, dementis**, adj., *out of one's senses, mad, insane*

antehac nefas depromere Caecubum   5
cellis avitis, dum Capitolio
   regina dementis ruinas
     funus et imperio parabat

contaminato cum grege turpium
morbo virorum, quidlibet inpotens   10
   sperare fortunaque dulci
     ebria; sed minuit furorem

---

dementis: accusative plural with **ruinas**; transferred epithet, in sense goes
    with **regina** as well
ruina, -ae, f., *collapse, ruin*

8   **funus, funeris**, n., *funeral, death, destruction*
    et: postposition; note the postponement of the conjunction until after **funus**.
    imperium, imperii, n., *power, command, government*
    parabat: imperfect with **dum**, rather than the more common present; under-
       stand this verb twice, once with **dementis ruinas** as direct object, then
       with **funus** as direct object

9   **contaminatus, -a, -um**, adj., *morally foul, impure*
    grex, gregis, m., *flock, herd, company, crowd*
    turpis, -e, adj., *ugly, shameful, disgraceful*

9–10   **contaminato...virorum**: contemptuous reference to Cleopatra's eunuchs
       who served as attendants at her court; note the use of the word "men" in
       connection with the eunuchs in light of the shifting vocabulary about
       gender roles in lines 22 and 32 below (**nec muliebriter, mulier**).

10   **morbus, -i**, m., *sickness, disease*
    morbo: ablative explaining **turpium**
    quilibet, quaelibet, quidlibet, pron., *anyone or anything whatever, whoever*
       or whatever you please
    inpotens, inpotentis, adj., *powerless, weak, wild, violent*

11   **sperare**: epexegetical infinitive explaining the adjective **inpotens**
    dulcis, -e, adj., *sweet*, (of persons) *dear, beloved*

12   **ebrius, -a, -um**, adj., *drunk*
    minuo, minuere, minui, minutum, *make smaller, reduce, weaken*
    minuit: perfect tense

13 **vix una sospes navis**: Horace exaggerates for effect; in fact, Cleopatra escaped with sixty ships. He continues his reworking of events in the poem by foreshortening the historical sequence. Almost a year elapsed between the battle of Actium and the final defeat of Antony and Cleopatra in Egypt.
   sospes, sospitis, adj., *safe and sound, unhurt*

14 **lymphatus, -a, -um**, adj., *frenzied, distracted, frantic*
   lymphatam: cf. notes on **nefas**, line 5, and **pede libero**, line 1, above. Here the displacement of the normal diaeresis underscores the distracted state of Cleopatra's mind.
   Mareoticum, -i, n., *wine from Mareotis*, area around Alexandria in Egypt

15 **redigo, redigere, redegi, redactum**, *drive back, reduce*

16 **Caesar, Caesaris**, m., *Caesar*, Octavian (later Augustus)
   ab Italia: literally, from Actium, not Italy; the idea is that she is compelled to flee from her goal
   Italia: the initial "i" is lengthened here

17 **remus, -i**, m., *oar*
   remis: synecdoche, "oars" for the whole ship
   adurgeo, adurgere, *press hard upon, pursue closely*
   accipiter, accipitris, m., *hawk*
   velut: introduces a simile; postposition, notice the placement of **velut** after **accipiter**, which begins the simile

18 **mollis, -e**, adj., *soft, gentle, flexible, voluptuous*
   columba, -ae, f., *dove, pigeon*
   lepus, leporis, m., *hare, rabbit*
   citus, -a, -um, adj., *swift, quick*

19 **venator, venatoris**, m., *hunter*
   campus, -i, m., *plain, level surface; plain, field*
   nivalis, -e, adj., *snowy*

20 **Haemonia, -ae**, f., *Thessaly*
   daret ut: subjunctive in purpose clause; postposition, **ut** placed after **daret**
   catena, -ae, f., *chain*

20–21 **daret ut catenis/fatale monstrum**: enjambment, emphasizes **fatale monstrum**

21 **fatalis, -e**, adj., *deadly, fatal*
   monstrum, -i, n., *portent, marvel, monster*

vix una sospes navis ab ignibus,
mentemque lymphatam Mareotico
    redegit in veros timores   15
       Caesar ab Italia volantem

remis adurgens, accipiter velut
mollis columbas aut leporem citus
    venator in campis nivalis
       Haemoniae, daret ut catenis   20

fatale monstrum, quae generosius
perire quaerens nec muliebriter
    expavit ensem, nec latentis
       classe cita reparavit oras,

---

fatale monstum: i.e., Cleopatra. Cleopatra VII (69 B.C.E.–30 B.C.E.)
quae: note the switch in gender to feminine from the neuter of the antecedent,
    monstrum
generose, adv., *nobly, with dignity*

22   **pereo, perire, perii, peritum**, *perish, die*
     muliebriter, adv., *like a woman*
     nec muliebriter: here, she is not "womanish"

23   **expavesco, expavescere, expavi**, *become frightened of, dread*
     ensis, ensis, m., *sword*
     lateo, latere, latui, *lie hidden*

24   **classis, classis**, f., *fleet, political class*
     reparo, reparare, reparavi, reparatum, *obtain in exchange for, recover*

23–24   **nec...reparavit**: the sense, here, is likely something like "did not reach"

25 **viso, visere, visi,** *look at, go and see*

26 **voltus, -us,** m., *face, expression*
    asper, aspera, asperum, adj., *fierce, rough*

27 **tracto, tractare, tractavi, tractatum,** *handle*
    tractare: epexegetical infinitive explaining the adjective **fortis**
    ater, atra, atrum, adj., *black, dark, gloomy*

28 **combibo, combibere, combibi,** *drink up, drink completely*
    combiberet: subjunctive in purpose clause
    venenum, -i, n., *poison, magical or medicinal potion*

29 **delibero, deliberare, deliberavi, deliberatum,** *consider carefully, deliber-*
    ate, decide

30 **Liburna, -ae,** f., *light, fast sailing warship, galley;* name taken from the
    Liburnians, a people of Illyricum
    scilicet, adv., *evidently, of course, surely*
    invideo, invidere, invidi, invisum, e*nvy, begrudge, refuse*

30–32 Some commentators take **saevis Liburnis** as ablative of means with **deduci**
    and **superbo...triumpho** as dative of purpose with **deduci**, while others
    take **saevis Liburnis** as dative with **invidens** and **deduci** as an infinitive
    dependent on **invidens** (epexegetical infinitive).

31 **privatus, -a, -um,** adj., *private, not in public life*
    deduco, deducere, deduxi, deductum, *lead away, lead down, escort, bring a*
    person or army back with one to Rome, bring home in procession as a
    bride, spin, compose, adapt

31–32 Note the portrayal of Cleopatra as well as the word order in these final
    two lines. She is described as a **non humilis mulier**. While **superbo**
    modifies **triumpho**, the placement of **mulier** directly before **triumpho,**
    in a kind of crescendo beginning with **non humilis,** lends a sense of
    triumph to the defeated queen. Some commentators have sensed an indi-
    rect admiration of Cleopatra here. On the other hand, the final word
    triumpho may look specifically towards Octavian, who celebrated a triple
    triumph in 29 B.C.E. for his victories in Illyricum, at Actium, and in Alex-
    andria.

32 **mulier**: cf. **mulier** with **nec muliebriter,** line 22 above

ausa et iacentem visere regiam   25
voltu sereno, fortis et asperas
    tractare serpentes, ut atrum
        corpore combiberet venenum,

deliberata morte ferocior:
saevis Liburnis scilicet invidens   30
    privata deduci superbo
        non humilis mulier triumpho.

Ode 1.38

The simplicity of this poem is deceptive. Everything is said indirectly; there is not a single positive statement. It can function on various levels: the metapoetic, symposiac, and, perhaps, even amatory.

Meter: Sapphic

Persicos odi, puer, apparatus,
displicent nexae philyra coronae;
mitte sectari, rosa quo locorum
    sera moretur.

---

1   **Persicus, -a, -um**, adj., *Persian*
    odi, odisse, osum, (perfect with present sense), *have an aversion to, hate*
    odi: cf. Ode 3.1.1, **odi profanum volgus et arceo**, for another example of Horace's method of delineating what he likes via what he does not like.
    puer, pueri, m., *boy, non-adult male, male beloved,* (young) *male slave*
    puer: It should be noted that here, as in Satire 1.9, discussed above, Horace is being attended by a slave.
    apparatus, -us, m., *preparation, show, sumptuousness, paraphernalia*
    Persicos...apparatus: yet cf. the previous poem, Ode 1.37, for an example of Horace's use of rather extravagant literary style. Cicero, *Orator* 83, makes an analogy (using the phrase **epularum apparatu**) between elaborate banquest preparations and elaborate literary style.

1–2 asyndeton: lack of connective between the clauses of lines 1 and 2, perhaps meant to underscore the idea of simplicity contained in the poem

2   **displiceo, displicere, displicui, displicitum**, *displease*
    necto, nectere, nexi, nexum, *tie, weave, bind, compose*
    philyra, -ae, f., *fibrous membrane under the bark of the linden or lime tree, bast;* used to bind together elaborate garlands of flowers
    corona, -ae, f., *crown, garland*

(notes contd. next page)

3   **mitto, mittere, misi, missum**, *release, let go, abandon, send*
    mitte sectari: the use of **mitte** makes this more vivid than a simple negative
        imperative would (**noli sectari**); cf. Horace's similar use of **fuge** in Ode
        1.9.13
    sector, sectari, sectatus sum, *pursue, chase*
    rosa, -ae, f., *rose*
    rosa: the rose is associated with Venus
    quo, adv., *where, for what purpose*
    locorum, partitive genitive with **quo**

3–4 **rosa quo locorum/sera moretur**: as often in Horace, the image of what is
        rejected contrasts with the rejection itself: the rose that is not to be pur-
        sued lingers in the mind's eye. Cf. the images of the tiger and lion in Ode
        1.23 above.

4   **serus, -a, -um**, adj., *late, blossoming after the normal time*
    moror, morari, moratus sum, *delay, linger, be late in appearing*
    moretur: subjunctive in indirect question
5   **simplex, simplicis**, adj., *simple, artless, plain*
    myrtus, -i, f., *myrtle*
    myrto: myrtle is associated with Venus
    simplici myrto: dative with **adlabores**
    adlaboro, adlaborare, *add to by taking trouble*

6   **sedulus, -a, -um**, adj., *attentive, diligent*
    sedulus: can modify either the speaker or the second person singular subject
        of **adlabores**; note its placement between the two words with which it
        can be construed
    curo, curare, curavi, curatum, *care about, take care of, attend to*
    curo: **curo** (**ut**) plus subjunctive in a substantive clause developed from the
        jussive subjunctive
    minister, ministri, m., *servant, assistant*

6–7 **neque...dedecet**: litotes

7   **dedecet, dedecere, dedecuit**, used in third person; *be unsuitable for, be un-
        becoming to*
    artus, -a, -um, adj., *close, thrifty, dense, economical*
    arta: this adjective has connotations of literary simplicity

8   **vitis, vitis**, f., *vine*
    bibo, bibere, bibi, *drink*

simplici myrto nihil adlabores   5
sedulus, curo: neque te ministrum
dedecet myrtus, neque me sub arta
    vite bibentem.

Ode 2.3

The themes of death, moderation, and enjoyment intertwine in this ode to Dellius. The generalizing statements and questions of the first three stanzas and the future, death-oriented, final three stanzas are divided by a central stanza (lines 13–16) which attempts to carve out a moment of physical and temporal immediacy that can be captured despite the universal human fact of death. The poem's final image of death as "exile" makes us want to return again to the immediacy of the sympotic moment which may be the only "home" that we can call our own for all time.

Meter: Alcaic

Aequam memento rebus in arduis
servare mentem, non secus in bonis
    ab insolenti temperatam
      laetitia, moriture Delli,

---

1   **aequus, -a, -um**, adj., *equal, even, impartial, fair*
    memini, meminisse, (perfect with present meaning), *remember, recollect*
    memento: future active imperative, second person singular, from **memini**
    arduus, -a, -um, adj., *steep, towering, lofty, high, difficult*
    aequam...arduis: note the contrast in images of "even" and "steep"

1–2 **aequam...mentem**: hyperbaton; cf. note on Ode 1.9.21–22

2   **secus**, adv., *otherwise, not so*
    non secus: litotes and asyndeton
    in bonis: understand **rebus**

3   **insolens, insolentis**, adj., *unaccustomed, excessive*
    tempero, temperare, temperavi, temperatum, *moderate, hold back*
    temperatam: understand **mentem**

(notes contd. next page)

4   **laetitia, -ae**, f., *happiness, joy*
     morior, mori, mortuus sum, *die*
     moriture: future active participle of **morior**, vocative
     Dellius, Dellii, m., *Quintus Dellius,* who first joined Dolabella, then Cassius, then Antony, and finally Octavian, right before Actium. He was called the **desultor bellorum civilium** "the circus rider of the civil wars" by Messalla. (A **desultor** is the circus rider who jumps from one horse to another.) His alternating allegiances to political figures make him an appropriate addressee for a poem that deals with changing circumstances.

5   **maestus, -a, -um**, adj., *sad, sorrowful, dejected, gloomy*
     omni tempore: ablative of time when
     vixeris: future perfect indicative

6   **removeo, removere, removi, remotum**, *move back, withdraw*
     gramen, graminis, n., *grass*

7   **festus, -a, -um**, adj., *festal, on holiday, festive*
     reclino, reclinare, reclinavi, reclinatum, *cause to lean back*
     reclinatum: perfect passive participle with middle sense; *having reclined*
     beo, beare, beavi, beatum, *bless, make happy*
     bearis: syncopated form of **bea(ve)ris**
     bearis: future perfect indicative, like **vixeris** (line 5)

8   **interior, interius**, adj., *inner, interior, private*
     interiore: a wine from the inner part of the wine cellar denoting an older, better wine
     nota, -ae, f., *mark, sign, wine of a specified quality or vintage*
     Falernum, -i, n., *Falernian wine,* wine from a district in northern Campania famous for its wine

9–12   The two questions that begin with **quo** and **quid** introduce contrasting personified images from nature of loving embrace and frenzied hurrying. The images suggest the erotic part of life (the trees embracing) as well as the brevity of life (the speed with which the water moves along). Cf. **fugerit invida/aetas**, Ode 1.11.7–8 for the "fleeing" quality of time. While the images portray a pleasant setting for the party called for in the next lines, they introduce a disquieting element as well.

9   **quo**, adv., *where, for what purpose*
     pinus, -us, f., *pine*
     albus, -a, -um, adj., *white, bright*
     populus, -i, f., *poplar tree*
     populus: the long "o" and the feminine gender distinguish this from the other, more common noun, **populus**, "people."

seu maestus omni tempore vixeris,   5
seu te in remoto gramine per dies
    festos reclinatum bearis
        interiore nota Falerni.

quo pinus ingens albaque populus
umbram hospitalem consociare amant   10
    ramis? quid obliquo laborat
        lympha fugax trepidare rivo?

---

pinus ingens albaque populus: chiasmus

10 **hospitalis, hospitale**, adj., *hospitable, belonging to a host or guest*
    consocio, consociare, consociavi, consociatum, *unite, connect, share*
    amant: cf. the use of this verb with an inanimate subject in Ode 1.25.3–4.

11 **ramus, -i**, m., *branch*
    quid, adv., *why*
    obliquus, -a, -um, adj., *slanting, zigzag*

11–12   **obliquo...rivo**: ablative of place where, **in** frequently omitted in poetry

12 **lympha, -ae**, f., *water*
    fugax, fugacis, adj., *swift, fugitive, elusive*
    trepido, trepidare, trepidavi, trepidatum, *be agitated, hurry*
    trepidare: infinitive with **laborat**
    rivus, -i, m., *stream*

13 **vina**: plural for singular
   unguentum, -i, n., *ointment, perfume*
   nimium, adv., *too, too much, very*
   nimium: modifies **brevis** (accusative plural), which modifies **flores**
   amoenus, -a, -um, adj., *charming, pleasing*
   rosa, rosae, f., *a rose*

13–14 tricolon crescendo: **vina, unguenta, nimium...rosae.** The length of the
   last element contrasts with the notion it contains of the brevity of the
   rose; the poet is extending through language what is desirable, but brief.

14 **ferre iube**: understand a word like **pueros** (slaves) as accusative with **iube**

15 **res**: recalls **rebus**, line 1
   aetas, aetatis, f., *time, age*

15–16 tricolon crescendo: **res, aetas, fila...** (with the phrase containing the last
   element (**fila...atra**) longer than the first two); **sororum...atra** refers to
   the image of the thread of each human life that the three Fates spin, mea-
   sure, and cut.

16 **filum, -i**, n., *thread*
   ater, atra, atrum, adj., *black, dark, gloomy*

17 **cedes...cedes** (line 19): anaphora; emphasizes the idea of loss
   coemo, coemere, coemi, coemptum, *buy up*
   saltus, -us, m., *forest or mountain pasture, forest or mountain pass*

17–18 **saltibus, domo, villa**: ablatives with **cedes**

18 **villa, -ae**, f., *country-house, estate, farm*
   flavos: earlier spelling for **flavus**
   flavus, -a, -um, adj., *yellow, golden, blonde, auburn*
   quam: postposition; **quam** is delayed to the second position in its clause
   Tiberis, Tiberis, m., *the river Tiber;* often described as yellowish because of
      the mud it contained
   lavo, lavare/lavere, lavi, lavatum/lautum/lotum, *wash*
   lavit: present tense; Horace treats the verb as third conjugation here.

19 **exstruo, exstruere, exstruxi, exstructum**, *heap up, pile up, construct*
   altum, -i, n., *high place or position, heaven, sea, the deep*

19–20 **exstructis...divitiis**: ablative with verb, **potior**

20 **divitiae, divitiarum**, f. pl., *wealth, riches*
   potior, potiri, potitus sum, *get possession of, obtain, possess*

huc vina et unguenta et nimium brevis
flores amoenae ferre iube rosae,
   dum res et aetas et sororum
     fila trium patiuntur atra.   15

cedes coemptis saltibus et domo
villaque, flavos quam Tiberis lavit,
   cedes, et exstructis in altum
     divitiis potietur heres.   20

divesne prisco natus ab Inacho,
nil interest, an pauper et infima
   de gente sub divo moreris,
     victima nil miserantis Orci:

---

heres, heredis, c., *heir*
heres: note the final, emphatic position of this word

21 **dives, divitis,** adj., *rich, wealthy*
    priscus, -a, -um, adj., *ancient, former*
    nascor, nasci, natus sum, *be born*
    Inachus, -i, m., *Inachus,* first king of Argos

21–22 **divesne...an pauper**: in apposition to the subject of **moreris**

22 **nil: nil = nihil;** cf. **nil** line 24; used adverbially here and in line 24, *not, not at all*
    intersum, interesse, interfui, when used impersonally, *it makes a difference, it matters, it is of importance*
    pauper, pauperis, adj., *poor*
    infimus, -a, -um, adj., *lowest, most humble*

23 **gens, gentis,** f., *clan, tribe, family*
    divum, -i, n., *sky*
    moror, morari, moratus sum, *delay, linger, be late in appearing*
    moreris: more vivid than "live" in the poem's context of the quick passing of time

24 **victima, -ae,** f., *victim, sacrifice*
    victima: understand **es**
    miseror, miserari, miseratus sum, *pity, lament*
    Orcus, Orci, m., *Orcus,* the god of the lower world, *the lower world, death*

omnes eodem cogimur, omnium   25
versatur urna serius ocius
   sors exitura et nos in aeternum
    exilium inpositura cumbae.

25 **eodem**, adv., *to the same place*
    cogo, cogere, coegi, coactum, *drive together, force*
    omnes...cogimur, omnium: the switch from second person singular to first
       person plural and the repetition of **omnes...omnium** (figura etymologica)
       generalize the situation to that of all human beings

26 **verso, versare, versavi, versatum**, *keep turning, stir*
    urna, -ae, f., *urn*
    urna: ablative of place where; cf. on **obliquo...rivo**, above, 11–12.
    serius, adv., *later*
    ocius, adv., *sooner, quicker*
    serius ocius: asyndeton

27 **sors, sortis**, f., *lot, share*
    exeo, exire, exii, exitum, *go out, come out, emerge*
    aeternus, -a, -um, adj., *eternal, everlasting*
    aeternum: hypermetric line; **aeternum** elides with **exilium** in the next line

28 **exilium, exilii**, n., *exile*
    inpono, inponere, inposui, inpositum, *place on or over, build on*
    cumba, -ae, f., *small boat,* especially that in which Charon ferries the dead
       across the river Styx
    cumbae: dative with **impositura**

Ode 2.7

When Horace was studying at the university in Athens he joined the republican forces and served under Brutus as a **tribunus militum**, a senior legionary officer, until Brutus' defeat at the battle of Philippi. This poem welcomes home Pompeius, who served along with Horace at Philippi. In the description of leaving behind his shield ignobly, Horace echoes a literary tradition that goes back to the Greek poets, Archilochus, Alcaeus, and Anacreon. There is a joyful sense to this poem of welcome (despite its reference to having been on the "wrong" side in the civil wars). In addition, there is an almost playful quality evinced by the frequent repetitions of the same or similar words: **deducte/duce**, **fregi/fracta**, **mecum/cum quo**, **celerem/celer**, **sustulit/tulit**, **coronatus/coronas**.

Meter: Alcaic

O saepe mecum tempus in ultimum
deducte Bruto militiae duce,
   quis te redonavit Quiritem
    dis patriis Italoque caelo,

---

1   **o**, interjection, *O* (with vocative)
    tempus: "danger" is the meaning here

2   **deduco, deducere, deduxi, deductum**, *lead away, lead down, escort, bring a person or army back with one to Rome, bring home in procession as a bride, spin, compose, adapt*
    deducte/duce: figura etymologica; cf. the other wordplay noted in the introduction to the poem, above
    Brutus, -i, m., *Marcus Iunius Brutus*, one of the leaders, along with Cassius, of the conspiracy to kill Julius Caesar. His forces were defeated by those of Antony, Octavian's then ally, at the second battle of Philippi in 42 B.C.E.
    Bruto...duce: ablative absolute

(notes contd. next page)

militia, -ae, f., *military service, war, army*

3   **redono, redonare, redonavi, redonatum**, *give back*
Quiris, Quiritis, m., *Roman citizen*
Quiritem: in apposition to **te**

4   **dis**: dative and ablative plural, alternate form for **deis**
patrius, -a, -um, adj., *of a father, ancestral, native, inherited, belonging to one's country*
Italus, -a, -um, adj., *Italian*

5   **Pompeius, Pompeii**, m., *Pompeius;* his identity is unknown
Pompei: vocative; disyllabic by synizesis
sodalis, sodalis, m., *companion*

6   **cum quo**: more frequently in Latin, **quocum**
moror, morari, moratus sum, *delay, linger, be late in appearing*
merus, -a, -um, adj., *pure, unmixed;* with **vinum** or with **vinum** understood, *wine not mixed with water*

7   **frango, frangere, fregi, fractum**, *break, crush*
corono, coronare, coronavi, coronatum, *put a garland on, crown*
niteo, nitere, nitui, *shine, be radiant with beauty*
nitentis: **-is** ending, alternate accusative plural ending for **-es**

7–8 **coronatus nitentis...capillos**: take as perfect passive participle with accusative of respect, or middle use of perfect passive participle with direct object

8   **malobathrum, -i**, n., *the tree Cinnamomum tamala or its oil*
Syrius, -a, -um, adj., *Syrian*

9   **Philippi, -orum**, m. pl., *Philippi,* town in eastern Macedonia where Brutus and Cassius were defeated
fuga, -ae, f., *flight, rout*

10   **non bene**: litotes
parmula, -ae, f., *little shield;* this particular shield was obsolete by Horace's time
relicta...parmula: ablative absolute
relicta...parmula: Horace places himself here in the Greek literary tradition of Archilochus, Alcaeus, and Anacreon, all of whom wrote poems in which they speak of leaving behind their shields shamefully.

11   **fracta**: see line 7

Pompei, meorum prime sodalium,   5
cum quo morantem saepe diem mero
    fregi coronatus nitentis
        malobathro Syrio capillos?

tecum Philippos et celerem fugam
sensi relicta non bene parmula,   10
    cum fracta virtus et minaces
        turpe solum tetigere mento.

---

fracta: understand **est**
minax, minacis, adj., *threatening, projecting*

11–12   **minaces...mento**: image of death or prostration

12 **turpis, -e**, adj., *ugly, shameful, disgraceful*
    solum, -i, n., *ground, floor, land*
    tango, tangere, tetigi, tactum, *touch*
    tetigere: alternate form of the third person plural perfect tense ending, **-erunt**
    mentum, -i, n., *chin*

13   **sed me...**: Horace is imitating the topos, found in Homeric epic, of the god
        whisking away a hero in a cloud.
     hostis, hostis, c., *enemy*
     hostis: **-is** ending, alternate accusative plural ending for **-es**
     Mercurius, Mercurii, m., *Mercury*, son of Jupiter and Maia
     Mercurius: perhaps Mercury because he is a protector of poets

14   **paveo, pavere**, *be frightened, be terrified*
     tollo, tollere, sustuli, sublatum, *lift, raise, extol, take away, destroy*
     aer, aeris, m., *air, weather, mist*
     aere: trisyllabic; "ae" is not a diphthong in the forms of **aer, aeris**

15   **rursus**, adv., *back, again*
     resorbeo, resorbere, *suck back, swallow again*

16   **unda, -ae**, f., *wave, water*
     fretum, -i, n., *strait, sea, violence*
     aestuosus, -a, -um, adj., *very hot, agitated*
     unda...aestuosis: notice the coincidence of meter and sense; the two dactyls that
        begin the fourth line of the Alcaic stanza play off the idea of a "wave"
     fretis...aestuosis: ablative of place where; **in** frequently omitted in poetry

17   **ergo**, particle, *then, consequently, therefore*
     obligo, obligare, obligavi, obligatum, *tie up, pledge, dedicate*
     daps, dapis, f., *feast, banquet*

18   **fessus, -a, -um**, adj., *tired, weary*
     militia: see line 2
     latus, lateris, n., *side, extreme part or region, flank, lungs, body*

19   **depono, deponere, deposui, depositum**, *lay down*
     laurus, -i/-us, f., *laurel tree*
     sub lauru mea: the laurel is associated both with those celebrating military
        triumphs and with poets

20   **parco, parcere, peperci, parsum**, *spare* (with dative)
     cadus, -i, m., *jar, flask* (especially for wine)
     destino, destinare, destinavi, destinatum, *fix, determine, intend, destine,*
        earmark

21   **obliviosus, -a, -um**, adj., *producing forgetfulness, forgetful*
     oblivioso: there may be an allusion here to the amnesty proclaimed by Octavian
        at the conclusion of the civil wars
     levis, -e, adj., *smooth, smooth* (from polishing)
     levia: note the long "e," which identifies this word as coming from the **levis, -e**
        given above, and not the other adjective, **levis, -e**, which has a short "e"

sed me per hostis Mercurius celer
denso paventem sustulit aere,
    te rursus in bellum resorbens   15
        unda fretis tulit aestuosis.

ergo obligatam redde Iovi dapem,
longaque fessum militia latus
    depone sub lauru mea, nec
        parce cadis tibi destinatis.   20

oblivioso levia Massico
ciboria exple, funde capacibus
    unguenta de conchis. quis udo
        deproperare apio coronas

Massicum, -i, n., *Massic wine, wine from the area of* **Massicus,** a mountain in Campania

22 **ciborium, ciborii**, n., *a kind of drinking cup*
     expleo, explere, explevi, expletum, *fill up*
     fundo, fundere, fudi, fusum, *pour, spread, scatter, defeat*
     capax, capacis, adj., *spacious, capable*

23 **unguentum, -i**, n., *ointment, perfume*
     concha, -ae, f., *shell fish, sea shell, perfume dish*
     udus, -a, -um, adj., *wet,* (here) *pliant*

24 **depropero, deproperare**, *hurry to complete*
     apium, apii, n., *parsley, celery*
     corona, -ae, f., *crown, garland*

curatve myrto? quem Venus arbitrum   25
dicet bibendi? non ego sanius
   bacchabor Edonis: recepto
      dulce mihi furere est amico.

---

25   **curo, curare, curavi, curatum**, *take care of, attend to, care about*
     myrtus, -i, f., *myrtle*
     venus, veneris, f., *Venus*, Roman goddess of love; *love, charm, sexual activity; best throw at dice*
     arbiter, arbitri, m., *judge, overseer*

25–26   **quem...bibendi**: the head of the drinking party was chosen by using dice; the Venus throw, or highest throw, determined the winner

26   **bibo, bibere, bibi**, *drink*
     sanus, -a, -um, adj., *healthy, sane*

27   **bacchor, bacchari, bacchatus sum**, *celebrate the festival of Bacchus, rave, rage*
     Edonus, -a, -um, adj., *Thracian;* the **Edoni** were a tribe celebrated for their orgiastic worship of Bacchus

28   **dulcis, -e**, adj., *sweet,* (of persons) *dear, beloved*
     furo, furere, *behave wildly, be crazy*

Ode 2.10

This poem, which advocates following a "golden mean," is built around a series of antitheses. Notice how Horace creates variation within this basic framework. For example, the balance of the pattern laying out alternatives in line 13 contrasts with the expansion (through the **dum** clause) upon the second alternative in the first stanza. It is this variation upon one basic theme that makes the poem seem both simple and carefully crafted.

Meter: Sapphic

Rectius vives, Licini, neque altum
semper urgendo, neque – dum procellas
cautus horrescis – nimium premendo
   litus iniquum.

---

1   **rectus, -a, -um**, adj., *straight, right, correct, proper*
    rectius: this comparative is echoed by the comparative, **saepius**, in line 9
    Licinius, Licinii, m., *Licinius;* this Licinius may have been Lucius Licinius Murena, brother-in-law of Maecenas, who was executed when trying to escape after his alleged participation in a conspiracy against Augustus. This Licinius was a patron of Athenaeus, a leading Peripatetic, or follower of Aristotle's school of philosophy. If this is the Licinius addressed, extra point is added to both the ethical and political advice Horace gives here.
    altum, -i, n., *high place or position, heaven, sea, the deep*
    altum: this nautical language introduces the metaphor of the "sea" of life or of politics

(notes contd. next page)

2   **urgeo, urgere, ursi**, *push, press upon*
    procella, -ae, f., *storm, trouble*

3   **cautus, -a, -um**, adj., *on one's guard, wary, cautious, prudent*
    horresco, horrescere, horrui, *shudder at, tremble at*
    nimium, adv., *too, too much, very*
    premo, premere, pressi, pressum, *press, follow closely*

4   **litus, litoris**, n., *shore, coast, beach*
    iniquus, -a, -um, adj., *uneven, unfavorable, treacherous, discontented*

5   **aureus, -a, -um**, adj., *golden, splendid*
    mediocritas, mediocritatis, f., *mean, moderation, keeping of a middle course*
    mediocritatem: Cf. Aristotle's notion in the *Nicomachean Ethics* that excellence in a particular thing lies somewhere (not necessarily midway) between the extremes of deficiency and excess.

6   **diligo, diligere, dilexi, dilectum**, *love, esteem, hold dear, have special regard for*
    tutus, -a, -um, adj., *safe, secure*
    careo, carere, carui, caritum, *lack, be without* (with ablative)
    obsoletus, -a, -um, adj., *worn out, shabby, ordinary*

6–8 Note the repetition of **caret**, which highlights the extremes, as well as the asyndeton, which makes the alternatives more stark.

7   **sordes, sordis**, f., often used in plural; *dirt, squalor, baseness*
    tectum, -i, n., *roof, house*
    caret: see line 6
    invideo, invidere, invidi, invisum, *envy, begrudge, refuse*

8   **sobrius, -a, -um**, adj., *sober, moderate, sensible*
    aula, aulae, f., *noble residence, palace, hall*

9   **agito, agitare, agitavi, agitatum**, *drive, agitate, excite*
    ingens, ingentis, adj., *huge*

10   **pinus, -us**, f., *pine*
   celsus, -a, -um, adj., *high, lofty, proud*
   casus, -us, m., *fall, event, misfortune, chance*

11   **decido, decidere, decidi**, *fall down, die*
   turris, -is, f., *tower*
   ferio, ferire, *strike, hit*

auream quisquis mediocritatem 5
diligit, tutus caret obsoleti
sordibus tecti, caret invidenda
    sobrius aula.

saepius ventis agitatur ingens
pinus et celsae graviore casu 10
decidunt turres feriuntque summos
    fulgura montis.

sperat infestis, metuit secundis
alteram sortem bene praeparatum
pectus. informis hiemes reducit 15
    Iuppiter, idem

submovet. non, si male nunc, et olim
sic erit: quondam cithara tacentem
suscitat Musam, neque semper arcum
    tendit Apollo. 20

---

12   **fulgur, fulguris**, n., *a flash of lightning, flash of light*
     montis: -**is** = -**es** (accusative plural)

13   **infestus, -a, -um**, adj., *dangerous, hostile, insecure*
     secundus, -a, -um, adj., *following, second, favorable*
     infestis...secundis: understand a word like **rebus** (circumstances); ablative
        of time when
     sperat...secundis: synchysis

14   **sors, sortis**, f., *lot, share*
     praeparo, praeparare, praeparavi, praeparatum, *prepare*

15   **pectus**: subject of **sperat** and **metuit** (13)
     informis, -e, adj., *shapeless, deformed, ugly*
     informis: -**is** = -**es** (accusative plural)
     hiems, hiemis, f., *winter, storm*

16–17   Note the enjambment between the fourth and fifth stanzas. All the other
        stanzas are end-stopped.

(notes contd. next page)

rebus angustis animosus atque
fortis appare: sapienter idem
contrahes vento nimium secundo
    turgida vela.

---

17 **submoveo, submovere, submovi, submotum**, *move away, remove, ward off, banish*
    olim, adv., *formerly, once, on an occasion, at some future date*

18 **quondam**, adv., *once, formerly, sometimes, in the future*
    cithara, -ae, f., *lyre*

19 **suscito, suscitare, suscitavi, suscitatum**, *rouse, awaken*
    Musa, -ae, f., *muse;* one of the nine Muses, goddesses who were daughters of Zeus and Mnemosyne and presided over the arts
    arcus, -us, m., *bow*

20 **tendo, tendere, tetendi, tentum/tensum**, *stretch out, extend, proceed*
    Apollo, Apollinis, m., *Apollo,* son of Jupiter and Latona, brother of Diana, god of archery, music, poetry, etc.

21 **rebus angustis**: ablative of time when
    angustus, -a, -um, adj., *narrow, limited, difficult* (of circumstances)
    animosus, -a, -um, adj., *spirited, bold*

22 **appareo, apparere, apparui, apparitum**, *appear*
    sapienter, adv., *wisely*

23 **contraho, contrahere, contraxi, contractum**, *draw together, narrow*
    nimium, adv., *too, too much, very*
    secundo: see line 13

24 **turgidus, -a, -um**, adj., *swollen, turgid*
    velum, -i, n., *sail*

Ode 2.14

While educated Romans of Horace's time were sceptical about the reality of the kinds of images of what occurs after death we find in this poem (cf., e.g., Cicero Tusculan Disputations 1.10–12), such images still functioned effectively at the imaginative level. Death's necessity is underscored through the poem's three gerundives (**enaviganda, visendus, linquenda**), which define the journey to the underworld, show what it contains, and explain what it leaves behind. The recklessness of Postumus' heir, who spills the wine he enjoys, intensifies the poem's gloom and may suggest that his behavior is a less than ideal alternative to Postumus' senseless hoarding. At the imaginative level, death overshadows the figure who is associated with the Epicurean injunction to enjoy the moment.

Meter: Alcaic

> Eheu fugaces, Postume, Postume,
> labuntur anni, nec pietas moram
>   rugis et instanti senectae
>   adferet indomitaeque morti,

---

1   **eheu**, interjection (expressing grief or pain), *alas*
     fugax, fugacis, adj., *swift, fugitive, elusive*
     Postumus, -i, m., *Postumus;* this name was often given to boys who were born after the death of their fathers; the identity of this Postumus is unknown; he may be the Postumus addressed by Propertius in Elegy 3.12.

2   **labor, labi, lapsus sum**, *glide, slip, pass*
     pietas, pietatis, f., *duty, devotion*
     mora, -ae, f., *delay, hindrance*

(notes contd. next page)

3   **ruga, -ae**, f., *wrinkle*
      instans, instantis, adj., *pressing, urgent*
      senecta, -ae, f., *old age*

4   **adfero, adferre, attuli, allatum**, *bring, add*
      indomitus, -a, -um, adj., *unconquered, unconquerable*

5   **treceni, trecenae, trecena**, pl. adj., *three hundred each, three hundred at a time*
      quotquot, indeclinable adj., *however many*

6   **placo, placare, placavi, placatum**, *appease, calm*
      places: note that this verb form is from **placo**, not **placeo**
      inlacrimabilis, -e, adj., *pitiless*

5–7 **trecenis...tauris**: this sacrifice would be three times as large as the traditional hecatomb, the sacrifice of one hundred cattle

7   **Pluto, Plutonis**, m., *Pluto,* king of the underworld
      taurus, -i, m., *bull*
      ter, adv., *three times*
      amplus, -a, -um, adj., *large, spacious*

8   **Geryon, Geryonis**, m., *Geryon;* triple-headed or triple-bodied king whom
      Hercules killed when carrying off his cattle.
      Tityos, -i, m., *Tityus;* giant primarily known for attempting to rape Latona, mother
      of Apollo and Diana; punished in the underworld by being stretched over
      nine acres while two vultures or snakes ate his heart or liver.
      Geryon and **Tityon**: Greek accusatives
      tristis, -e, adj., *sad*

9   **compesco, compescere, compescui**, *confine, restrain, check*
      unda, -ae, f., *wave, water*
      unda: ablative with **enaviganda** (11)
      scilicet, adv., *evidently, of course, surely*
      omnibus: dative of agent with gerundive

10   **munus, muneris**, n., *service, duty, gift, entertainment*
      vescor, vesci, *enjoy, feed on, eat* (with ablative)

11   **enavigo, enavigare, enavigavi, enavigatum**, *sail across, sail forth*
      enaviganda, visendus (17), **linquenda** (21): gerundives

12   **inops, inopis**, adj., *lacking wealth, poor*
      colonus, -i, m., *farmer, settler*

13   **frustra**, adv., *in vain, to no purpose*

non, si trecenis, quotquot eunt dies,   5
amice, places inlacrimabilem
    Plutona tauris, qui ter amplum
        Geryonen Tityonque tristi

conpescit unda, scilicet omnibus,
quicumque terrae munere vescimur,   10
    enaviganda, sive reges,
        sive inopes erimus coloni.

frustra cruento Marte carebimus
fractisque rauci fluctibus Hadriae,
    frustra per autumnos nocentem   15
        corporibus metuemus Austrum:

---

cruentus, -a, -um, adj., *bloody, gory, cruel*
Mars, Martis, m., *Mars*, god of war
Marte: *war*, by metonymy
careo, carere, carui, caritum, *lack, be without* (with ablative)

14 **frango, frangere, fregi, fractum**, *break, crush*
raucus, -a, -um, adj., *hoarse, noisy, raucous*
Hadria, -ae, m., *Adriatic Sea*
fractisque...Hadriae: synchysis

15 **frustra**: see line 13
autumnus, -i, m., *autumn*
autumnos: autumn was traditionally an unhealthy season in Italy
noceo, nocere, nocui, nocitum, *harm* (with dative)

16 **Auster, Austri**, m., *south wind*

17 **viso, visere, visi,** *look at, go and see*
    visendus: takes its number and gender from **Cocytos** (masculine singular);
        genus and **Sisyphus** should be taken with it as well
    ater, atra, atrum, adj., *black, dark, gloomy*
    flumen, fluminis, n., *river, waters of a river*
    languidus, -a, -um, adj., *languid, sluggish, slow*

18 **Cocytos, Cocyti,** m., *Cocytus,* one of the rivers of the underworld
    Danaus, -i, m., *Danaus;* all but one of his fifty daughters, the Danaids, on
        instructions from their father, killed their husbands on their wedding
        night; they are punished in the underworld by having continuously to fill
        up leaky jars; story portrayed by Polygnotus at Delphi as well as at
        Augustus' Temple of Apollo on the Palatine.

19 **infamis, -e,** adj., *infamous, disreputable*
    damno, damnare, damnavi, damnatum, *condemn, sentence*
    longi: litotes

19–20 **longi...laboris**: genitive of penalty with **damnatus**

20 **Sisyphus, -i,** m., *Sisyphus;* son of Aeolus, committed various crimes and is
        punished in the underworld by forever having to roll a rock up a steep hill
        only to have it roll down again.
    Aeolides, Aeolidae, m., *a son or more remote descendant of Aeolus*

21 **linquo, linquere, liqui,** *go away from, abandon, leave behind*
    tellus, telluris, f., *land, earth, country, ground*
    placeo, placere, placui, placitum, *please*

22 **colo, colere, colui, cultum,** *cultivate, cherish*

23 **praeter,** preposition with accusative, *except, beyond*
    invisus, -a, -um, adj., *hateful, odious*
    cupressus, -i, f., *cypress;* the cypress had funereal associations

24 **dominus, -i,** m., *master, lord, ruler*

25 **absumo, absumere, absumpsi, absumptum,** *spend, consume*
    heres, heredis, c., *heir*
    Caecubum, -i, n., *choice wine from Caecubum,* a district in south Latium
    dignus, -a, -um, adj., *worthy, worthy of, deserving* (with ablative)
    dignior: because he uses and enjoys the wine rather than hoarding it, how-
        ever there may be irony here

26 **clavis, clavis,** f., *key*

visendus ater flumine languido
Cocytos errans et Danai genus
   infame damnatusque longi
      Sisyphus Aeolides laboris. 20

linquenda tellus et domus et placens
uxor, neque harum, quas colis, arborum
   te praeter invisas cupressos
      ulla brevem dominum sequetur,

absumet heres Caecuba dignior 25
servata centum clavibus et mero
   tinguet pavimentum superbo,
      pontificum potiore cenis.

---

merus, -a, -um, adj., *pure, unmixed;* with **vinum** or with **vinum** understood, *wine not mixed with water*

27 **tinguo, tinguere, tinxi, tinctum**, *wet, stain*
pavimentum, -i, n., *pavement, floor*
superbo: suggests both an excellent wine and perhaps arrogant disregard for wasting some wine while enjoying life's pleasures

28 **pontifex, pontificis**, m., *high priest, pontiff*
potior, potius, adj., *better, preferable*
pontificum potiore cenis: elliptical; wine being compared to *the wine* served at the dinners of the pontiffs

Ode 3.1

Some see in this ode an attempt to discourage personal ambition and to encourage contentment with one's situation. Whatever grand power and wealth one seeks does not differentiate one from the powerless and poor in the long run — all are subject to divinity and Necessity, powers beyond human control. Yet, it is in Horace's ambitous role as "priest of the Muses" that he makes these pronouncements, leading the reader to the paradoxical conclusion that it is his poetry (surely the product of intense ambition) that allows him to make these very pronouncements against personal ambition.

Meter: Alcaic

Odi profanum volgus et arceo.
favete linguis: carmina non prius
   audita Musarum sacerdos
      virginibus puerisque canto.

1–4 These lines function as an introduction to this poem and to the so-called Roman Odes (Book 3.1–6), a group of poems set apart by their Alcaic meter, solemn style, closely related themes, lack of individual addressees, and interest in the values necessary for a successful Augustan Rome. The **carmina non prius/audita** (2–3) refer to Latin lyric used for national song. Horace as "priest of the Muses" initiates the next generation into the sacral space of his song.

1   **odi, odisse, osum**, (perfect with present sense), *have an aversion to, hate*
    profanus, -a, -um, adj., *profane, secular, impious, uninitiated*
    volgus, -i, n., *the common people, the general public, crowd*
    arceo, arcere, arcui, *contain, keep away, spurn*

(notes contd. next page)

2   **faveo, favere, favi, fautum,** *favor;* with **linguis** (ablative), *avoid words of ill omen, be silent*
    carmen, carminis, n., *solemn or ritual utterance, song, poem, lyric poetry*

3   **Musa, -ae,** f., *muse;* one of the nine Muses, goddesses who were daughters of Zeus and Mnemosyne and presided over the arts
    sacerdos, sacerdotis, c., *priest or priestess*

4   **puer, pueri,** m., *boy, non-adult male, male beloved,* (young) *male slave*
    canto, cantare, cantavi, cantatum, *sing, sing about, recite*

5–8 The kings who evince fear (**regum timendorum**) quickly give way to Jupiter who rules them in turn (**reges in ipsos imperium est Iovis**). Lines 7–8 expand upon the description of the power of Jupiter who rules with a nod of his head.

5   **regum timendorum:** understand **imperium est** from the next line
    proprius, -a, -um, adj., *one's own, personal*
    grex, gregis, m., flock, *herd, company, crowd*

5–6 **in: in** plus accusative in these two lines has the sense of "over"
    regum/reges: figura etymologica

6   **imperium, imperii,** n., *power, command, government*

6–7 With **imperium** and **triumpho** Horace uses words from the Roman political vocabulary to describe the power structure of the world.

7   **Giganteus, -a, -um,** adj., *of the Giants,* a mythical race, who fought and were defeated by the Olympian gods
    clari: modifies **Iovis**
    Giganteo triumpho: the adjective functions like an objective genitive with the noun; for more on Jupiter's victory over the Giants, cf. Ode 3.4.42–80

8   **supercilium, supercilii,** n., *eyebrow, nod*
    moventis: modifies **Iovis**

9–16 A successful landowner (**vir**) and three candidates for political office (**hic, hic, illi**) who excel, respectively, in noble birth, character and fame, and number of clients are shown to be subject to the impartial law of Necessity that determines the fates of high and low alike.

9–14 **Est, ut** introduces four subordinate verbs in the subjunctive in substantive clauses of result: **ordinet...descendat...contendat...sit**

regum timendorum in proprios greges,   5
reges in ipsos imperium est Iovis,
   clari Giganteo triumpho,
    cuncta supercilio moventis.

est, ut viro vir latius ordinet
arbusta sulcis, hic generosior   10
   descendat in campum petitor,
    moribus hic meliorque fama

9   **ordino, ordinare, ordinavi, ordinatum**, *set in order, arrange*

10   **arbustum, -i**, n., *wood, plantation,* (plural) *trees*
      sulcus, -i, m., *a furrow, trench, track*
      generosus, -a, -um, adj., *of noble birth, noble*

11   **descendo, descendere, descendi, descensum**, *come or go down, descend*
      campus, -i, m., *plain, level surface; plain, field;* often refers specifically to
         the Campus Martius in Rome; elections took place in the Campus Martius
      petitor, petitoris, m., *seeker, candidate*

12   **mos, moris**, m., *custom, tradition;* (plural) *character, habits*
      moribus and **fama**: ablatives of respect with **melior**

12–13   Notice the enjambment. The structure of the poem is as follows: 1–4
        (introduction to this poem and the Roman Odes as a whole); 5–8; then
        pairs of stanzas joined by enjambment: 9–16; 17–24; 25–32; 33–40; 41–48.

13 **contendo, contendere, contendi, contentum,** *stretch, hasten, compete, contend*
   turba, -ae, f., *crowd*
   cliens, clientis, m., *client;* one who attaches himself to a person of greater
      influence or political power (**patronus**) for protection

14 **aequus, -a, -um,** adj., *equal, even, impartial, fair*
   The personifications of **Necessitas** (14), **Timor** (37), **Minae** (37), and **Cura**
      (40) create very strong images.

15 **sortior, sortiri, sortitus sum,** *cast lots over, choose*
   sortitur: a significant verb to use directly following a political context where
      winners were not chosen by lot
   insignis, -e, adj., *distinguished*
   imus, -a, -um, adj., *lowest*

16 **capax, capacis,** adj., *spacious, capable*
   urna, -ae, f., *urn*
   capax...urna: cf. Ode 2.3.25 ff. where fortunes are also tossed about in an urn
   omne capax movet urna nomen: a golden line, i.e., two adjectives and two
      nouns with a verb between, in this case arranged chiastically, adj. a, adj.
      b, verb, noun b, noun a

17–24 Those who possess power and wealth cannot enjoy them because of the
      threat of their loss; sleep eludes them unlike the humble farmer, and
      those who enjoy the shady bank and the wind-stirred valley.

17–19 These lines are a reference to the story of the sword of Damocles. Dionysius,
      tyrant of Syracuse (430–367 B.C.E.), shows his subject, Damocles, that the life
      of the tyrant is not the total enjoyment Damocles thinks it is by placing before
      him a magnificent banquet only to suspend over his head a sword. In this
      story, Dionysius teaches Damocles a lesson about the anxieties inherent in
      power and wealth. Horace, in turn, uses the story for his own moral purpose,
      which seems to be to show the tyrant's greedy use of power. The description of
      the neck as **impia** suggests a grasping after things beyond what is good. The
      wise ruler, presumably, would not be worried about what he personally has to
      lose.

17 **destringo, destringere, destrinxi, destrictum,** *strip off, scrape lightly, draw*
      or unsheathe (a weapon)
   ensis, ensis, m., *sword*
   cui: dative of reference
   impius, -a, -um, adj., *impious, undutiful, disloyal*

18 **cervix, cervicis,** f., *neck*

contendat, illi turba clientium
sit maior: aequa lege Necessitas
    sortitur insignis et imos,   15
        omne capax movet urna nomen.

destrictus ensis cui super impia
cervice pendet, non Siculae dapes
    dulcem elaborabunt saporem,
        non avium citharaeque cantus   20

---

pendeo, pendere, pependi, *hang, hover, hang down, be suspended*
Siculus, -a, -um, adj., *Sicilian*
daps, dapis, f., *feast, banquet*

19 **elaboro, elaborare, elaboravi, elaboratum**, *strive, work out, develop, perfect*
    sapor, saporis, m., *taste, flavor*

20 **avis, avis**, f., *bird*
    cithara, -ae, f., *lyre*
    cantus, -us, m., *singing, song, poetry*

21 **somnus, -i**, m., *sleep*
   agrestis, -e, adj., *of the country, rustic, rural*

22 **lenis, -e**, adj., *smooth, gentle, mild, soft*
   humilis, -e, adj., *humble, low*
   humilis: **-is** = **-es** (accusative plural)

23 **fastidio, fastidire, fastidivi, fastiditum**, *show aversion to, scorn*
   umbrosus, -a, -um, adj., *shady*
   ripa, -ae, f., *bank of a river, shore*

24 **zephyrus, -i**, m., *west wind, zephyr*
   agito, agitare, agitavi, agitatum, *stir, drive, agitate, excite*
   Tempe, n. pl., (here, accusative), *Tempe,* valley of the Peneus river between
     Ossa and Olympus in Thessaly noted for its beauty; *any beautiful valley*

25-32 The one who desires just what is enough is not bothered by various
     forces of nature that pose a danger to one's livelihood, whether merchant
     or farmer.

26 **tumultuosus, -a, -um**, adj., *full of commotion, turbulent*
   sollicito, sollicitare, sollicitavi, sollicitatum, *rouse, excite, shake up, disturb*
     with repeated attacks

27-28 Haedus and Arcturus are constellations that appear in October, the stormy
     season.

27 **Arcturus, -i**, m., *Arcturus,* the brightest star of the constellation Boötes
   cadentis: the verb **cado** is used of the setting of heavenly bodies

28 **impetus, -us**, m., *attack, onset, rapid motion*
   orior, oriri, ortus sum, *rise, be born*
   Haedus, -i, m., *young goat, kid;* two stars in the constellation **Auriga**

29 **verbero, verberare, verberavi, verberatum**, *beat, lash*
   grando, grandinis, f., *hail*
   vinea, -ae, f., *vineyard*

30-32 The farm and tree are personified; the farm is deceitful (**mendax**), while
     the tree (**arbore**) blames (**culpante**) the water, stars, and winters, pre-
     sumably for its lack of productivity. Notice the repetition of **nunc** with
     each new reason for complaint.

30 **fundus, -i**, m., *bottom, farm, estate*
   mendax, mendacis, adj., *lying, false*

somnum reducent: somnus agrestium
lenis virorum non humilis domos
   fastidit umbrosamque ripam,
     non Zephyris agitata Tempe.

desiderantem quod satis est neque   25
tumultuosum sollicitat mare,
   nec saevus Arcturi cadentis
     impetus aut orientis Haedi,

non verberatae grandine vineae
fundusque mendax, arbore nunc aquas   30
   culpante, nunc torrentia agros
     sidera, nunc hiemes iniquas.

---

31 **culpo, culpare, culpavi, culpatum**, *blame*
   torreo, torrere, torrui, tostum, *burn, parch*

32 **sidus, sideris**, n., *star; sky* (plural)
   hiems, hiemis, f., *winter, storm*
   iniquus, -a, -um, adj., *uneven, unfavorable, treacherous, discontented*

33–40   The rich build houses out into the sea, overstepping natural bounds, with the master disdainful of the land. Yet fear and threats and concern follow the master wherever he goes.

33   **contraho, contrahere, contraxi, contractum**, *draw together, narrow*
piscis, piscis, m., *fish*
aequor, aequoris, n., *a flat level surface, the flat surface of the sea,* (often used in plural)

34   **iacio, iacere, ieci, iactum**, *throw, lay foundations*
altum, -i, n., *high place or position, heaven, sea, the deep*
moles, molis, f., *mass, bulk, massive structure*
frequens, frequentis, adj., *crowded, assiduous, constant, regular*

35   **caementum, -i**, n., *small stones, rubble*
demitto, demittere, demisi, demissum, *let down, sink, lower*
redemptor, redemptoris, m., *contractor*

36   **famulus, -i**, m., *servant, attendant, slave*
dominus, -i, m., *master, lord, ruler*

37   **fastidiosus, -a, -um**, adj., *critical, exacting, disdainful*
timor, timoris, m., *fear*
minae, -arum, f. pl., *threats, warning signs*

38   **scando, scandere**, *climb, ascend, mount*
eodem, adv., *to the same place*
quo, adv., *where, for what purpose*
dominus: see line 36

39   **decedo, decedere, decessi, decessum**, *go away, depart, withdraw* (with ablative)
aeratus, -a, -um, adj., *made of or fitted with bronze or brass*
triremis, triremis, f., *ship having three banks of oars; trireme*

39–40   The rich man engages in leisure activities by riding (**equitem**) and going out on a fancy boat (**aerata triremi**).

40   **eques, equitis**, m., *horseman, rider, member of the cavalry, member of the equestrian order*
ater, atra, atrum, adj., *black, dark, gloomy*
cura, -ae, f., *care, concern, worry, a person or thing constituting an object of care*

41–48   If excessive elaborateness does nothing to alleviate pain and entails excessive toil (**divitias operosiores**), how could it be preferable to the poet's

contracta pisces aequora sentiunt
iactis in altum molibus: huc frequens
   caementa demittit redemptor   35
      cum famulis dominusque terrae

fastidiosus, sed Timor et Minae
scandunt eodem, quo dominus, neque
   decedit aerata triremi et
      post equitem sedet atra Cura.   40

quodsi dolentem nec Phrygius lapis,
nec purpurarum sidere clarior
   delenit usus, nec Falerna
      vitis Achaemeniumque costum,

Sabine home? These lines echo the first person singular used in the opening lines of the poem.

41 **quodsi**, conj., *but if*
    doleo, dolere, dolui, dolitum, *suffer mental or physical pain, be in pain, grieve*
    Phrygius, -a, -um, adj., *Phrygian*
    lapis, lapidis, m., *stone*
    Phrygius lapis: a kind of marble

42 **purpura, -ae**, f., *shellfish yielding a purple dye, the purple dye from the shellfish, purple-dyed cloth, purple*
    sidere: (see line 32)
    clarior: transferred epithet; grammatically modifies **usus** (43), but goes in sense with **purpurarum**

43 **delenio, delenire, delenivi, delenitum**, *soothe*
    usus, -us, m., *use, enjoyment*
    Falernus, -a, -um, adj., *Falernian,* of a district in northern Campania famous for its wine

44 **vitis, vitis**, f., *vine*
    Achaemenius, -a, -um, adj., *Persian, Parthian*
    costum, -i, n., *an aromatic plant*

cur invidendis postibus et novo   45
sublime ritu moliar atrium?
  cur valle permutem Sabina
    divitias operosiores?

---

45 **invideo, invidere, invidi, invisum**, *envy, begrudge, refuse*
    postis, postis, m., *door-post, door*

46 **sublimis, -e**, adj., *high, raised, elevated, sublime, lofty*
    ritus, -us, m., *ritual, custom, manner, style*
    molior, moliri, molitus sum, *labor at, build*
    moliar: deliberative subjunctive
    atrium, atrii, n., *hall, first main room in a Roman-style house*

47 **valles, vallis**, f., *valley*
    permuto, permutare, permutavi, permutatum, *exchange, receive in ex-*
        change for (accusative of thing received and ablative of thing given up)
    permutem: deliberative subjunctive, like **moliar** above
    Sabinus, -a, -um, adj., *Sabine;* the Sabines were a people of central Italy.
    valle...Sabina: where Horace had his Sabine farm

48 **divitiae, divitiarum**, f. pl., *wealth, riches*
    operosus, -a, -um, adj., *toilsome, laborious, painstaking, industrious*
    operosiores: Cf. Ode 4.2.31–32, where Horace describes his own poems as
      operosa...carmina.

Ode 3.9

This conversation between two lovers (former lovers, present lovers? future lovers?) is Horace's only lyric poem in dialogue form. Each of the lovers speaks the same number of lines. Each tries to outdo the other's previous words. Some see the woman each time outdoing the man; others see the man, who speaks first, as the one who gets to set the terms of the conversation. Some see the end of the poem as the lovers' reconciliation; others, more sceptical, see the competitive and tempestuous nature of the relationship as a sign that any reconciliation would contain the elements of its own destruction. This poem is frequently compared with Catullus 45, the Acme and Septimius poem. There, too, critics debate the believability of what seems to be an ideal love.

Meter: second Asclepiadean

❦ ❦ ❦

> Donec gratus eram tibi,
>   nec quisquam potior brachia candidae
> cervici iuvenis dabat,
>   Persarum vigui rege beatior.

---

1   **donec**, conj., *as long as, while*
    gratus, -a, -um: adj., *pleasing*

2   **potior, potius**, adj., *more able, more powerful, preferable*
    brachium, brachii, n., *arm*
    candidus, -a, -um, adj., *bright, radiant, white*

3   **cervix, cervicis**, f., *neck*
    iuvenis, iuvenis, m., (f.), *young man, young woman*

4   **Persae, Persarum**, m. pl., *Persians*
    vigeo, vigere, vigui, *flourish, thrive*

5   **alia**: note the meter requires this to be a long **a**; ablative with **ardeo**, not ablative of comparison

6   **ardeo, ardere, arsi**, *be on fire, burn, be in love* (with ablative)
    Lydia, -ae, f., *Lydia*, woman's name
    post: after, in sense of "second to"
    Chloe, Chloes, f., *Chloe*, Greek woman's name; the **oe** is not a diphthong here.
    Chloen: Greek accusative singular; two syllables

7   **Lydia**: note how the repetition of the name **Lydia** from the previous line enacts the sense of **multi nominis**; the male speaker's name never appears in the poem; the names Chloe and Lydia each occur three times
    multi nominis: genitive of quality

8   **Ilia, -ae**, f., *Ilia* or *Rhea Silvia*, mother of Romulus and Remus
    Romana...Ilia: ablative of comparison

9   **Thressa, -ae**, f., *a Thracian woman;* here, as feminine adjective, *Thracian*

10   **dulcis**: **-is** = **-es** (accusative plural)
    doctus, -a, -um, *learned, taught*
    dulcis...modos: accusative of respect with **docta**
    modus, -i, m., *limit, way, rhythmic pattern;* in plural, *poetry*
    cithara, -ae, f., *lyre*
    citharae: genitive of reference (cf. notes to Ode 1.22.1) with **sciens**; here, the participle functions as an adjective, "knowing" plus the genitive

11   **metuam**: the form can be either future indicative or present subjunctive; probably best taken as future, considering the future tense of **parcent** (line 12)
    morior, mori, mortuus sum, *die*

12   **parco, parccre, peperci, parsum**, *spare* (with dative)
    anima, -ae, f., *breath, life, darling*
    fatum, -i, n., *fate*, pl., *the Fates*
    superstes, superstitis, adj., *standing over, surviving*
13   **torreo, torrere, torrui, tostum**, *burn, parch*
    fax. facis, f., *torch, torch used at funerals and marriages, marriage, death*
    mutuus, -a, -um, adj., *mutual, reciprocal*

14   **Thurinus, -a, -um**, adj., *pertaining to the town of Thurii in southern Italy*
    Calais, Calais, m., *Calais*, man's name
    Ornytus, -i, m., *Ornytus*, man's name
    Thurini...Ornyti: Lydia makes important the "naming" of her current flame; cf. lines 7–8 where she makes her own name important

'donec non alia magis   5
    arsisti, neque erat Lydia post Chloen,
multi Lydia nominis
    Romana vigui clarior Ilia.'

me nunc Thressa Chloe regit,
    dulcis docta modos et citharae sciens,   10
pro qua non metuam mori,
    si parcent animae fata superstiti.

'me torret face mutua
    Thurini Calais filius Ornyti,
pro quo bis patiar mori,   15
    si parcent puero fata superstiti.'

quid si prisca redit Venus
    diductosque iugo cogit aeneo,
si flava excutitur Chloe,
    reiectaeque patet ianua Lydiae?   20

---

15 **bis**, adv., *twice*
    patior, pati, passus sum, *suffer, undergo, experience, endure, allow*
    patiar: cf. **metuam**, line 11, for the form
    mori: see line 11

16 **parcent**: see line 12
    puer, pueri, m., *boy, non-adult male, male beloved,* (young) *male slave*
    fata: see line 12
    superstiti: see line 12

17 **priscus, -a, -um**, adj., *ancient, former*
    redeo, redire, redii, reditum, *go back, come back, return*
    venus, veneris, f., *Venus,* Roman goddess of love; *love, charm, sexual activity; best throw at dice*

18 **diduco, diducere, diduxi, diductum**, *separate, split*
    iugum, -i, n., *yoke, bond*
    cogo, cogere, coegi, coactum, *drive together, force*
    aeneus, -a, -um, adj., *of bronze;* the **ae** is not a diphthong here

(notes contd. next page)

'quamquam sidere pulchrior
   ille est, tu levior cortice et inprobo
iracundior Hadria,
    tecum vivere amem, tecum obeam libens.'

19 **flavus, -a, -um**, adj., *yellow, golden, blonde, auburn*
    excutio, excutere, excussi, excussum, *shake out, drive out, banish*
    Chloe: see line 6

20 **reicio, reicere, reieci, reiectum**, *throw back, drive back, reject*
    pateo, patere, patui, *be open*
    ianua, -ae, f., *door*
    Lydiae: see line 6
    reiectae...Lydiae: dative, rather than genitive, in the context

21 **quamquam**, conj., *although*
    sidus, sideris, n., *star; sky* (plural)

22 **levis, -e**, adj., *light, swift, gentle, unimportant, fickle*
    cortex, corticis, m., *bark, rind, cork*
    inprobus, -a, -um, adj., *unprincipled, immoderate, unruly, relentless, shameless*

23 **iracundus, -a, -um**, adj., *angry, hot-tempered, prone to anger*
    Hadria, -ae, m., *Adriatic Sea*

24 **amem, obeam**: potential subjunctive
    obeo, obire, obii, obitum, *go to, meet, die*
    libens, libentis, adj., *willing*
    tecum: note the repetition of this word in the last line of the poem

Ode 3.13

This hymn to a spring celebrates the complexity of the site of poetic creativity. On the one hand, a hymn involving a proposed dedication, the poem also functions as vehicle for the poet's self-praise. How do humility and pride operate in the poem? What is gained and lost in the sacrifice of the kid to the spring? What, finally, is the relationship between the spring and the poet?

Meter: fourth Asclepiadean

O fons Bandusiae splendidior vitro,
dulci digne mero non sine floribus,
   cras donaberis haedo,
      cui frons turgida cornibus

---

1   **o**, interjection, *O* (with vocative)
    fons, fontis, m., *spring, source*
    Bandusia, -ae, f., *Bandusia*, name of a spring perhaps at Horace's Sabine farm or near Apulia, the area on which his hometown bordered; Horace mentions a spring on his Sabine farm elsewhere, but not by name.
    Bandusiae: appositional genitive, with **fons**
    splendidus, -a, -um, adj., *bright, brilliant, glittering, illustrious*
    vitrum, -i, n., *glass*

2   **dulcis, -e**, adj., *sweet*, (of persons) *dear, beloved*
    dignus, -a, -um, adj., *worthy, worthy of, deserving* (with ablative)
    digne: vocative with **fons**
    merus, -a, -um, adj., *pure, unmixed;* with **vinum** or with **vinum** understood, *wine not mixed with water*
    non sine: litotes
    flos, floris, m., *flower*

(notes contd. next page)

mero, floribus: wine as a libation to the gods; flowers, perhaps in the form of garlands, which were used to decorate springs at the festival of the Fontinalia, the festival of the **Fons**

3 **dono, donare, donavi, donatum**, *present, endow, reward* (with), with ablative of thing given
haedus, -i, m., *young goat, kid;* two stars in the constellation **Auriga**

4 **cui**: dative of reference
frons, frontis, f., *forehead, brow, front*
turgidus, -a, -um, adj., *swollen, turgid*
cornu, -us, n., *horn, anything horn-shaped*

4–5 **cornibus/primis**: horns just beginning to grow

5 **venus, veneris**, f., *Venus,* Roman goddess of love; *love, charm, sexual activity; best throw at dice*
proelium, proelii, n., *battle*
destino, destinare, destinavi, destinatum, *fix, determine, intend, destine, earmark*
et Venerem et proelia destinat: "destines (him) for," with accusative of what he is destined for; **Venerem et proelia**, love and battles may be taken separately, or may refer to battling with rivals over sex (hendiadys)

6 **frustra**, adv., *in vain, to no purpose*
gelidus, -a, -um, adj., *cold, icy*
inficio, inficere, infeci, infectum, *dye, imbue, taint, stain*

7 **ruber, rubra, rubrum**, adj., *red*
sanguis, sanguinis, m., *blood*
rivus, -i, m., *stream*

8 **lascivus, -a, -um**, adj., *playful, frisky, wanton*
suboles, subolis, f., *offspring*
grex, gregis, m., *flock, herd, company, crowd*

9 **te, tu** (10, 13): the repetition in asyndeton of the personal pronoun is typical in outlining the characteristics of the divinity in a hymn
flagrans, flagrantis, adj., *hot, blazing, passionate*
atrox, atrocis, adj., *dreadful, fierce, cruel*
canicula, -ae, f., *the Dog Star, Sirius,* in the constellation Canis Major, brightest star in the sky, thought to bring hot weather

10 **nescio, nescire, nescivi, nescitum**, *not know, be ignorant of, not to know how to, not to be able to*

primis et Venerem et proelia destinat,   5
frustra: nam gelidos inficiet tibi
    rubro sanguine rivos
        lascivi suboles gregis.

te flagrantis atrox hora Caniculae
nescit tangere, tu frigus amabile   10
    fessis vomere tauris
        praebes et pecori vago.

---

tango, tangere, tetigi, tactum, *touch*
frigus, frigoris, n., *cold*

11 **fessus, -a, -um**, adj., *tired, weary*
    vomer, vomeris, m., *plowshare;* by metonymy, *the plow*
    taurus, -i, m., *bull*

12 **praebeo, praebere, praebui, praebitum**, *give, supply, provide*
    pecus, pecoris, n., *farm animal;* singular as collective, *farm animals, live-*
        stock, especially sheep and cattle
    vagus, -a, -um, adj., *roaming, wandering*

fies nobilium tu quoque fontium
me dicente cavis inpositam ilicem
   saxis, unde loquaces   15
      lymphae desiliunt tuae.

---

13 **fontium**: see line 1

     nobilium...fontium: ellipsis of **unus** and genitive of the whole; the fountain will become famous, like Hippocrene, Arethusa, Castalia

14 **me dicente**: causal ablative absolute

     cavus, -a, -um, adj., *hollow, concave*

     inpono, inponere, inposui, inpositum, *place on or over, build on*

     inpositam, desiliunt (16): both these verbs can have sexual meanings in descriptions of the animal world; **inpono** can mean to place a male to a female for purposes of copulation (cf. *OLD* 8), while **desilio** can be used of an animal jumping or leaping down after copulation (cf. *OLD*).

     ilex, ilicis, f., *holm oak, ilex*

     ilicem: direct object of **dicente**

14–15 **cavis...saxis**: dative with **inpositam**

15 **saxum, -i**, n., *rock*

     loquax, loquacis, adj., *talkative, loquacious, talking*

     loquaces: personification; also, cf. the sense of **me dicente** above

15–16 The alliteration of the liquid consonant "l" in **loquaces, lymphae, desiliunt** imitates the sense of the lines

16 **lympha, -ae**, f., *water*

     desilio, desilire, desilui, *leap or jump down*

Ode 3.30

With this ode Horace closes the lyric collection he published in 23 B.C.E. He frames the collection by repeating only here the first Asclepiadean meter he used in the first poem of the collection. In this poem he takes on a tone of supreme confidence and lays claim to an enduring literary achievement: the adaptation to the Latin language of the genre of Greek lyric poetry. There is a grandeur to this ode that gives one a sense of how much pride Horace must have had in his own work. This almost excessive pride is balanced by the reference to humble beginnings and the prayer-like address to the Muse whom he indirectly asks to approve of his work. It is difficult to read this ode without incorporating our knowledge that, in fact, Horace's work has endured, long past the time of Roman rule.

Meter: first or lesser Asclepiadean

Exegi monumentum aere perennius
regalique situ pyramidum altius,

---

1   **exigo, exigere, exegi, exactum**, *drive out, complete, execute*
     monumentum, -i, n., *monument, memorial*
     monumentum: anything that "reminds or tells" (the root in the word is the
         verb **moneo**); often refers to inscriptions in bronze or stone
     aes, aeris, n., *copper, bronze, money*
     perennis, -e, adj., *lasting throughout the year, lasting for many years, enduring*

2   **regalis, -e**, adj., *royal, regal*
     situs, -us, m., *site*
     situs, -us, m., *deterioration, neglect*
     situ: can be from either **situs**; since both words make sense it is best to keep
         the ambiguity.
     pyramis, pyramidis, f., *pyramid*
     regali...pyramidum: the pyramids of Egypt; while the pyramids were very
         old there may be an allusion here to the end of Cleopatra's rule and threat
         to Roman power; cf. Ode 1.37

3   **non...non**: anaphora with asyndeton
    imber, imbris, m., *rain, rain shower, water*
    edax, edacis, adj., *greedy, devouring, destructive*
    Aquilo, Aquilonis, m., *the north wind*
    inpotens, inpotentis, adj., *powerless, weak, wild, violent*

3–4 The Greek lyric poet, Pindar, also speaks in Pythian 6 of poems that cannot be
    destroyed by wind and rain.

4   **possit**: potential subjunctive
    diruo, diruere, dirui, dirutum, *cause to fall in ruin, demolish*
    innumerabilis, -e, adj., *countless, numberless*

5   **series, (-ei)**, f., *series, sequence, succession*
    fuga, -ae, f., *flight, rout*

6   **omnis**: all, "completely"; English would use an adverb here where Latin uses
    an adjective; contrasts with **pars**
    morior, mori, mortuus sum, *die*
    mei: partitive genitive

7   **vito, vitare, vitavi, vitatum**, *avoid, shun*
    Libitina, -ae, f., *Libitina, the goddess of funerals; funeral couch*
    Libitinam: death, by metonymy; however, her specificity may wittily coun-
    teract some of the grandiosity of these lines, for it reminds us of the
    details of burial
    usque, adv., *continuously, continually, all the way*
    posterus, -a, -um, adj., *next, following, future, later*

8   **cresco, crescere, crevi, cretum**, *arise, multiply, expand, increase*
    recens, recentis, adj., *fresh, recent, modern*
    Capitolium, Capitolii, n., *Capitolium*, the Capitoline hill in Rome on which
    the Capitoline gods, Jupiter, Juno, and Minerva, were worshipped

8–9 **dum...pontifex**: The Pontifex Maximus, or chief priest, and the Vestal Virgins
    represent Rome's state religion. Their continued walk up the Capitolium
    symbolizes the continuity of Roman culture and institutions. Cf. note on
    Satire 1.9.35.

9   **scando, scandere**, *climb, ascend, mount*
    tacitus, -a, -um, adj., *silent*
    tacita: Note the contrast between the Vestal Virgin's silence and the roaring
    Aufidus of the next line as well as Horace's voice as poet and the voice of
    posterity which will increase his fame.
    pontifex, pontificis, m., *high priest, pontiff*

quod non imber edax, non Aquilo inpotens
possit diruere aut innumerabilis

annorum series et fuga temporum.   5
non omnis moriar, multaque pars mei

vitabit Libitinam: usque ego postera
crescam laude recens, dum Capitolium

scandet cum tacita virgine pontifex.
dicar, qua violens obstrepit Aufidus   10

et qua pauper aquae Daunus agrestium
regnavit populorum, ex humili potens

---

10 **qua**, adv., *where*
    violens, violentis, adj., *violent, vehement*
    obstrepo, obstrepere, obstrepui, obstrepitum, *make a loud noise, roar, drown*
        by louder noise
    Aufidus, -i, m., *Aufidus*, river in Apulia

10–12 He is powerful, although from humble origins (a reference, perhaps, both
       to his status as a freedman's son and his small town beginnings), and his
       fame will exist in the Apulian area of his childhood.

11 **pauper, pauperis**, adj., *poor* (with genitive of reference; cf. notes to Ode
        1.22.1)
    Daunus, -i, m., *Daunus*, legendary king of Apulia
    agrestis, -e, adj., *of the country, rustic, rural*

11–12 **agrestium...populorum**: genitive with **regnavit** (a Greek construction
       for verbs of ruling)

12 **humilis, -e**, adj., *humble, low;* neuter as noun, *low position;* masculine as
        noun, *humble person*
    potens, potentis, *able, powerful, potent*

13 **princeps, principis**, adj., *first in time, leading, first*
   princeps: suggests temporal priority as well as leadership. **Princeps** is also the title Augustus officially used of himself, so the term has Roman political resonance as well.
   Aeolius, -a, -um, adj., *Aeolian, Aeolic;* referring to Aeolia, the Greek area of Asia Minor, including the island of Lesbos where the Greek poets Sappho and Alcaeus lived, as well as to the dialect of Greek in which they wrote.
   carmen, carminis, n., *solemn or ritual utterance, song, poem, lyric poetry*
   Italus, -a, -um, adj., *Italian*
   Italos: Some take **Italos** as proleptic, in that the lyric meters were not "Italian" until Horace adapted them from the Greek. The initial "i" is long here.

13–14 **princeps...modos**: This is Horace's claim that he, first, adapted Aeolic poetry, that is, the Greek lyric poetry of Sappho and Alcaeus, to the Latin language. Of course, Catullus did write two poems in the Sapphic meter (11 and 51), but clearly Horace's accomplishment in this area is on a far greater scale.

14 **deduco, deducere, deduxi, deductum**, *lead away, lead down, escort, bring a person or army back with one to Rome, bring home in procession as a bride, spin, compose, adapt*
   deduxisse: the verb **deducere** can have the sense of "to settle" (leading down people to the ships to embark on a journey to the new colony) and therefore Horace is establishing an image of his being the leader of a Greek colonization of Italy (**ad Italos...**).
   modus, -i, m., *limit, way, rhythmic pattern;* in plural, *poetry*
   modos: The word **modos** operates on many levels, as "poetry," "rhythmic patterns or verse," and "ways."
   sumo, sumere, sumpsi, sumptum, *take, take on*
   superbia, -ae, f., *pride, arrogance*
   superbiam: The Muse, Melpomene, deserves to be proud because of Horace's poetic achievement.

15 **meritum, -i**, n., *that which one deserves, due reward, service, meritorious action*
   meritis: by not using a possessive adjective with this word, Horace leaves open whose "meritorious actions" have earned Melpomene her pride. Are they Horace's actions as evidenced in his lyric achievement or are they the "services" of inspiration provided by the Muse?
   Delphicus, -a, -um, adj., *Delphic, of Delphi* (the site of the oracle of Apollo, god of poetry and the arts, among other things)

15–16 **Delphica...comam**: cf. Ode 1.1.29: **doctarum hederae praemia frontium**

16 **laurus, -i/-us**, f., *laurel tree*

princeps Aeolium carmen ad Italos
deduxisse modos. sume superbiam

quaesitam meritis et mihi Delphica   15
lauro cinge volens, Melpomene, comam.

---

lauro: the laurel tree was sacred to Apollo; cf. the story of Apollo and Daphne
(Greek for laurel); triumphant Roman generals were crowned with laurel
cingo, cingere, cinxi, cinctum, *surround, encircle*
volens, volentis, adj., *willing*
volens: see note on **omnis** (line 6) above
Melpomene, Melpomenes, f., *Melpomene*, one of the Muses

Ode 4.7

In this poem thoughts of spring give way to thoughts of death. Here Horace articulates, perhaps more powerfully than in any other poem of his, the difference between what time means for nature and what it means for humankind: the repeated, cyclical, motion of time versus the inexorable one-way progression of time from human birth to human death.

Meter: first Archilochian

Diffugere nives, redeunt iam gramina campis
    arboribusque comae,
mutat terra vices et decrescentia ripas
    flumina praetereunt,

---

1   **diffugio, diffugere, diffugi,** *flee in several directions, disperse, scatter*
    diffugere: alternate form of the third person plural perfect tense ending, **-erunt**
    nix, nivis, f., *snow*
    redeo, redire, redii, reditum, *go back, come back, return*
    gramen, graminis, n., *grass*
    campus, -i, m., *plain, level surface; plain, field*

1–2 **gramina campis/arboribusque comae**: chiasmus

2   **comae**: *hair;* by extension, *leaves*

3   **mutat vices**: **mutare vices,** pass through one's cycle of changes
    vicis (genitive), f., *turn, succession, alternation*
    decresco, decrescere, decrevi, decretum, *decrease, grow smaller, shrink*
    ripa, -ae, f., *bank of a river, shore*

4   **flumen, fluminis,** n., *river, waters of a river*
    praetereo, praeterire, praeterii, praeteritum, *go by, go past, pass by, go
      beyond, omit*

5   **gratia, -ae**, f., *goodwill, kindness charm, attraction*, plural personified, *the Graces*, goddesses (usually three in number) embodying charm and beauty
     nympha, -ae, f., *nymph*, semi-divine female spirit of nature
     geminus, -a, -um, adj., *twin, double*
     soror, sororis, f., *sister*

6   **nudus, -a, -um**, adj., *naked, bare, plain*
     chorus, -i, m., *choral dance, people singing and dancing, crowd, troop*
     ne speres: subjunctive in indirect command introduced by **monet**

7   **almus, -a, -um**, adj., *providing nurture, kindly, gracious*

7–8 **almum**: postposition, **quae** placed after **almum**; also, hyperbaton, with the separation of **almum...diem**; the postponement of the antecedent, **hora**, so that it follows rather than precedes the relative pronoun, **quae**, is an example of postposition, verging on hyperbaton. Compare the length of the statement and the complexity of the word order from **monet** to **diem** with the simplicity of **rapit hora diem**, which in a sense sums up the idea expressed from **monet** to **diem**.

9–12 The word order and vocabulary choice of this stanza are particularly note-worthy; summer is trampling on spring, so **ver** comes first and is gone by the time **aestas** is reached; but the fact that summer is about to die is immediately introduced by **interitura**, and **simul** makes this even more immediate; the quickness of the change in seasons is heightened by **recurrit**, with its root "to run," while the emphasis on time is continued through the use of the word **bruma** for winter, rather than **hiems**, which refers to the shortest day of the year and is the superlative of the adjective **brevis, -e**, as well; **iners**, with its sense of inactivity effectively brings the cycle to a halt.

9   **frigus, frigoris**, n., *cold*
     mitesco, mitescere, *become mild, soft, or ripe*
     zephyrus, -i, m., *west wind, zephyr*
     ver, veris, n., *spring*
     protero, proterere, protrivi, protritum, *trample down, crush*
     aestas, aestatis, f., *summer*

10   **intereo, interire, interii, interitum**, *perish, die*

11   **pomifer, pomifera, pomiferum**, adj., *fruit-bearing, fruitful*
     autumnus, -i, m., *autumn*
     frux, frugis, f. usually in plural, *fruit, crops*
     effundo, effundere, effudi, effusum, *pour out, pour forth*

Gratia cum Nymphis geminisque sororibus audet   5
    ducere nuda choros.
inmortalia ne speres, monet annus et almum
    quae rapit hora diem.

frigora mitescunt Zephyris, ver proterit aestas
    interitura, simul   10
pomifer autumnus fruges effuderit, et mox
    bruma recurrit iners.

---

12 **bruma, -ae**, f., *the shortest day, winter, wintry weather*
    recurro, recurrere, recurri, recursum, *run back, return*
    iners, inertis, adj., *lacking skill, inactive, lazy, impotent*

13 **damnum, -i**, n., *loss*
reparo, reparare, reparavi, reparatum, *obtain in exchange for, recover*
caelestis, -e, adj., *of the sky, celestial, divine*
lunae: the use of the plural emphasizes the endless repeatability of nature as opposed to the "end" of human existence
damna...celeres...caelestia lunae: synchysis
damna...lunae: Horace is referring to the monthly cycle of the moon; his terminology of loss and recovery comes from the financial world; cf. the focus on material goods in lines 19–20 below.

13–16 Cf. Catullus 5.4–6 with these lines and with **cum semel occideris** (21), below, for a similar contrast between time in nature and in the human condition and the use of some similar vocabulary: **Soles occidere et redire possunt;/nobis cum semel occidit brevis lux,/nox est perpetua una dormienda.**

14 **decido, decidere, decidi**, *fall down, die*

15 **quo**, adv., *where, for what purpose*
Aeneas, Aeneae, m., *Aeneas,* son of Venus and Anchises, Trojan leader who brought his followers to Italy after the Trojan War and founded what would become the Roman state; hero of Vergil's *Aeneid*; cf. note to lines 25–28 below.
Tullus, -i, m., *Tullus Hostilius,* third king of Rome
dives, divitis, adj., *rich, wealthy*
dives: cf. the notes to lines 13 and 19–20 on financial language and material possessions
Ancus, -i, m., *Ancus Martius,* fourth king of Rome

16 **pulvis, pulveris**, m., *dust*
umbra: the use of the singular with the plural **sumus** is particularly effective here; the plural of **umbra** (shades, ghosts) would suggest at least individual continuity after death, whereas the singular gives the sense of all people becoming one undifferentiated mass of shade and dust.

17 **adicio, adicere, adieci, adiectum**, *throw to, add*
adiciant: subjunctive in indirect question; the tense of the subjunctive denotes either present or future time
hodiernus, -a, -um, adj., *of today*
crastinus, -a, -um, adj., *of tomorrow*
summa, -ae, f., *sum, the whole*

17–18 **hodiernae crastina summae/tempora**: synchysis

18 **di**: alternate form of **dei**, nominative plural of **deus**

damna tamen celeres reparant caelestia lunae:
   nos ubi decidimus,
quo pater Aeneas, quo Tullus dives et Ancus,   15
   pulvis et umbra sumus.

quis scit, an adiciant hodiernae crastina summae
   tempora di superi?
cuncta manus avidas fugient heredis, amico
   quae dederis animo.   20

---

superus, -a, -um, adj., *upper, higher*

19 **cunctus, -a, -um**, adj., *the whole of, all*
    avidus, -a, -um, adj., *greedy, avaricious, eager*
    heres, heredis, c., *heir*
    amico: imitation of the use of the Greek adjective, **philos** (beloved, dear),
       which is comparable to **amicus, -a, -um**, as "one's own."

19–20 **amico/quae**: postposition, **quae** placed after **amico**
    The sense, here, is that whatever material goods you do not enjoy now will
       just go to your greedy heir.

20 **animus, -i**, m., *mind; mind, as standing for the whole person*

21 **semel**, adv., *once, once and for all*
   occido, occidere, occidi, occasum, *fall, die*
   splendidus, -a, -um, adj., *bright, brilliant, glittering, illustrious*
   Minos, Minois/Minonis, m., *Minos*, king of Crete, and later a judge in the
   underworld

22 **arbitrium, arbitrii**, n., *decision, judgement*

23 **Torquatus, -i**, m., *Torquatus;* identity uncertain; a Torquatus, an orator, also
   appears as addressee of Horace Epistle 1.5; may be a son of Lucius Manlius
   Torquatus, consul in 65 B.C.E., the year in which Horace was born; the
   Manlii Torquati were a famous family.
   facundia, -ae, f., *eloquence*

23–24 **non...non...non**: the anaphora makes emphatic the finality of death; note,
   though, that the repetition calls attention to the very qualities (**genus,
   facundia, pietas**) that will not be of help

24 **restituo, restituere, restitui, restitutum**, *restore, revive*
   pietas, pietatis, f., *duty, devotion*

25–28 These extremely compact lines need some elucidation. Chaste Hippolytus
   rejects love as represented by Venus and embraces the worship of chaste
   Diana. Theseus and Pirithous swear lifelong friendship and, among other
   things, attempt to steal Persephone from the underworld as wife for
   Pirithous. When Pirithous is compelled to stay in the underworld, Theseus
   attempts to save him. Theseus functions in these stories as intimate friend
   of Pirithous and as father who causes the death of his son, Hippolytus.
   There is a contrast between love by a divinity, Diana, and love by a
   mortal, Theseus. In lines 25–26 the pair involves male and female, in
   lines 27–28, male and male. Hippolytus is a symbol of chastity, Pirithous
   of lechery.
   It should be noted that there are other versions in which Hippolytus is saved
   by Diana (cf. Vergil *Aeneid* 7.761 ff., esp., 769, **revocatum...amore
   Dianae**) and in which Theseus remains in the underworld (cf. Vergil
   Aeneid 6.617–18, but contrast 6.122). Horace's particular use of these
   stories underscores the notion of the finality of death and its accompany-
   ing end to love. The reference to **pater Aeneas** in line 15 suggests that
   Horace may be responding here to the *Aeneid*, which had recently been
   published.
   Ode 4.7 is often compared with Ode 1.4 because they both deal with spring.
   The tone of 4.7 is much more grim and it is interesting to note that 1.4,
   which expresses much more ambivalence than grimness, ends with the
   next generation loving Lycidas who will be lost to Sestius after Sestius
   dies (cf. Ode 1.4.14–20).

cum semel occideris, et de te splendida Minos
    fecerit arbitria,
non, Torquate, genus, non te facundia, non te
    restituet pietas:

infernis neque enim tenebris Diana pudicum   25
    liberat Hippolytum,
nec Lethaea valet Theseus abrumpere caro
    vincula Pirithoo.

---

25 **infernus, -a, -um**, adj., *lower, of the lower world, infernal*
    tenebrae, -arum, f. pl., *darkness*
    infernis...tenebris: ablative of separation
    Diana, -ae, f., *Diana*, the goddess, daughter of Jupiter and Latona
    pudicus, -a, -um, adj., *having a sense of modesty or shame, modest, honor-*
        able, chaste

26 **Hippolytus, -i**, m., *Hippolytus,* son of Theseus, whose rejection of the sexual
    advances of his stepmother, Phaedra, resulted in his death

27 **Lethaeus, -a, -um**, adj., *relating to Lethe or the underworld;* Lethe is a place
    or river in the underworld whose waters, if drunk, were supposed to
    induce sleepiness or forgetfulness
    valeo, valere, valui, valitum, *be powerful, be strong enough to, be well*
    Theseus, Thesei/Theseos, m., *Theseus,* son of Aegeus or Poseidon; national
    hero of Athens; **Theseus** is disyllabic.
    abrumpo, abrumpere, abrupi, abruptum, *break, break apart*
    carus, -a, -um, adj., *dear, beloved*

27-28 **caro...Pirithoo**: ablative with **abrumpere** or dative of personal interest

28 **vinculum, -i**, n., *chain, bond*
    Pirithous, -i, m., *Pirithous,* a king of the Lapiths who fights with the Cen-
    taurs; son by Dia of Zeus or Ixion
    Pirithoo: on Pirithous, cf. Horace Ode 3.4.79-78: **trecentae/Pirithoum**
    cohibent catenae.

Map of Rome
❧ ❧ ❧

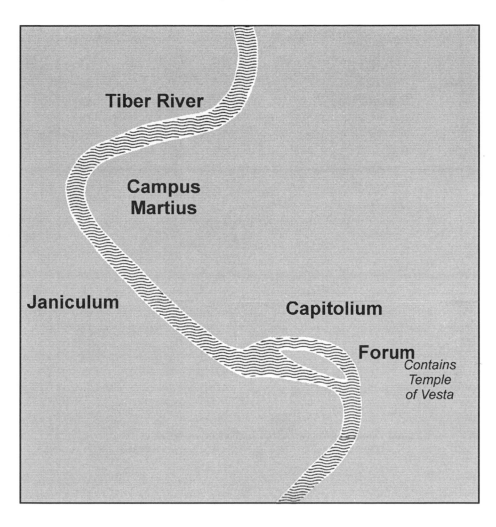

The Via Sacra, or Sacred Way, went through the Forum and on to the Capitolium.

Campus Martius (Odes 1.9 and 3.1)

Tiber River (Satire 1.9 and Ode 2.3)

Temple of Vesta (Satire 1.9)

Via Sacra (Satire 1.9)

Capitolium (Ode 1.37 and 3.30)

Map of Italy

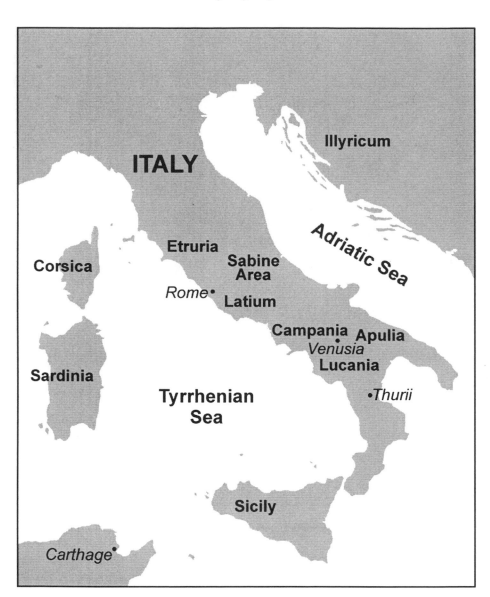

Map of Greece
❧ ❧ ❧

Map of the Mediterranean and Beyond

❧ ❧ ❧

Meters of the Poems

In English poetry metrical patterns are based on which syllables in a word are *stressed*, or said more emphatically. In Latin poetry, however, the metrical patterns are based on the *length* of the syllables in the Latin words, not on their stress. While the stress accent played some role in how Latin poetry sounded, the *length* of the syllables determined the particular meter being used in a given poem. For this reason the meters are called *quantitative meters*, that is, they are based on the length or *quantity* of the syllables. The student or teacher should consult the prosody or versification section in a basic Latin grammar or text for rules about determining syllable length, and, more generally, for rules about figuring out Latin meter.

The metrical patterns consist of arrangements of short syllables (∪) and long syllables (—). A syllable marked (X) is called *anceps* ("double-headed") and can be long or short. When pronounced, long syllables are said for a longer time than short ones.

The student should learn to write out the *scansion*, or the marking of the long and short syllables and elisions, of the poems. (Students taking the Advanced Placement Latin Exam will be *required* to do this on the exam.) After gaining competence in writing out the scansion, the student should become familiar with the *sound* of the Latin poetry. The best way to accomplish this is to write out the scansion of a particular passage, e.g., about four lines that make sense as a metrical and grammatical unit, to practice reading it with the appropriate long and short syllables, elisions etc., and then to *memorize* it. Having such a "chunk" of Latin in one's head or on one's lips is the best way to reinforce the particular metrical patterns.

The following nine meters occur in the poems in this text: dactylic hexameter, Alcaic, Sapphic, first or lesser Asclepiadean, second Asclepiadean, third Asclepiadean, fourth Asclepiadean, fifth or greater Asclepiadean, and first Archilochian. (It should be noted that scholars have not adopted a consistent method for numbering the Asclepiadean meters in Horace. For example, what is called third Asclepiadean here may be called fourth Asclepiadean elsewhere. I have adopted the system that is used most commonly.)

Dactylic Hexameter
This meter occurs in Satire 1.9.

Horace's satires are composed in dactylic hexameter, the same meter used in Latin for Vergil's *Aeneid* and Ovid's *Metamorphoses,* and in Greek for Homer's *Iliad* and *Odyssey.* While perhaps best known as an epic meter, dactylic hexameter fits well the conversational style of satire.

There are six feet ("hex" is Greek for six) in a line or verse of dactylic hexameter poetry. (A foot is the smallest metrical unit of verse with a given sequence and number of short and long syllables.) The first five feet are either dactyls (— ∪ ∪) or spondees (— —) or any combination of these (i.e., the first foot could be a dactyl, the second a spondee etc.). A dactyl is one long syllable followed by two short syllables. A spondee is two long syllables. The sixth foot is treated as a spondee (— —), but the second syllable of the spondee is actually anceps (— X). The fifth foot is almost always a dactyl.

This is the metrical pattern of the line:

$$\underset{\textstyle - \,-}{\cup\cup} \quad \underset{\textstyle - \,-}{\cup\cup} \quad \underset{\textstyle - \,-}{\cup\cup} \quad \underset{\textstyle - \,-}{\cup\cup} \quad \underset{\textstyle - \,-}{\cup\cup} \quad -X$$

The major pause in the line, called the principal caesura—a caesura (//) is a pause or break between words within a foot—usually occurs after the first syllable of the third foot or after the first syllable of the fourth foot.

example (Satire 1.9.1)

```
——    — ∪ ∪—    — —    — —    ∪ ∪  —    X
Ibam  forte  via   sacra,  sicut meus  est mos,
```

Alcaic
This meter is used in the following poems: Odes 1.9, 1.37, 2.3, 2.7, 2.14, 3.1.

The Alcaic meter is used in the *Odes* more often than any other meter. It is named after Alcaeus, the Greek lyric poet from the island of Lesbos.

This is the metrical pattern of the Alcaic stanza:

X — ∪ — — // — ∪ ∪ — ∪ X

X — ∪ — — // — ∪ ∪ — ∪ X

X — ∪ — — — ∪ — X

— ∪ ∪ — ∪ ∪ — ∪ — X

The first two lines have the same meter. Horace prefers to start the first three lines with a long syllable, but does not always do so. (Cf., e.g., Ode 1.9.1). (Students taking the Advanced Placement Latin Exam *will not* be tested on Alcaic lines that begin with a short syllable.) There is typically a diaeresis (//), or pause and break between words, after the fifth syllable in the first two lines, but cf. Ode 1.37.5 and 14.

example (Ode 1.9.22-24)

— — ∪ — — — ∪∪— ∪ X
nunc et latentis proditor intumo
— — ∪ — — — ∪ ∪ — ∪X
gratus puellae risus ab angulo
— — ∪ — — — ∪ — X
pignusque dereptum lacertis
— ∪∪— ∪∪ — ∪—X
aut digito male pertinaci

Sapphic

This meter is used in the following poems: Odes 1.22, 1.25, 1.38, 2.10.

The Sapphic meter is named after Sappho, the Greek lyric poet from the island of Lesbos.

The following is the metrical pattern of the Sapphic stanza. The pattern is written as four lines, although the fourth line originally may have been thought of as just a lengthening of the third line:

$$— \cup — — — // \cup \cup — \cup — X$$

$$— \cup — — — // \cup \cup — \cup — X$$

$$— \cup — — — // \cup \cup — \cup — X$$

$$— \cup \cup — X$$

Occasionally the diaeresis will occur after the sixth syllable rather than the fifth (cf. Ode 1.25.11).

example (Ode 1.22.1-4)

$$— \cup — — — \quad \cup \cup — \quad \cup \quad — X$$
Integer vitae scelerisque purus
$$— \quad \cup — \quad — — \cup \ \cup — \quad \cup \qquad — X$$
non eget Mauris iaculis nequ(e) arcu,
$$— \quad \cup — — — \quad \cup \ \cup — \cup — X$$
nec venenatis gravida sagittis,
$$— \quad \cup \quad \cup — X$$
   Fusce, pharetra,

First or Lesser Asclepiadean
This meter is used in Odes 1.1 and 3.30.

This meter is named after the Hellenistic poet Asclepiades, who revived these meters used earlier by Sappho and Alcaeus.

This is the pattern for the first Asclepiadean line:

$$- - -\, - \cup \cup - // - \cup \cup - \cup\, x\, \underset{\smile}{}$$

The first Asclepiadean line is a Glyconic (see under second Asclepiadean) lengthened through a choriamb ($- \cup \cup -$) placed between its sixth and seventh syllables.The diaeresis after the sixth foot does not appear in Ode 3.30.1, 7, and 12.

example (Ode 3.30.16)

$$- \,- -\quad \cup\ \cup-\quad - \cup\ \cup - \cup\ x$$
lauro cinge volens, Melpomene, comam.

Second Asclepiadean
This meter is used in Odes 1.13 and 3.9.

$$- - - \cup \cup - \cup\, x$$

$$- - - \cup \cup - // - \cup \cup - \cup\, x$$

The first line is called a Glyconic. The Glyconic or a version of it is found in all the Asclepiadean meters. The second of the two lines is a first Asclepiadean line.

example (Ode 3.9.1–2)

$$- -\quad - \cup\ \cup-\quad \cup\, x$$
Donec gratus eram tibi,
$$-\ \ -\ \ -\quad \cup \cup-\ -\ \cup \cup -\ \cup\ x$$
    nec quisquam potior brachia candidae

Third Asclepiadean
This meter occurs in Ode 1.24.

The following is the pattern for the third Asclepiadean stanza:

———∪∪—//—∪∪—∪X

———∪∪—//—∪∪—∪X

———∪∪—//—∪∪—∪X

———∪∪—∪X

This stanza is composed of three first Asclepiadean lines followed by a Glyconic.

example (Ode 1.24.1–4)

Quis desiderio sit pudor aut modus
tam cari capitis? praecipe lugubris
cantus, Melpomene, cui liquidam pater
    vocem cum cithara dedit.

Fourth Asclepiadean
This meter occurs in Odes 1.5, 1.23, 3.13.

The pattern of the fourth Asclepiadean meter is as follows:

$$———\cup\cup—/\!/—\cup\cup—\cup X$$

$$———\cup\cup—/\!/—\cup\cup—\cup X$$

$$———\cup\cup—X$$

$$———\cup\cup—\cup X$$

The stanza consists of two first Asclepiadean lines, followed by a Pherecratean and a Glyconic.

example (Ode 1.23.1–4)

Vitas inuleo me similis, Chloe,

quaerenti pavidam montibus aviis

matrem non sine vano

aurar(um) et siluae metu.

(note that "siluae" is trisyllabic here)

Fifth or Greater Asclepiadean

This meter occurs in Ode 1.11

This is the pattern for the fifth Asclepiadean meter:

$$———\cup\cup—//—\cup\cup—//—\cup\cup—\cup\text{X}$$

example (Ode 1.11.8)

$$——\quad—\cup\cup—\quad—\quad\cup\cup—\quad—\cup\cup—\cup\text{X}$$
aetas: carpe diem, quam minimum credula postero.

First Archilochian

This meter occurs in Ode 4.7.

Archilochian meters are named after the Greek iambic and elegiac poet, Archilochus.

The pattern for the first Archilochian meter is as follows:

The first line is a dactylic hexameter. The second line is a hemiepes; the hemiepes repeats the dactylic hexameter line up to the caesura, but has two dactyls rather than dactyls or spondees.

example (Ode 4.7.1–2)

$$——\,—\cup\,\cup—\quad\cup\,\cup—\quad—\quad—\cup\cup—\quad\text{X}$$
Diffugere nives, redeunt iam gramina campis
$$—\,\cup\cup—\quad\cup\,\cup\,\text{X}$$
  arboribusque comae,

Metrical Terms, Tropes, and Rhetorical Figures or Figures of Speech

The following is a list of definitions for terms used in this book that are important for (1) meter and (2) the figurative use of language, whether a departure from the standard meaning of a word (a trope) or a departure from the standard order of words (a rhetorical figure). References in parentheses are to examples from poems in this book.

alliteration: repetition of the same sound, usually initial, in two or more words. The term usually applies to consonants. (Ode 3.13.15–16)

anaphora: repetition of a word, often at the beginning of successive clauses or phrases. (Ode 4.7.23–24)

asyndeton: lack of a conjunction between words or clauses. (Ode 2.3.26)

caesura: pause or break between words within a metrical foot.

chiasmus: arrangement of words parallel in syntax with corresponding words reversed in an A B B A pattern like the Greek letter *chi* (X). (Ode 1.22.1)

diaeresis: pause or break between words that coincides with the end of a metrical unit; except for those in the dactylic hexameter line, the pauses indicated in this book are diaereses. The same symbol (//) is used here to indicate either kind of pause.

elision: suppression, partial suppression, or blending of a final syllable of a word ending in a vowel (or a vowel followed by the letter "m") before another word beginning with a vowel (or the letter "h" followed by a vowel). Elision is indicated in scansion by writing the symbol (∪) from the end of the first word to the beginning of the second word as well as by crossing through with a single line (/) or putting in parentheses ( ) the elided letter(s).

ellipsis: omission of a word or words that must be understood from the context. (Satire 1.9.2)

enjambment: running over of a phrase, clause, or sentence from one line to the next. (Ode 1.37.20–21)

foot: the smallest metrical unit of verse with a given sequence and number of short and long syllables.

figura etymologica: the repetition of a word in a somewhat different form. (Ode 1.24.9–10)

golden line: two adjectives and two nouns with a verb between. (Ode 3.1.16)

hendiadys: one idea expressed through two. (Ode 3.13.5)

hiatus: lack of elision. (Ode 1.1.2)

hyperbaton: disruption of normal prose word order, for example, through wide separation of noun and modifier. (Ode 1.9.21–22)

hyperbole: extravagant exaggeration. (Satire 1.9.38)

hypermetric line: elision from one line to the next. (Ode 2.3.27)

irony: statement in which implied meaning is different from explicitly stated meaning. (Satire 1.9.54)

litotes: understatement, usually involving the assertion of something by denying its opposite. (Ode 1.23.3)

metaphor: implied comparison in the form of an identity. The "tenor" is the subject to which the metaphoric language is applied, while the "vehicle" is the metaphoric language itself. (In Ode 1.25.17–19 the tenor consists of particular times of life, while the vehicle consists of the ivy, myrtle, or dry leaves.)

metonymy: application of a term for one thing to another with which it is closely associated. (Ode 1.1.5)

oxymoron: paradox expressed through juxtaposition of seemingly contradictory words. (Ode 1.22.16)

personification: application to inanimate objects of human qualities. (Ode 3.13.15)

postposition: placement of a word later than the location expected in prose; often, the placement of a word second rather than first in its clause. (Ode 1.25.17)

simile: explicit comparison between two distinct things introduced by a word like **velut** (just as). (Ode 1.37.17 ff.)

stanza: division of a poem containing a series of lines repeating in a pattern.

strophe: stanza

synapheia: the joining together of two lines as if they were one. (Ode 1.25.11–12)

synchysis or interlocked word order: arrangement of words parallel in syntax with an interlocking of the corresponding words in an A B A B pattern. (Ode 1.5.6–7)

synecdoche: part of something used to signify the whole. (Ode 1.37.17)

synizesis: the joining of two successive vowels within a word into one long syllable. (Ode 2.7.5)

tmesis: separation of a compound word. (Satire 1.9.33)

transferred epithet (or hypallage): transfer of an adjective from the noun with which it goes "in sense" to another related noun. (Ode 1.1.5)

tricolon crescendo: arrangement of three phrases, clauses etc. with increasing length. (Ode 2.3.13–14)

Latin Text Without Notes and Vocabulary

Satire 1.9

Ibam forte via sacra, sicut meus est mos,
nescio quid meditans nugarum, totus in illis.
accurrit quidam notus mihi nomine tantum,
arreptaque manu: 'quid agis, dulcissime rerum?'
'suaviter, ut nunc est' inquam, 'et cupio omnia, quae vis.'   5
cum adsectaretur: 'numquid vis?' occupo, at ille
'noris nos' inquit, 'docti sumus.' hic ego: 'pluris
hoc' inquam 'mihi eris.' misere discedere quaerens
ire modo ocius, interdum consistere, in aurem
dicere nescio quid puero, cum sudor ad imos   10
manaret talos. 'o te, Bolane, cerebri
felicem' aiebam tacitus, cum quidlibet ille
garriret, vicos, urbem laudaret. ut illi
nil respondebam: 'misere cupis' inquit 'abire;
iam dudum video. sed nil agis; usque tenebo.   15
persequar hinc, quo nunc iter est tibi.' 'nil opus est te
circumagi: quendam volo visere non tibi notum;
trans Tiberim longe cubat is prope Caesaris hortos.'
'nil habeo, quod agam, et non sum piger: usque sequar te.'
demitto auriculas, ut iniquae mentis asellus,   20
cum gravius dorso subiit onus. incipit ille:
'si bene me novi, non Viscum pluris amicum,
non Varium facies: nam quis me scribere pluris
aut citius possit versus? quis membra movere
mollius? invideat quod et Hermogenes ego canto.'   25
interpellandi locus hic erat: 'est tibi mater,
cognati, quis te salvo est opus?' 'haud mihi quisquam;
omnis composui.' 'felices! nunc ego resto.
confice! namque instat fatum mihi triste, Sabella
quod puero cecinit divina mota anus urna: 30
hunc neque dira venena, nec hosticus auferet ensis,
nec laterum dolor aut tussis, nec tarda podagra:

garrulus hunc quando consumet cumque. loquaces,
si sapiat, vitet, simul atque adoleverit aetas.'
ventum erat ad Vestae, quarta iam parte diei   35
praeterita, et casu tum respondere vadato
debebat, quod ni fecisset, perdere litem.
'si me amas' inquit, 'paulum hic ades.' 'interim, si
aut valeo stare aut novi civilia iura,
et propero, quo scis.' 'dubius sum, quid faciam' inquit,   40
'tene relinquam, an rem.' 'me, sodes.' 'non faciam' ille
et praecedere coepit. ego, ut contendere durum
cum victore, sequor. 'Maecenas quomodo tecum?'
hinc repetit, 'paucorum hominum et mentis bene sanae;
nemo dexterius fortuna est usus. haberes   45
magnum adiutorem, posset qui ferre secundas,
hunc hominem velles si tradere. dispeream, ni
summosses omnis.' 'non isto vivimus illic,
quo tu rere, modo. domus hac nec purior ulla est,
nec magis his aliena malis. nil mi officit, inquam,   50
ditior hic aut est quia doctior: est locus uni
cuique suus.' 'magnum narras, vix credibile.' 'atqui
sic habet.' 'accendis, quare cupiam magis illi
proxumus esse.' 'velis tantummodo: quae tua virtus,
expugnabis, et est, qui vinci possit, eoque   55
difficilis aditus primos habet.' 'haud mihi dero:
muneribus servos corrumpam; non, hodie si
exclusus fuero, desistam; tempora quaeram,
occurram in triviis, deducam. nil sine magno
vita labore dedit mortalibus.' haec dum agit, ecce   60
Fuscus Aristius occurrit, mihi carus et illum
qui pulchre nosset. consistimus. 'unde venis?' et
'quo tendis?' rogat et respondet. vellere coepi
et pressare manu lentissima brachia, nutans,
distorquens oculos, ut me eriperet. male salsus   65
ridens dissimulare, meum iecur urere bilis:
'certe nescio quid secreto velle loqui te
aiebas mecum.' 'memini bene, sed meliore
tempore dicam: hodie tricesima sabbata. vin tu
curtis Iudaeis oppedere?' 'nulla mihi' inquam   70
'religio est.' 'at mi! sum paulo infirmior, unus
multorum. ignosces; alias loquar.' huncine solem
tam nigrum surrexe mihi! fugit inprobus ac me
sub cultro linquit. casu venit obvius illi
adversarius et 'quo tu, turpissime?' magna   75
inclamat voce, et 'licet antestari?' ego vero
oppono auriculam. rapit in ius: clamor utrimque,
undique concursus. sic me servavit Apollo.

Ode 1.1

❊ ❊ ❊

Maecenas atavis edite regibus,
o et praesidium et dulce decus meum:

sunt, quos curriculo pulverem Olympicum
collegisse iuvat metaque fervidis

evitata rotis palmaque nobilis   5
terrarum dominos evehit ad deos;

hunc, si mobilium turba Quiritium
certat tergeminis tollere honoribus,

illum, si proprio condidit horreo,
quicquid de Libycis verritur areis.   10

gaudentem patrios findere sarculo
agros Attalicis condicionibus

numquam demoveas, ut trabe Cypria
Myrtoum pavidus nauta secet mare;

luctantem Icariis fluctibus Africum   15
mercator metuens otium et oppidi

laudat rura sui, mox reficit rates
quassas indocilis pauperiem pati.

est, qui nec veteris pocula Massici
nec partem solido demere de die   20

spernit, nunc viridi membra sub arbuto
stratus, nunc ad aquae lene caput sacrae;

multos castra iuvant et lituo tubae
permixtus sonitus bellaque matribus

detestata; manet sub Iove frigido   25
venator tenerae coniugis inmemor,

seu visa est catulis cerva fidelibus,
seu rupit teretes Marsus aper plagas.

me doctarum hederae praemia frontium
dis miscent superis, me gelidum nemus   30

Nympharumque leves cum Satyris chori
secernunt populo, si neque tibias

Euterpe cohibet, nec Polyhymnia
Lesboum refugit tendere barbiton.

quodsi me lyricis vatibus inseres,   35
sublimi feriam sidera vertice.

Ode 1.5

❦ ❦ ❦

Quis multa gracilis te puer in rosa
perfusus liquidis urget odoribus
   grato, Pyrrha, sub antro?
     cui flavam religas comam

simplex munditiis? heu quotiens fidem   5
mutatosque deos flebit et aspera
   nigris aequora ventis
     emirabitur insolens,

qui nunc te fruitur credulus aurea,
qui semper vacuam, semper amabilem   10
   sperat, nescius aurae
     fallacis. miseri, quibus

intemptata nites. me tabula sacer
votiva paries indicat uvida
   suspendisse potenti   15
     vestimenta maris deo.

Ode 1.9

❦ ❦ ❦

Vides, ut alta stet nive candidum
Soracte, nec iam sustineant onus
   silvae laborantes, geluque
      flumina constiterint acuto?

dissolve frigus ligna super foco   5
large reponens atque benignius
   deprome quadrimum Sabina,
      o Thaliarche, merum diota.

permitte divis cetera, qui simul
stravere ventos aequore fervido   10
   deproeliantis, nec cupressi
      nec veteres agitantur orni.

quid sit futurum cras, fuge quaerere, et
quem Fors dierum cumque dabit, lucro
   adpone, nec dulcis amores   15
      sperne puer neque tu choreas,

donec virenti canities abest
morosa. nunc et campus et areae
   lenesque sub noctem susurri
      composita repetantur hora,   20

nunc et latentis proditor intumo
gratus puellae risus ab angulo
   pignusque dereptum lacertis
      aut digito male pertinaci.

Ode 1.11

❧ ❧ ❧

Tu ne quaesieris (scire nefas), quem mihi, quem tibi
finem di dederint, Leuconoe, nec Babylonios

temptaris numeros. ut melius, quidquid erit, pati!
seu pluris hiemes, seu tribuit Iuppiter ultimam,

quae nunc oppositis debilitat pumicibus mare   5
Tyrrhenum: sapias, vina liques et spatio brevi

spem longam reseces. dum loquimur, fugerit invida
aetas: carpe diem, quam minimum credula postero.

Ode 1.13

❧ ❧ ❧

Cum tu, Lydia, Telephi
   cervicem roseam, cerea Telephi
laudas brachia, vae meum
   fervens difficili bile tumet iecur.

tunc nec mens mihi, nec color   5
   certa sede manet, umor et in genas
furtim labitur arguens,
   quam lentis penitus macerer ignibus.

uror, seu tibi candidos
   turparunt umeros inmodicae mero   10
rixae, sive puer furens
   inpressit memorem dente labris notam.

non, si me satis audias,
   speres perpetuum dulcia barbare
laedentem oscula, quae Venus   15
   quinta parte sui nectaris imbuit.

felices ter et amplius,
   quos inrupta tenet copula, nec malis
divolsus querimoniis
   suprema citius solvet amor die.   20

Ode 1.22

⁜ ⁜ ⁜

Integer vitae scelerisque purus
non eget Mauris iaculis neque arcu,
nec venenatis gravida sagittis,
    Fusce, pharetra,

sive per Syrtis iter aestuosas   5
sive facturus per inhospitalem
Caucasum, vel quae loca fabulosus
    lambit Hydaspes.

namque me silva lupus in Sabina,
dum meam canto Lalagen et ultra   10
terminum curis vagor expeditis,
    fugit inermem,

quale portentum neque militaris
Daunias latis alit aesculetis,
nec Iubae tellus generat, leonum   15
    arida nutrix.

pone me, pigris ubi nulla campis
arbor aestiva recreatur aura,
quod latus mundi nebulae malusque
    Iuppiter urget,   20

pone sub curru nimium propinqui
solis in terra domibus negata:
dulce ridentem Lalagen amabo,
    dulce loquentem.

Ode 1.23
❀ ❀ ❀

Vitas inuleo me similis, Chloe,
quaerenti pavidam montibus aviis
   matrem non sine vano
      aurarum et siluae metu.

nam seu mobilibus veris inhorruit   5
adventus foliis, seu virides rubum
   dimovere lacertae,
      et corde et genibus tremit.

atqui non ego te tigris ut aspera
Gaetulusve leo frangere persequor: 10
   tandem desine matrem
      tempestiva sequi viro.

Ode 1.24

Quis desiderio sit pudor aut modus
tam cari capitis? praecipe lugubris
cantus, Melpomene, cui liquidam pater
    vocem cum cithara dedit.

ergo Quintilium perpetuus sopor   5
urget? cui Pudor et Iustitiae soror,
incorrupta Fides nudaque Veritas
    quando ullum inveniet parem?

multis ille bonis flebilis occidit,
nulli flebilior, quam tibi, Vergili.   10
tu, frustra pius, heu, non ita creditum
    poscis Quintilium deos.

quid, si Threicio blandius Orpheo
auditam moderere arboribus fidem,
num vanae redeat sanguis imagini,   15
    quam virga semel horrida

non lenis precibus fata recludere
nigro compulerit Mercurius gregi?
durum, sed levius fit patientia,
    quicquid corrigere est nefas.   20

Ode 1.25

❦ ❦ ❦

Parcius iunctas quatiunt fenestras
iactibus crebris iuvenes protervi,
nec tibi somnos adimunt, amatque
    ianua limen,

quae prius multum facilis movebat   5
cardines. audis minus et minus iam:
'me tuo longas pereunte noctes,
    Lydia, dormis?'

invicem moechos anus adrogantis
flebis in solo levis angiportu,   10
Thracio bacchante magis sub inter-
    lunia vento,

cum tibi flagrans amor et libido,
quae solet matres furiare equorum,
saeviet circa iecur ulcerosum,   15
    non sine questu,

laeta quod pubes hedera virenti
gaudeat pulla magis atque myrto,
aridas frondes hiemis sodali
    dedicet Hebro.   20

Ode 1.37

✥ ✥ ✥

Nunc est bibendum, nunc pede libero
pulsanda tellus, nunc Saliaribus
   ornare pulvinar deorum
     tempus erat dapibus, sodales.

antehac nefas depromere Caecubum   5
cellis avitis, dum Capitolio
   regina dementis ruinas
     funus et imperio parabat

contaminato cum grege turpium
morbo virorum, quidlibet inpotens   10
   sperare fortunaque dulci
     ebria; sed minuit furorem

vix una sospes navis ab ignibus,
mentemque lymphatam Mareotico
   redegit in veros timores   15
     Caesar ab Italia volantem

remis adurgens, accipiter velut
mollis columbas aut leporem citus
   venator in campis nivalis
     Haemoniae, daret ut catenis   20

fatale monstrum, quae generosius
perire quaerens nec muliebriter
   expavit ensem, nec latentis
     classe cita reparavit oras,

ausa et iacentem visere regiam   25
voltu sereno, fortis et asperas
   tractare serpentes, ut atrum
     corpore combiberet venenum,

deliberata morte ferocior:
saevis Liburnis scilicet invidens   30
   privata deduci superbo
     non humilis mulier triumpho.

Ode 1.38

Persicos odi, puer, apparatus,
displicent nexae philyra coronae;
mitte sectari, rosa quo locorum
   sera moretur.

simplici myrto nihil adlabores   5
sedulus, curo: neque te ministrum
dedecet myrtus, neque me sub arta
   vite bibentem.

Ode 2.3

❀ ❀ ❀

Aequam memento rebus in arduis
servare mentem, non secus in bonis
 ab insolenti temperatam
  laetitia, moriture Delli,

seu maestus omni tempore vixeris,   5
seu te in remoto gramine per dies
 festos reclinatum bearis
  interiore nota Falerni.

quo pinus ingens albaque populus
umbram hospitalem consociare amant   10
 ramis? quid obliquo laborat
  lympha fugax trepidare rivo?

huc vina et unguenta et nimium brevis
flores amoenae ferre iube rosae,
 dum res et aetas et sororum   15
  fila trium patiuntur atra.

cedes coemptis saltibus et domo
villaque, flavos quam Tiberis lavit,
 cedes, et exstructis in altum
  divitiis potietur heres.   20

divesne prisco natus ab Inacho,
nil interest, an pauper et infima
 de gente sub divo moreris,
  victima nil miserantis Orci:

omnes eodem cogimur, omnium   25
versatur urna serius ocius
 sors exitura et nos in aeternum
  exilium inpositura cumbae.

Ode 2.7

❀ ❀ ❀

O saepe mecum tempus in ultimum
deducte Bruto militiae duce,
   quis te redonavit Quiritem
     dis patriis Italoque caelo,

Pompei, meorum prime sodalium,   5
cum quo morantem saepe diem mero
   fregi coronatus nitentis
     malobathro Syrio capillos?

tecum Philippos et celerem fugam
sensi relicta non bene parmula,   10
   cum fracta virtus et minaces
     turpe solum tetigere mento.

sed me per hostis Mercurius celer
denso paventem sustulit aere,
   te rursus in bellum resorbens   15
     unda fretis tulit aestuosis.

ergo obligatam redde Iovi dapem,
longaque fessum militia latus
   depone sub lauru mea, nec
     parce cadis tibi destinatis.   20

oblivioso levia Massico
ciboria exple, funde capacibus
   unguenta de conchis. quis udo
     deproperare apio coronas

curatve myrto? quem Venus arbitrum   25
dicet bibendi? non ego sanius
   bacchabor Edonis: recepto
     dulce mihi furere est amico.

Ode 2.10

Rectius vives, Licini, neque altum
semper urgendo, neque – dum procellas
cautus horrescis – nimium premendo
 litus iniquum.

auream quisquis mediocritatem   5
diligit, tutus caret obsoleti
sordibus tecti, caret invidenda
 sobrius aula.

saepius ventis agitatur ingens
pinus et celsae graviore casu   10
decidunt turres feriuntque summos
 fulgura montis.

sperat infestis, metuit secundis
alteram sortem bene praeparatum
pectus. informis hiemes reducit   15
 Iuppiter, idem

submovet. non, si male nunc, et olim
sic erit: quondam cithara tacentem
suscitat Musam, neque semper arcum
 tendit Apollo.   20

rebus angustis animosus atque
fortis appare: sapienter idem
contrahes vento nimium secundo
 turgida vela.

Ode 2.14

&❦ &❦ &❦

Eheu fugaces, Postume, Postume,
labuntur anni, nec pietas moram
   rugis et instanti senectae
     adferet indomitaeque morti,

non, si trecenis, quotquot eunt dies,   5
amice, places inlacrimabilem
   Plutona tauris, qui ter amplum
     Geryonen Tityonque tristi

conpescit unda, scilicet omnibus,
quicumque terrae munere vescimur,   10
   enaviganda, sive reges,
     sive inopes erimus coloni.

frustra cruento Marte carebimus
fractisque rauci fluctibus Hadriae,
   frustra per autumnos nocentem   15
     corporibus metuemus Austrum:

visendus ater flumine languido
Cocytos errans et Danai genus
   infame damnatusque longi
     Sisyphus Aeolides laboris.   20

linquenda tellus et domus et placens
uxor, neque harum, quas colis, arborum
   te praeter invisas cupressos
     ulla brevem dominum sequetur,

absumet heres Caecuba dignior   25
servata centum clavibus et mero
   tinguet pavimentum superbo,
     pontificum potiore cenis.

Ode 3.1

❧ ❧ ❧

Odi profanum volgus et arceo.
favete linguis: carmina non prius
   audita Musarum sacerdos
      virginibus puerisque canto.

regum timendorum in proprios greges,   5
reges in ipsos imperium est Iovis,
   clari Giganteo triumpho,
      cuncta supercilio moventis.

est, ut viro vir latius ordinet
arbusta sulcis, hic generosior   10
   descendat in campum petitor,
      moribus hic meliorque fama

contendat, illi turba clientium
sit maior: aequa lege Necessitas
   sortitur insignis et imos,   15
      omne capax movet urna nomen.

destrictus ensis cui super impia
cervice pendet, non Siculae dapes
   dulcem elaborabunt saporem,
      non avium citharaeque cantus   20

somnum reducent: somnus agrestium
lenis virorum non humilis domos
   fastidit umbrosamque ripam,
      non Zephyris agitata Tempe.

desiderantem quod satis est neque   25
tumultuosum sollicitat mare,
   nec saevus Arcturi cadentis
      impetus aut orientis Haedi,

non verberatae grandine vineae
fundusque mendax, arbore nunc aquas   30
   culpante, nunc torrentia agros
      sidera, nunc hiemes iniquas.

contracta pisces aequora sentiunt
iactis in altum molibus: huc frequens
    caementa demittit redemptor   35
        cum famulis dominusque terrae

fastidiosus, sed Timor et Minae
scandunt eodem, quo dominus, neque
    decedit aerata triremi et
        post equitem sedet atra Cura.   40

quodsi dolentem nec Phrygius lapis,
nec purpurarum sidere clarior
    delenit usus, nec Falerna
        vitis Achaemeniumque costum,

cur invidendis postibus et novo   45
sublime ritu moliar atrium?
    cur valle permutem Sabina
        divitias operosiores?

Ode 3.9

❀ ❀ ❀

Donec gratus eram tibi,
   nec quisquam potior brachia candidae
cervici iuvenis dabat,
   Persarum vigui rege beatior.

'donec non alia magis   5
   arsisti, neque erat Lydia post Chloen,
multi Lydia nominis
   Romana vigui clarior Ilia.'

me nunc Thressa Chloe regit,
   dulcis docta modos et citharae sciens,   10
pro qua non metuam mori,
   si parcent animae fata superstiti.

'me torret face mutua
   Thurini Calais filius Ornyti,
pro quo bis patiar mori,   15
   si parcent puero fata superstiti.'

quid si prisca redit Venus
   diductosque iugo cogit aeneo,
si flava excutitur Chloe,
   reiectaeque patet ianua Lydiae?   20

'quamquam sidere pulchrior
   ille est, tu levior cortice et inprobo
iracundior Hadria,
   tecum vivere amem, tecum obeam libens.'

Ode 3.13

❀ ❀ ❀

O fons Bandusiae splendidior vitro,
dulci digne mero non sine floribus,
   cras donaberis haedo,
      cui frons turgida cornibus

primis et Venerem et proelia destinat,   5
frustra: nam gelidos inficiet tibi
   rubro sanguine rivos
      lascivi suboles gregis.

te flagrantis atrox hora Caniculae
nescit tangere, tu frigus amabile   10
   fessis vomere tauris
      praebes et pecori vago.

fies nobilium tu quoque fontium
me dicente cavis inpositam ilicem
   saxis, unde loquaces   15
      lymphae desiliunt tuae.

Ode 3.30

❧ ❧ ❧

Exegi monumentum aere perennius
regalique situ pyramidum altius,

quod non imber edax, non Aquilo inpotens
possit diruere aut innumerabilis

annorum series et fuga temporum.   5
non omnis moriar, multaque pars mei

vitabit Libitinam: usque ego postera
crescam laude recens, dum Capitolium

scandet cum tacita virgine pontifex.
dicar, qua violens obstrepit Aufidus   10

et qua pauper aquae Daunus agrestium
regnavit populorum, ex humili potens

princeps Aeolium carmen ad Italos
deduxisse modos. sume superbiam

quaesitam meritis et mihi Delphica   15
lauro cinge volens, Melpomene, comam.

Ode 4.7

❦ ❦ ❦

Diffugere nives, redeunt iam gramina campis
    arboribusque comae,
mutat terra vices et decrescentia ripas
    flumina praetereunt,

Gratia cum Nymphis geminisque sororibus audet   5
    ducere nuda choros.
inmortalia ne speres, monet annus et almum
    quae rapit hora diem.

frigora mitescunt Zephyris, ver proterit aestas
    interitura, simul   10
pomifer autumnus fruges effuderit, et mox
    bruma recurrit iners.

damna tamen celeres reparant caelestia lunae:
    nos ubi decidimus,
quo pater Aeneas, quo Tullus dives et Ancus,   15
    pulvis et umbra sumus.

quis scit, an adiciant hodiernae crastina summae
    tempora di superi?
cuncta manus avidas fugient heredis, amico
    quae dederis animo.   20

cum semel occideris, et de te splendida Minos
    fecerit arbitria,
non, Torquate, genus, non te facundia, non te
    restituet pietas:

infernis neque enim tenebris Diana pudicum   25
    liberat Hippolytum,
nec Lethaea valet Theseus abrumpere caro
    vincula Pirithoo.

Vocabulary

In general, only long vowels in metrically indeterminate positions are marked. For example, the length of the "a" in "accipiter" need not be marked as long or short because the syllable in which it is contained must be long, regardless of the length of the vowel, because the vowel is followed by two consonants, "cc," (not a combination like "tr" which can create indeterminacy), while the "a" in "beātus" must be marked long because it occurs in a position where metrical rules cannot determine the length of the syllable in which it occurs.

A

ā/ab, prep. with abl., *from, by*

abeō, abīre, abiī, abitum, *go away, depart*

abrumpō, abrumpere, abrūpī, abruptum, *break, break apart*

absum, abesse, āfuī, āfutūrus, *be away, be absent*

absūmō, absūmere, absumpsī, absumptum, *spend, consume*

ac, conj., *and*

accendō, accendere, accendī, accensum, *kindle, arouse, ignite*

accipiter, accipitris, m., *hawk*

accurrō, accurrere, accurrī/ accucurrī, accursum, *run or hurry up to*

Achaemenius, -a, -um, adj., *Persian, Parthian*

acūtus, -a, -um, adj., *sharp, severe*

ad, prep. with acc., *to, towards, near*

adferō, adferre, attulī, allātum, *bring, add*

adiciō, adicere, adiēcī, adiectum, *throw to, add*

adimō, adimere, adēmī, ademptum, *take away*

aditus, -ūs, m., *approach, access*

adiūtor, adiūtōris, m., *helper*

adlabōrō, adlabōrāre, *add to by taking trouble*

adolescō, adolescere, adolēvī, adultum, *grow up,* (of a season or time) *reach its peak*

adpōnō, adpōnere, adposuī, adpositum, *add; treat as, count as* (with **lucrum**)

adrogans, adrogantis, adj., *arrogant, insolent*

adsector, adsectārī, adsectātus sum, *follow closely, attend, escort*

adsum, adesse, adfuī, *be present;* in technical sense, *be present in court as a friend or adviser*

adurgeō, adurgēre, *press hard upon, pursue closely*

adventus, -ūs, m., *arrival, approach*

adversārius, adversāriī, m., *adversary, opponent*

Aenēās, Aenēae, m., *Aeneas,* son of Venus and Anchises, Trojan leader who brought his followers to Italy after the Trojan War and founded what would become the Roman state; hero of Veṙgil's *Aeneid*

aēneus, -a, -um, adj., *of bronze*

Aeolidēs, Aeolidae, m., *a son or more remote descendant of Aeolus*

Aeolius, -a, -um, adj., *Aeolian, Aeolic;* referring to Aeolia, the Greek area of Asia Minor, including the island of Lesbos where the Greek poets Sappho and Alcaeus lived, as well as to the dialect of Greek in which they wrote

aequor, aequoris, n., *a flat level surface, the flat surface of the sea,* (often used in pl.)

aequus, -a, -um, adj., *equal, even, impartial, fair*

āēr, āeris, m., *air, weather, mist*

aerātus, -a, -um, adj., *made of or fitted with bronze or brass*

aes, aeris, n., *copper, bronze, money*

aesculētum, -ī, n., *oak forest*

aestās, aestātis, f., *summer*

aestīvus, -a, -um, adj., *summer*

aestuōsus, -a, -um, adj., *very hot, agitated*

aetās, aetātis, f., *time, age*

aeternus, -a, -um, adj., *eternal, everlasting*

Āfricus, -a, -um, *African*

ager, agrī, m., *field, territory*

agitō, agitāre, agitāvī, agitātum, *stir, drive, agitate, excite*

agō, agere, ēgī, actum, *do, drive*

agrestis, -e, adj., *of the country, rustic, rural*

āiō, defective verb, *say yes, say*

albus, -a, -um, adj., *white, bright*

aliās, adv., *at another time*

aliēnus, -a, -um, adj., *of another, alien, strange* (with abl. or dat.)

alius, alia, aliud, adj., *other, another*

almus, -a, -um, adj., *providing nurture, kindly, gracious*

alō, alere, aluī, altum, *nourish*

alter, altera, alterum, adj., *another, one of two, the one, the other*

altum, -ī, n., *high place or position, heaven, sea, the deep*

altus, -a, -um, adj., *high, deep, tall*

amābilis, -e, adj., *lovable, delightful*

amīcus, -ī, m., *friend*

amō, amāre, amāvī, amātum, *love*

amoenus, -a, -um, adj., *charming, pleasing*

amor, amōris, m., *love*

amplius, adv., *more*

amplus, -a, -um, adj., *large, spacious*

an, conj., *whether, or*

Ancus, -ī, m., *Ancus Martius,* fourth king of Rome

angiportus, -ūs, m., *alley*

angulus, -ī, m., *angle, corner*

angustus, -a, -um, adj., *narrow, limited, difficult* (of circumstances)

anima, -ae, f., *breath, life, darling*

animōsus, -a, -um, adj., *spirited, bold*

animus, -ī, m., *mind; mind, as standing for the whole person*

annus, -ī, m., *year*

antehāc, adv., *previously*

antestor, antestārī, antestātus sum, *call as a witness*

antrum, -ī, n., *cave, hollow space*

anus, -ūs, f., *old woman*

aper, aprī, m., *wild boar*

apium, apiī, n., *parsley, celery*

Apollō, Apollinis, m., *Apollo,* son of Jupiter and Latona, brother of Diana, god of archery, music, poetry, etc.

apparātus, -ūs, m., *preparation, show, sumptuousness, paraphernalia*

appāreō, appārēre, appāruī, appāritum, *appear*

aqua, -ae, f., *water, body of water*

Aquilō, Aquilōnis, m., *the north wind*

arbiter, arbitrī, m., *judge, overseer*

arbitrium, arbitriī, n., *decision, judgement*

arbor, arboris, f., *tree*

arbustum, -ī, n., *wood, plantation,* (pl.) *trees*

arbutus, -ī, f., *the wild strawberry or arbutus tree*

arceō, arcēre, arcuī, *contain, keep away, spurn*

Arctūrus, -ī, m., *Arcturus, the brightest star of the constellation Boötes*

arcus, -ūs, m., *bow*

ardeō, ardēre, arsī, *be on fire, burn, be in love* (with abl.)

arduus, -a, -um, adj., *steep, towering, lofty, high, difficult*

ārea, -ae, f., *open space, threshing floor*

arguō, arguere, arguī, argūtum, *prove, show*

āridus, -a, -um, adj., *dry*

Aristius, Aristiī, m., *Aristius Fuscus, Horace's literary friend; cf. Satire 1.9 and Ode 1.22*

arripiō, arripere, arripuī, arreptum, *seize, take hold of, arrest, bring before a court*

artus, -a, -um, adj., *close, thrifty, dense, economical*

asellus, -ī, m., *young ass, young donkey*

asper, aspera, asperum, adj., *fierce, rough*

at, conj., *but*

atavus, -ī, m., *a great-great-great grandfather, or remote ancestor*

āter, ātra, ātrum, adj., *black, dark, gloomy*

atque, conj., *and; after comparatives, than; also,* cf. **simul**

atquī, conj., *but, nevertheless*

ātrium, ātriī, n., *hall, first main room in a Roman-style house*

atrox, atrōcis, adj., *dreadful, fierce, cruel*

Attalicus, -a, -um, adj., *of King Attalus or his dynasty, rich, splendid*

audeō, audēre, ausus sum, *dare, wish*

audiō, audīre, audīvī, audītum, *hear, heed*

auferō, auferre, abstulī, ablātum, *take away, carry off, kill*

Aufidus, -ī, m., *Aufidus, river in Apulia*

aula, aulae, f., *noble residence, palace, hall*

aura, -ae, f., *breeze*

aureus, -a, -um, adj., *golden, splendid*

auricula, -ae, f., *ear*

auris, auris, f., *ear*

Auster, Austrī, m., *south wind*

aut, conj., *or;* **aut...aut,** *either...or*

autumnus, -ī, m., *autumn*

avidus, -a, -um, adj., *greedy, avaricious, eager*

avis, avis, f., *bird*

avītus, -a, -um, adj., *of a grandfather, ancestral*

āvius, -a, -um, adj., *pathless, remote*

B

Babylōnius, -a, -um, adj., *Babylonian*

bacchor, bacchārī, bacchātus sum, *celebrate the festival of Bacchus, rave, rage*

Bandusia, -ae, f., *Bandusia, name of a spring, perhaps at Horace's Sabine farm or near Apulia, the area on which his hometown bordered*

barbarē, adv., *roughly, cruelly*

barbitos, barbitī, m., *lyre*

beātus, -a, -um, adj., *happy, fortunate*

bellum, -ī, n., *war*

bene, adv., *well;* with adj. or adv., *quite*

benignē, adv., *lavishly, liberally*

beō, beāre, beāvī, beātum, *bless, make happy*

bibō, bibere, bibī, *drink*

bīlis, bīlis, f., *gall, bile, anger*

bis, adv., *twice*

blandus, -a, -um, adj., *charming, persuasive, seductive*

Bōlānus, -ī, m., *Bolanus, Roman cognomen*

bonus, -a, -um, adj., *good*

brāchium, brāchiī, n., *arm*

brevis, -e, adj., *short, brief*

brūma, -ae, f., *the shortest day, winter, wintry weather*

Brūtus, -ī, m., *Marcus Iunius Brutus,* one of the leaders, along with Cassius, of the conspiracy to kill Julius Caesar.

C

cadō, cadere, cecidī, cāsum, *fall, die, set* (of heavenly bodies)

cadus, -ī, m., *jar, flask* (especially for wine)

Caecubum, -ī, n., *choice wine from Caecubum,* a district in south Latium

caelestis, -e, adj., *of the sky, celestial, divine*

caelum, -ī, n., *sky, heavens, weather, world*

caementum, -ī, n., *small stones, rubble*

Caesar, Caesaris, m., *Caesar;* Octavian (later Augustus), in Ode 1.37; in Satire 1.9, Julius Caesar, (100–44 B.C.E.), Roman general who defeated Pompey at the battle of Pharsalus in 48 B.C.E. and was made dictator for life in 44 B.C.E., shortly before his assassination in the conspiracy led by Brutus and Cassius.

Calais, Calais, m., *Calais,* man's name

campus, -ī, m., *plain, level surface; plain, field;* often refers specifically to the Campus Martius in Rome

candidus, -a, -um, adj., *bright, radiant, white*

canīcula, -ae, f., *the Dog Star, Sirius,* in the constellation Canis Major, brightest star in the sky, thought to bring hot weather

canitiēs, canitiēī, f., *white or grey coloring, grey or white hair*

canō, canere, cecinī, cantum, *sing, sing about, recite, prophesy, foretell*

cantō, cantāre, cantāvī, cantātum, *sing, sing about, recite*

cantus, -ūs, m., *singing, song, poetry*

capax, capācis, adj., *spacious, capable*

Capitōlium, Capitōliī, n., *Capitolium,* the Capitoline hill in Rome on which the Capitoline gods, Jupiter, Juno, and Minerva, were worshipped

caput, capitis, n., *head, top, source, person, person's life*

cardō, cardinis, m., *hinge*

careō, carēre, caruī, caritum, *lack, be without* (with abl.)

carmen, carminis, n., *solemn or ritual utterance, song, poem, lyric poetry*

carpō, carpere, carpsī, carptum, *pluck, seize*

cārus, -a, -um, adj., *dear, beloved*

castra, castrōrum, n. pl., *military camp*

cāsus, -ūs, m., *fall, event, misfortune, chance*

catēna, -ae, f., *chain*

catulus, -ī, m., *a young animal,* especially *a young dog*

Caucasus, -ī, m., *Caucasus mountains*

cautus, -a, -um, adj., *on one's guard, wary, cautious, prudent*

cavus, -a, -um, adj., *hollow, concave*

cēdō, cēdere, cessī, cessum, *go, yield, withdraw*

celer, celeris, celere, adj., *swift, quick*

cella, -ae, f., *storeroom, wine cellar*

celsus, -a, -um, adj., *high, lofty, proud*

cēna, -ae, f., *dinner*

centum, indecl.adj., *a hundred*

cerebrum, -ī, n., *brain, seat of intelligence, seat of anger, anger*

cēreus, -a, -um, adj., *waxen, supple*

certō, certāre, certāvī, certātum, *contend, strive*

certus, -a, -um, adj., *certain, definite*

cerva, -ae, f., *deer, female deer*

cervix, cervīcis, f., *neck*

cēterus, -a, -um, adj., *the rest,* usually found in plural

Chloē, Chloēs, f., *Chloe,* Greek woman's name

chorēa, -ae, f., *dance*

chorus, -ī, m., *choral dance, people singing and dancing, crowd, troop*

cibōrium, cibōriī, n., *a kind of drinking cup*

cingō, cingere, cinxī, cinctum, *surround, encircle*

circā, prep. with acc., *around*

circumagō, circumagere, circumēgī, circumactum, *drive or lead around, lead around in circles*

cithara, -ae, f., *lyre*

citius, adv., *quicker, sooner*

citus, -a, -um, adj., *swift, quick*

cīvīlis, -e, adj., *civil*

clāmor, clāmōris, m., *shout, shouting, clamor*

clārus, -a, -um, adj., *clear, bright, famous*

classis, classis, f., *fleet, political class*

clāvis, clāvis, f., *key*

cliens, clientis, m., *client;* one who attaches himself to a person of greater influence or political power (**patrōnus**) for protection

Cōcȳtos, Cōcȳtī, m., *Cocytus,* one of the rivers of the underworld

coemō, coemere, coēmī, coemptum, *buy up*

coepī, coepisse, coeptum (typically appears in perfect system), *begin*

cognātus, -a, -um, adj., *related*

cōgō, cōgere, coēgī, coactum, *drive together, force*

cohibeō, cohibēre, cohibuī, cohibitum, *hold together, hold back, confine*

colligō, colligere, collēgī, collectum, *to gather or bring together, collect*

colō, colere, coluī, cultum, *cultivate, cherish*

colōnus, -ī, m., *farmer, settler*

color, colōris, m., *color*

columba, -ae, f., *dove, pigeon*

coma, -ae, f., *hair*

combibō, combibere, combibī, *drink up, drink completely*

compellō, compellere, compulī, compulsum, *bring together, drive together, round up*

compescō, compescere, compescuī, *confine, restrain, check*

compōnō, compōnere, composuī, compositum, *put together, arrange, compose, calm, bury*

concha, -ae, f., *shell fish, sea shell, perfume dish*

concursus, -ūs, m., *running to and fro*

condiciō, condiciōnis, f., *condition, term, agreement*

condō, condere, condidī, conditum, *found, establish, store up*

conficiō, conficere, confēcī, confectum, *complete, destroy, finish off, kill*

coniunx, coniugis, c., *spouse, wife, husband*

consistō, consistere, constitī, *stop, pause, stand still, take a position*

consociō, consociāre, consociāvī, consociātum, *unite, connect, share*

constō, constāre, constitī, *stand together, stand still*

consūmō, consūmere, consumpsī, consumptum, *consume, destroy, kill*

contāminātus, -a, -um, adj., *morally foul, impure*

contendō, contendere, contendī, contentum, *stretch, hasten, compete, contend*

contrahō, contrahere, contraxī, contractum, *draw together, narrow*

cōpula, -ae, f., *bond, link*

cor, cordis, n., *heart*

cornū, -ūs, n., *horn, anything horn-shaped*

corōna, -ae, f., *crown, garland*
corōnō, corōnāre, corōnāvī, corōnātum, *put a garland on, crown*
corpus, corporis, n., *body*
corrigō, corrigere, correxī, correctum, *make straight, correct, remedy*
corrumpō, corrumpere, corrūpī, corruptum, *damage, spoil, bribe, seduce*
cortex, corticis, m., *bark, rind, cork*
costum, -ī, n., *an aromatic plant*
crās, adv., *tomorrow*
crastinus, -a, -um, adj., *of tomorrow*
crēber, crēbra, crēbrum, adj., *crowded together, frequent*
crēdibilis, -e, adj., *believable*
crēdō, crēdere, crēdidī, crēditum, *trust, believe, entrust*
crēdulus, -a, -um, adj., *credulous, trustful*
crescō, crescere, crēvī, crētum, *arise, multiply, expand, increase*
cruentus, -a, -um, adj., *bloody, gory, cruel*
cubō, cubāre, cubuī, cubitum, *lie down or be lying down, recline, be in bed or on one's couch, be confined to bed by illness, recline at table*
culpō, culpāre, culpāvī, culpātum, *blame*
culter, cultrī, m., *knife*
cum, prep. with abl., *with;* conj. *when, since, although*
cumba, -ae, f., *small boat,* especially that in which Charon ferries the dead across the river Styx
cunctus, -a, -um, adj., *the whole of, all*
cupiō, cupere, cupīvī, cupītum, *wish, desire, long for*
cupressus, -ī, f., *cypress*
cūr, adv., *why*
cūra, -ae, f., *care, concern, worry, a person or thing constituting an object of care*

cūrō, cūrāre, cūrāvī, cūrātum, *care about, take care of, attend to*
curriculum, -ī, n., *a running, course, race, racing chariot*
currus, -ūs, m., *chariot*
curtus, -a, -um, adj., *having a part missing, mutilated, circumcized*
Cyprius, -a, -um, adj., *Cyprian, of the island of Cyprus*

D

damnō, damnāre, damnāvī, damnātum, *condemn, sentence*
damnum, -ī, n., *loss*
Danaus, -ī, m., *Danaus;* all but one of his fifty daughters, the Danaids, on instructions from their father, killed their husbands on their wedding night; they are punished in the underworld by having continuously to fill up leaky jars
daps, dapis, f., *feast, banquet*
Daunias, Dauniadis, f., *Apulia,* region of southeastern Italy
Daunus, -ī, m., *Daunus,* legendary king of Apulia
dē, prep. with abl., *about, concerning, down from, from*
dēbeō, dēbēre, dēbuī, dēbitum, *owe, ought, should, must*
dēbilitō, dēbilitāre, dēbilitāvī, dēbilitātum, *weaken*
dēcēdō, dēcēdere, dēcessī, dēcessum, *go away, depart, withdraw* (with abl.)
dēcidō, dēcidere, dēcidī, *fall down, die*
dēcrescō, dēcrescere, dēcrēvī, dēcrētum, *decrease, grow smaller, shrink*
decus, decoris, n., *that which adorns or beautifies, honor, glory*
dēdecet, dēdecēre, dēdecuit, used in third person, *be unsuitable for, be unbecoming to*

dēdicō, dēdicāre, dēdicāvī,
dēdicātum, *dedicate*
dēdūcō, dēdūcere, dēduxi,
dēductum, *lead away, lead
down, escort, bring a person or
army back with one to Rome,
bring home in procession as a
bride, spin, compose, adapt*
dēlēniō, dēlēnīre, dēlēnīvī,
dēlēnītum, *soothe*
dēlīberō, dēlīberāre, dēlīberāvī,
dēlīberātum, *consider carefully,
deliberate, decide*
Dellius, Delliī, m., *Quintus Dellius,*
who first joined Dolabella, then
Cassius, then Antony, and finally
Octavian, right before Actium
Delphicus, -a, -um, adj., *Delphic, of
Delphi* (the site of the oracle of
Apollo, god of poetry and the arts,
among other things)
dēmens, dēmentis, adj., *out of one's
senses, mad, insane*
dēmittō, dēmittere, dēmīsī,
dēmissum, *let down, let fall,
lower, sink*
dēmō, dēmere, dempsī, demptum,
take away, subtract
dēmoveō, dēmovēre, dēmōvī,
dēmōtum, *remove, drive out*
dens, dentis, m., *tooth*
densus, -a, -um, adj., *thick, dense*
dēpōnō, dēpōnere, dēposuī,
dēpositum, *lay down*
dēproelior, dēproeliārī, *fight fiercely,
struggle violently*
dēprōmō, dēprōmere, dēprompsī,
dēpromptum, *bring out, produce*
dēproperō, dēproperāre, *hurry to
complete*
dēripiō, dēripere, dēripuī,
dēreptum, *tear down, snatch away*
descendō, descendere, descendī,
descensum, *come or go down,
descend*

dēsīderium, desideriī, n., *desire,
longing* (for something or some-
one lost or absent)
dēsīderō, dēsīderāre, dēsīderāvī,
dēsīderātum, *desire, want, long for*
dēsiliō, dēsilīre, dēsiluī, *leap or
jump down*
dēsinō, dēsinere, dēsiī, dēsitum,
stop, cease
dēsistō, dēsistere, destitī, *cease, desist*
destinō, destināre, destināvī,
destinātum, *fix, determine,
intend, destine, earmark*
destringō, destringere, destrinxī,
districtum, *strip off, scrape
lightly, draw or unsheathe* (a
weapon)
dēsum, dēesse, dēfuī, *be missing,
fail* (with dat. of person)
dētestor, dētestārī, dētestātus sum,
pray against, curse
deus, -ī, m., *god;* dī, alternate form of
deī, nom. pl., dīs, alternate form
of deīs, dat. and abl. pl.
dexter, dextra, dextrum, adj., *right,
skillful*
Diāna, -ae, f., *the goddess Diana,*
daughter of Jupiter and Latona
dīcō, dīcere, dixī, dictum, *say, tell,
call*
dīdūcō, dīdūcere, dīduxī, dīductum,
separate, split
diēs, diēī, m., (f.) *day*
difficilis, -e, adj., *difficult, trouble-
some, hard to manage*
diffugiō, diffugere, diffūgī, *flee in
several directions, disperse, scatter*
digitus, -ī, m., *finger*
dignus, -a, -um, adj., *worthy, worthy
of, deserving* (with abl.)
dīligō, dīligere, dīlexī, dīlectum,
*love, esteem, hold dear, have
special regard for*
dīmoveō, dīmovēre, dīmōvī,
dīmōtum, *move apart, separate*

diōta, -ae, f., *two-handled wine jar*
dīruō, dīruere, dīruī, dīrutum,
    cause to fall in ruin, demolish
dīrus, -a, -um, adj., *terrible, awful, dire*
dīs, dītis, adj., *rich, wealthy*
discēdō, discēdere, discessi,
    discessum, *go away, depart*
dispereō, disperīre, disperiī, *perish,*
    be destroyed (frequently hyperbolic)
displiceō, displicēre, displicuī,
    displicitum, *displease*
dissimulō, dissimulāre, dissimulāvī,
    dissimulātum, *pretend that*
    something is not what it is, pretend
    not to notice, ignore
dissolvō, dissolvere, dissolvī,
    dissolūtum, *dissolve, free*
distorqueō, distorquēre, distorsī,
    distortum, *twist this way and*
    that, distort, torment
dīvellō, dīvellere, dīvellī, dīvolsum,
    tear apart
dīves, dīvitis, adj., *rich, wealthy*
dīvīnus, -a, -um, adj., *divine*
dīvitiae, dīvitiārum, f. pl., *wealth,*
    riches
dīvum, -ī, n., *sky*
dīvus, -a, -um, adj., *divine*
dīvus, -ī, m., *god*
dō, dare, dedī, datum, *give*
doctus, -a, -um, *learned, taught*
doleō, dolēre, doluī, dolitum, *suffer*
    mental or physical pain, be in
    pain, grieve
dolor, dolōris, m., *pain, anguish, grief*
dominus, -ī, m., *master, lord, ruler*
domus, -ūs/-ī, f., *house, home*
dōnec, conj., *as long as, while*
dōnō, dōnāre, dōnāvī, dōnātum,
    present, endow, reward (with),
    with abl. of thing given
dormiō, dormīre, dormīvī,
    dormītum, *sleep*
dorsum, -ī, n., *back*

dubius, -a, -um, adj., *uncertain,*
    indecisive
dūcō, dūcere, duxī, ductum, *lead,*
    take, consider
dudum, adv., *some time ago, previously,*
    just now; for a long time (with **iam**)
dulce, adv., *sweetly*
dulcis, -e, adj., *sweet,* (of persons)
    dear, beloved
dum, conj., *while, as long as,*
    provided that, if only, until
dūrus, -a, -um, adj., *hard, harsh*
dux, ducis, m., *leader, general,*
    commander

E

ē/ex, prep. with abl., *out of, from*
ēbrius, -a, -um, adj., *drunk*
ecce, interj., *look, behold*
edax, edācis, adj., *greedy, devouring,*
    destructive
ēditus, -a, -um, adj. (from **ēdo**),
    descended from
ēdō, ēdere, ēdidī, ēditum, *put forth,*
    give out, give birth to
Ēdōnus, -a, -um, adj., *Thracian;* the
    Ēdōnī were a tribe celebrated for
    their orgiastic worship of Bacchus
effundō, effundere, effūdī, effūsum,
    pour out, pour forth
egeō, egēre, eguī, *need, want* (with abl.)
ego, meī, mihi/mī, mē, mē, pron., *I, me*
ēheu, interj. (expressing grief or pain), *alas*
ēlabōrō, ēlabōrāre, ēlabōrāvī,
    ēlabōrātum, *strive, work out,*
    develop, perfect
ēmīror, ēmīrārī, *wonder at exceedingly,*
    be astonished at
ēnāvigō, ēnāvigāre, ēnāvigāvī,
    ēnāvigātum, *sail across, sail forth*
enim, conj., *for, truly*
ensis, ensis, m., *sword*
eō, adv., abl. of **is,** *therefore*
eō, īre, īvī/iī, itum, *go*

eōdem, adv., *to the same place*

eques, equitis, m., *horseman, rider, member of the cavalry, member of the equestrian order*

equus, -ī, m., *horse*

ergō, particle, *then, consequently, therefore*

ēripiō, ēripere, ēripuī, ēreptum, *snatch away, rescue*

errō, errāre, errāvī, errātum, *wander, make a mistake*

et, conj., *and, even;* **et...et,** *both...and*

Euterpē, Euterpēs, f., *Euterpe,* one of the Muses.

ēvehō, ēvehere, ēvexī, ēvectum, *carry out, lift up, raise*

ēvītō, ēvītāre, ēvītāvī, ēvītātum, *avoid*

exclūdō, exclūdere, exclūsī, exclūsum, *shut out, exclude*

excutiō, excutere, excussī, excussum, *shake out, drive out, banish*

exeō, exīre, exiī, exitum, *go out, come out, emerge*

exigō, exigere, exēgī, exactum, *drive out, complete, execute*

exilium, exiliī, n., *exile*

expavescō, expavescere, expāvī, *become frightened of, dread*

expediō, expedīre, expedīvī, expedītum, *free, extricate, release*

expleō, explēre, explēvī, explētum, *fill up*

expugnō, expugnāre, expugnāvī, expugnātum, *storm, conquer, overcome*

exstruō, exstruere, exstruxī, exstructum, *heap up, pile up, construct*

F

fābulōsus, -a, -um, adj., *legendary, storied*

facilis, -e, adj., *easy, quick*

faciō, facere, fēcī, factum, *make, do, regard*

fācundia, -ae, f., *eloquence*

Falernum, -ī, n., *Falernian wine,* wine from a district in northern Campania famous for its wine

Falernus, -a, -um, adj., *Falernian, of* a district in northern Campania famous for its wine

fallax, fallācis, adj., *deceitful, deceptive*

fāma, -ae, f., *fame, reputation*

famulus, -ī, m., *servant, attendant, slave*

fastīdiō, fastīdīre, fastīdīvī, fastīdītum, *show aversion to, scorn*

fastīdiōsus, -a, -um, adj., *critical, exacting, disdainful*

fātālis, -e, adj., *deadly, fatal*

fātum, -ī, n., *fate,* pl., *the Fates*

faveō, favēre, fāvī, fautum, *favor;* with **linguīs** (abl.), *avoid words of ill omen, be silent*

fax, facis, f., *torch, torch used at funerals and marriages, marriage, death*

fēlix, fēlīcis, adj., *happy, fortunate*

fenestra, -ae, f., *window*

feriō, ferīre, *strike, hit*

ferō, ferre, tulī, lātum, *bear, bring, carry, play* (a part, role)

ferox, ferōcis, adj., *bold*

fervens, ferventis, adj., *boiling, seething*

fervidus, -a, -um, adj., *boiling, burning, hot, impetuous*

fessus, -a, -um, adj., *tired, weary*

festus, -a, -um, adj., *festal, on holiday, festive*

fidēlis, -e, adj., *faithful*

fidēs, fideī, f., *trust, belief, faith, honesty, honor*

fidēs, fidis, f., *lyre*

filius, filiī, m., *son*

fīlum, -ī, n., *thread*

findō, findere, fidī, fissum, *split, separate, divide*

fīnis, fīnis, m., *boundary, limit, end*

fīō, fīerī, factus sum, be made, become

flagrans, flagrantis, adj., hot, blazing, passionate

flāvus, -a, -um, adj., yellow, golden, blonde, auburn

flēbilis, -e, adj., worthy of tears, lamentable

fleō, flēre, flēvī, flētum, weep for, lament

flōs, flōris, m., flower

fluctus, -ūs, m., a flowing, wave, disturbance

flūmen, flūminis, n., river, waters of a river

focus, -ī, m., hearth, fireplace

folium, foliī, n., leaf

fons, fontis, m., spring, source

fors, fortis, f., chance, luck

forte, adv., by chance, as luck would have it, as it so happened

fortis, -e, adj., brave

fortūna, -ae, f., fortune, chance, luck

frangō, frangere, frēgī, fractum, break, crush

frequens, frequentis, adj., crowded, assiduous, constant, regular

fretum, -ī, n., strait, sea, violence

frīgidus, -a, -um, cold

frīgus, frigoris, n., cold

frons, frondis, f., leaf

frons, frontis, f., forehead, brow, front

fruor, fruī, fructus sum, enjoy (with abl.)

frustrā, adv., in vain, to no purpose

frux, frūgis, f., usually in pl., fruit, crops

fuga, -ae, f., flight, rout

fugax, fugācis, adj., swift, fugitive, elusive

fugiō, fugere, fūgī, fugitum, flee, flee from, avoid

fulgur, fulguris, n., a flash of lightning, flash of light

fundō, fundere, fūdī, fūsum, pour, spread, scatter, defeat

fundus, -ī, m., bottom, farm, estate

fūnus, fūneris, n., funeral, death, destruction

furens, furentis, adj., mad, wild

furiō, furiāre, furiāvī, furiātum, madden

furō, furere, behave wildly, be crazy

furor, furōris, m., madness, frenzy, fury

furtim, adv., secretly

Fuscus, -ī, m., Aristius Fuscus, Horace's literary friend; cf. Satire 1.9 and Ode 1.22

G

Gaetūlus, -a, -um, adj., Gaetulian, of Gaetulia, region of northwest Africa known for its lions

garriō, garrīre, garrīvī, talk rapidly, chatter, (do this in writing)

garrulus, -a, -um, adj., talkative, loquacious

gaudeō, gaudēre, gāvīsus sum, rejoice, delight in (with abl.)

gelidus, -a, -um, adj., cold, icy

gelū, -ūs, n., frost, cold, chill

geminus, -a, -um, adj., twin, double

gena, -ae, f., cheek

generō, generāre, generāvī, generātum, produce, create

generōsē, adv., nobly, with dignity

generōsus, -a, -um, adj., of noble birth, noble

gens, gentis, f., clan, tribe, family

genū, -ūs, n., knee

genus, generis, n., birth, race, kind, offspring

Gēryōn, Gēryonis, m., Geryon; triple-headed or triple-bodied king whom Hercules killed when carrying off his cattle

Gigantēus, -a, -um, adj., of the Giants, a mythical race, who fought and were defeated by the Olympian gods

gracilis, -e, adj., slender, thin

grāmen, grāminis, n., *grass*
grandō, grandinis, f., *hail*
grātia, -ae, f., *goodwill, kindness, charm, attraction,* pl. personified, *the Graces,* goddesses (usually three in number) embodying charm and beauty
grātus, -a, -um, adj., *pleasing*
gravidus, -a, -um, adj., *laden, weighed down*
gravis, -e, adj., *heavy, weighty, serious*
grex, gregis, m., *flock, herd, company, crowd*

H

habeō, habēre, habuī, habitum, *have, hold, consider, keep*
Hadria, -ae, m., *Adriatic Sea*
haedus, -ī, m., *young goat, kid;* two stars in the constellation Auriga
Haemonia, -ae, f., *Thessaly*
haud, adv., *not*
Hebrus, -ī, m., *Hebrus,* river in Thrace
hedera, -ae, f., *ivy*
hērēs, hērēdis, c., *heir*
Hermogenēs, Hermogenis, m., *Hermogenes;* in Satire 1.10.80 Horace places a Hermogenes Tegellius in a group of people whose opinions do not matter to him as opposed to those of his literary friends.
heu, interj., expressing grief or pain, *oh, alas*
hīc, adv., *here, at this point*
hic, haec, hoc, demonstr. pron. and adj., *this, the latter*
hiems, hiemis, f., *winter, storm*
hinc, adv., *from here, here*
Hippolytus, -ī, m., *Hippolytus,* son of Theseus, whose rejection of the sexual advances of his stepmother, Phaedra, resulted in his death.
hodiē, adv., *today*
hodiernus, -a, -um, adj., *of today*

homō, hominis, m., *person, human being*
honor (honōs), honōris, m., *honor, office*
hōra, -ae, f., *hour, time, season*
horrescō, horrescere, horruī, *shudder at, tremble at*
horreum, -ī, n., *storehouse, granary*
horridus, -a, -um, adj., *rough, harsh, dreadful*
hortus, -ī, m., *garden;* usually in pl., *pleasure grounds or gardens*
hospitālis, -e, adj., *hospitable, belonging to a host or guest*
hosticus, -a, -um, adj., *belonging to an enemy*
hostis, hostis, c., *enemy*
hūc, adv., *to here, here*
humilis, -e, adj., *humble, low;* neuter as noun, *low position*
Hydaspēs, Hydaspis, m., *Hydaspes,* tributary of river Indus, the Jhelum

I

iaceō, iacēre, iacuī, *lie, be in ruins*
iaciō, iacere, iēcī, iactum, *throw, lay foundations*
iactus, -ūs, m., *throwing, hurling*
iaculum, -ī, n., *javelin*
iam, adv., *already, now*
iānua, -ae, f., *door*
Īcarius, -a, -um, adj., *of Icarus, Icarian*
īdem, eadem, idem, pron. and adj., *the same, too, likewise*
iecur, iecoris, n., *liver, the seat of the feelings*
ignis, ignis, m., *fire*
ignoscō, ignoscere, ignōvī, ignōtum, *forgive, pardon*
īlex, īlicis, f., *holm oak, ilex*
Īlia, -ae, f., *Ilia or Rhea Silvia,* mother of Romulus and Remus
ille, illa, illud, demonstr. pron. and adj., *that, the former*

illīc, adv., *there*

imāgō, imāginis, f., *image, likeness, shape*

imber, imbris, m., *rain, rain shower, water*

imbuō, imbuere, imbuī, imbūtum, *wet, fill, inspire*

imperium, imperiī, n., *power, command, government*

impetus, -ūs, m., *attack, onset, rapid motion*

impius, -a, -um, adj., *impious, undutiful, disloyal*

īmus, -a, -um, adj., *lowest, bottom of*

īn(n)uleus, -ī, m., *fawn*

in, prep. with abl., *in, on;* prep. with acc., *into, onto, against, over*

Īnachus, -ī, m., *Inachus,* first king of Argos

incipiō, incipere, incēpī, inceptum, *begin*

inclāmō, inclāmāre, inclāmāvī, inclāmātum, *call out, cry out*

incorruptus, -a, -um, adj., *uncorrupted, upright*

indicō, indicāre, indicāvī, indicātum, *point out, show, declare*

indocilis, -e, adj., *untrained, hard to instruct*

indomitus, -a, -um, adj., *unconquered, unconquerable*

inermis, -e, adj., *unarmed*

iners, inertis, adj., *lacking skill, inactive, lazy, impotent*

infāmis, -e, adj., *infamous, disreputable*

infernus, -a, -um, adj., *lower, of the lower world, infernal*

infestus, -a, -um, adj., *dangerous, hostile, insecure*

inficiō, inficere, infēcī, infectum, *dye, imbue, taint, stain*

infimus, -a, -um, adj., *lowest, most humble*

infirmus, -a, -um, adj., *weak, lacking strength of purpose, not resolute*

informis, -e, adj., *shapeless, deformed, ugly*

ingens, ingentis, adj., *huge*

inhorrescō, inhorrescere, inhorruī, *begin to tremble, bristle, become stiffly erect*

inhospitālis, -e, adj., *inhospitable*

inīquus, -a, -um, adj., *uneven, unfavorable, treacherous, discontented*

inlacrimābilis, -e, adj., *pitiless*

inmemor, inmemoris, adj., *forgetful, unmindful*

inmodicus, -a, -um, adj., *immoderate*

inmortālis, -e, adj., *immortal*

innumerābilis, -e, adj., *countless, numberless*

inops, inopis, adj., *lacking wealth, poor*

inpōnō, inpōnere, inposuī, inpositum, *place on or over, build on*

inpotens, inpotentis, adj., *powerless, weak, wild, violent*

inprimō, inprimere, inpressī, inpressum, *press upon*

inprobus, -a, -um, adj., *unprincipled, immoderate, unruly, relentless, shameless*

inquam, inquit, defective verb, only a few forms occur, most often used parenthetically or before or after a quotation, *say*

inruptus, -a, -um, *broken into, interrupted; unbroken*

inserō, inserere, inseruī, insertum, *introduce, insert, put in or among*

insignis, -e, adj., *distinguished*

insolens, insolentis, adj., *unaccustomed, excessive*

instans, instantis, adj., *pressing, urgent*

instō, instāre, institī, *be pressing, loom, threaten*

integer, integra, integrum, adj., *whole, untouched, upright*

intemptātus, -a, -um, adj., *untried, unattempted*

interdum, adv., *at times*
intereō, interīre, interiī, interitum, *perish, die*
interior, interius, adj., *inner, interior, private*
interlūnium, interlūniī, n., *the period between the old moon and the new*
interpellō, interpellāre, interpellāvī, interpellātum, *interrupt, break in on, impede*
intersum, interesse, interfuī, when used impersonally, *it makes a difference, it matters, it is of importance*
intumus, -a, -um, adj., *innermost, most secret*
inveniō, invenīre, invēnī, inventum, *find*
invicem, adv., *in turn*
invideō, invidēre, invīdī, invīsum, *envy, begrudge, refuse*
invidus, -a, -um, adj., *envious, jealous*
invīsus, -a, -um, adj., *hateful, odious*
ipse, ipsa, ipsum, pron., adj., *himself, herself, itself, oneself* etc.
īrācundus, -a, -um, adj., *angry, hot-tempered, prone to anger*
is, ea, id, pron. and adj., *he, she, it, this, that*
iste, ista, istud, pron. and adj., *that of yours, this, that* (often with derogatory sense)
ita, adv., *thus, so*
Italia, -ae, f., *Italy*
Italus, -a, -um, adj., *Italian*
iter, itineris, n., *journey*
Iuba, -ae, m., *Juba;* Juba I, Numidian king who supported Pompey in the civil war; Juba II, son of Juba I, fought for Octavian (Augustus) at the battle of Actium, made king of Mauretania by Augustus, known for his learning
iubeō, iubēre, iussī, iussum, *order, command, bid*
Iūdaeus, -ī, m., *Jew*
iugum, -ī, n., *yoke, bond*

iungō, iungere, iunxī, iunctum, *join, yoke, mate*
Iuppiter, Iovis, m., *Jupiter,* supreme god of the Romans, god of sky and weather
iūs, iūris, n., *law, right, court*
iustitia, -ae, f., *justice*
iuvenis, iuvenis, m., (f.), *young man, young woman*
iuvō, iuvāre, iūvī, iūtum, *please, delight, help*

L

lābor, lābī, lapsus sum, *glide, slip, pass*
labor, labōris, m., *work, effort, task*
labōrō, labōrāre, labōrāvī, labōrātum, *work, suffer, labor*
labrum, -ī, n., *lip*
lacerta, -ae, f., *lizard*
lacertus, -ī, m., *upper arm*
laedō, laedere, laesī, laesum, *harm, strike*
laetitia, -ae, f., *happiness, joy*
laetus, -a, -um, adj., *happy, glad, fertile*
Lalagē, Lalagēs, f., *Lalage,* woman's name; Greek for "chatterer"
lambō, lambere, lambī, *lick, wash*
languidus, -a, -um, adj., *languid, sluggish, slow*
lapis, lapidis, m., *stone*
largē, adv., *generously, plentifully*
lascīvus, -a, -um, adj., *playful, frisky, wanton*
lateō, latēre, latuī, *lie hidden*
lātus, -a, -um, adj., *wide*
latus, lateris, n., *side, extreme part or region, flank, lungs, body*
laudō, laudāre, laudāvī, laudātum, *praise*
laurus, -ī/-ūs, f., *laurel tree*
laus, laudis, f., *praise*
lavō, lavāre/lavere, lāvī, lavātum/ lautum/lōtum, *wash*

lēnis, -e, adj., *smooth, gentle, mild, soft*

lentus, -a, -um, adj., *slow, lingering, unresponsive*

leō, leōnis, m., *lion*

lepus, leporis, m., *hare, rabbit*

Lesbōus, -a, -um, adj., *Lesbian, of the Greek island of Lesbos*

Lēthaeus, -a, -um, adj., *relating to Lethe or the underworld;* Lethe is a place or river in the underworld whose waters, if drunk, were supposed to induce sleepiness or forgetfulness.

Leuconoē, Leuconoēs, f., *Leuconoe,* woman's name

levis, -e, adj., *light, swift, gentle, unimportant, fickle*

lēvis, -e, adj., *smooth, smooth* (from polishing)

lex, lēgis, f., *law, rule, particular condition or term*

libens, libentis, adj., *willing*

līber, lībera, līberum, adj., *free*

līberō, līberāre, līberāvī, līberātum, *free*

libīdō, libīdinis, f., *desire, lust*

Libitīna, -ae, f., *Libitina,* the goddess of funerals, *funeral couch*

Liburna, -ae, f., *light, fast sailing warship, galley;* name taken from the Liburnians, a people of Illyricum

Libycus, -a, -um, adj., *Libyan,* sometimes *African,* in general

licet, licēre, licuit/licitum est, impersonal verb, *it is permitted*

Licinius, Liciniī, m., *Licinius;* maybe Lucius Licinius Murena, brother-in- law of Maecenas, who was executed when trying to escape after his alleged participation in a conspiracy against Augustus.

lignum, -ī, n., *wood* (often in pl.)

līmen, līminis, n., *threshold*

lingua, -ae, f., *tongue, language*

linquō, linquere, līquī, *go away from, abandon, leave behind*

liquidus, -a, -um, adj., *flowing, clear, melodious, liquid*

liquō, liquāre, liquāvī, liquātum, *melt, strain*

līs, lītis, f., *quarrel, lawsuit*

lītus, lītoris, n., *shore, coast, beach*

lituus, lituī, m., *curved cavalry trumpet*

locus, -ī, m., *place, occasion;* m. pl., **-ī;** n. pl., **-a**

longē, adv., *far, far off, far away in time*

longus, -a, -um, adj., *long*

loquax, loquācis, adj., *talkative, loquacious, talking*

loquor, loquī, locūtus sum, *speak*

lucrum, -ī, n., *profit, gain*

luctor, luctārī, luctātus sum, *wrestle, struggle, contend*

lūgubris, -e, adj., *mournful*

lūna, -ae, f., *moon*

lupus, -ī, m., *wolf*

Lȳdia, -ae, f., *Lydia,* woman's name

lympha, -ae, f., *water*

lymphātus, -a, -um, adj., *frenzied, distracted, frantic*

lyricus, -a, -um, adj., *of the lyre, lyric*

M

mācerō, mācerāre, mācerāvī, mācerātum, *soften, make weak, torment*

Maecēnās, Maecēnātis, m., *Gaius Cilnius Maecenas,* friend and supporter of Horace and of other contemporary poets, including Vergil

maestus, -a, -um, adj., *sad, sorrow-ful, dejected, gloomy*

magis, adv., *more*

magnus, -a, -um, adj., *large, big, great*
maior, maius, adj., *greater, larger*
male, adv., *badly, insufficiently, wickedly, scarcely*
mălobathrum, -ī, n., *the tree Cinnamomum tamala or its oil*
malus, -a, -um, adj., *bad, nasty, hostile, unfavorable*
maneō, manēre, mansī, mansum, *remain, stay, endure*
mānō, mānāre, mānāvī, mānātum, *flow, spread*
manus, -ūs, f., *hand, band*
mare, maris, n., *sea*
Mareōticum, -ī, n., *wine from Mareotis, area around Alexandria in Egypt*
Mars, Martis, m., *Mars, god of war*
Marsus, -a, -um, adj., *Marsian, of the* **Marsī,** a people of central Italy
Massicum, -ī, n., *Massic wine, wine from the area of* **Massicus,** a mountain in Campania
Massicus, -a, -um, adj., *Massic*
māter, mātris, f., *mother*
Maurus, -a, -um, adj., *Moorish, African*
mēcum = cum mē
mediocritās, mediocritātis, f., *mean, moderation, keeping of a middle course*
meditor, meditārī, meditātus sum, *think over, contemplate, practice*
melior, melius, adj., *better*
Melpomenē, Melpomenēs, f., *Melpomene, one of the Muses*
membrum, -ī, n., *limb or member of the body, limb, member, part of anything*
meminī, meminisse (perf. with pres. meaning), *remember, recollect*
memor, memoris, adj., *mindful, remembering*
mendax, mendācis, adj., *lying, false*
mens, mentis, f., *mind*
mentum, -ī, n., *chin*

mercātor, mercātōris, m., *merchant*
Mercurius, Mercuriī, m., *Mercury, son of Jupiter and Maia*
meritum, -ī, n., *that which one deserves, due reward, service, meritorious action*
merus, -a, -um, adj., *pure, unmixed;* with **vīnum** or with **vīnum** understood, *wine not mixed with water*
mēta, -ae, f., *turning point, end*
metuō, metuere, metuī, metūtum, *fear, be afraid of, be afraid*
metus, -ūs, m., *fear*
meus, -a, -um, adj., *my*
mī = mihi
mīlitāris, -e, adj., *military*
mīlitia, -ae, f., *military service, war, army*
minae, -ārum, f. pl., *threats, warning signs*
minax, minācis, adj., *threatening, projecting*
minimus, -a, -um, adj., *smallest, least*
minister, ministrī, m., *servant, assistant*
Mīnōs, Mīnōis/Minōnis, m., *Minos, king of Crete, and later a judge in the underworld*
minuō, minuere, minuī, minūtum, *make smaller, reduce, weaken*
minus, adv., *less*
misceō, miscēre, miscuī, mixtum, *mix, mingle*
miser, misera, miserum, adj., *unhappy, pitiful*
miserē, adv., *pitifully, desperately*
miseror, miserārī, miserātus sum, *pity, lament*
mītescō, mītescere, *become mild, soft, or ripe*
mittō, mittere, mīsī, missum, *release, let go, abandon, send*
mōbilis, -e, adj., *moveable, changeable, inconstant, pliant*

**moderor, moderārī, moderātus
sum,** *handle, control, play*
modo, adv., *only, just now*
modus, -ī, m., *limit, way, rhythmic
pattern;* in pl., *poetry*
moechus, -ī, m., *adulterer*
mōlēs, mōlis, f., *mass, bulk, massive
structure*
mōlior, mōlīrī, mōlītus sum, *labor
at, build*
mollis, -e, adj., *soft, gentle, flexible,
voluptuous*
moneō, monēre, monuī, monitum,
*bring to the notice of, remind, tell
(of), warn*
mons, montis, m., *mountain*
monstrum, -ī, n., *portent, marvel,
monster*
monumentum, -ī, n., *monument,
memorial*
mora, -ae, f., *delay, hindrance*
morbus, -ī, m., *sickness, disease*
morior, morī, mortuus sum, *die*
moror, morārī, morātus sum, *delay,
linger, be late in appearing*
mōrōsus, -a, -um, adj., *difficult*
mors, mortis, f., *death*
mortālis, -e, adj., *mortal*
mōs, mōris, m., *custom, tradition;*
(pl.) *character, habits*
moveō, movēre, mōvī, mōtum, *move*
mox, adv., *soon*
muliebriter, adv., *like a woman*
mulier, mulieris, f., *woman, wife*
multum, adv., *much*
multus, -a, -um, *much, many, large*
(with sing. noun)
munditia, -ae, f., *neatness, elegance*
mundus, -ī, m., *world*
mūnus, mūneris, n., *service, duty,
gift, entertainment*
Mūsa, -ae, f., *muse;* one of the nine
Muses, goddesses who were
daughters of Zeus and Mnemosyne
and presided over the arts

mūtō, mūtāre, mūtāvī, mūtātum,
change
mūtuus, -a, -um, adj., *mutual, reciprocal*
Myrtōus, -a, -um, adj., *Myrtoan*
myrtus, -ī, f., *myrtle*

N

nam, conj., *for, because*
namque, conj., *for, because*
narrō, narrāre, narrāvī, narrātum,
tell
nascor, nascī, nātus sum, *be born*
nauta, -ae, m., *sailor*
nāvis, nāvis, f., *ship*
nē, negative adv. and conj., *not, that
not, so that not, lest;* used in
negative purpose clauses and
prohibitions, among other
constructions
-ne, interr. particle, in direct ques-
tions; in indirect questions with
alternatives, often used with **an,**
whether...or; affirmative particle
often used with infinitive in
exclamations, *indeed*
nebula, -ae, f., *mist, fog*
nec, conj., *and not;* **nec...nec,**
neither...nor
nectar, nectaris, n., *nectar,* drink of
the gods
nectō, nectere, nexī, nexum, *tie,
weave, bind, compose*
nefās, n., indecl., *crime, offense
against divine law, sacrilege*
negō, negāre, negāvī, negātum, *say
no, deny, refuse*
nēmō, nēminis, m., pron., *no one,
nobody*
nemus, nemoris, n., *grove, forest*
neque, conj., *and not;*
neque...neque, *neither...nor*
nesciō, nescīre, nescīvī, nescītum,
*not know, be ignorant of, not to
know how to, not to be able to*

nescius, -a, -um, adj., *ignorant, unaware*

niger, nigra, nigrum, adj., *black, dark, gloomy, black as a color of ill omen, evil*

nihil, n., indecl., *nothing*

nīl = nihil

nimium, adv., *too, too much, very*

nisi, conj., *if not, unless*

niteō, nitēre, nituī, *shine, be radiant with beauty*

nivālis, -e, adj., *snowy*

nix, nivis, f., *snow*

nōbilis, -e, adj., *noble*

noceō, nocēre, nocuī, nocitum, *harm* (with dat.)

nōmen, nōminis, n., *name*

nōn, adv., *not*

nōs, nostrī/nostrum, nōbīs, nōs, nōbīs, pron., *we, us*

noscō, noscere, nōvī, nōtum, *get to know learn; know* (in perfect tense)

nota, -ae, f., *mark, sign, wine of a specified quality or vintage*

nōtus, -a, -um, adj., *known, familiar*

novus, -a, -um, adj., *new, strange*

nox, noctis, f., *night*

nūdus, -a, -um, adj., *naked, bare, plain*

nūgae, -ārum, f. pl., *trifles, nonsense, things of no importance*

nullus, -a, -um, adj., *no, not any*

num, interr. particle, *certainly not*

numerus, -ī, m., *number*

numquam, adv., *never*

numquid, interr. particle, introduces question where a negative answer is expected, *surely...not; you don't, do you?*

nunc, adv., *now*

nūtō, nūtāre, nūtāvī, nūtātum, *nod with the head, nod, hesitate*

nūtrix, nūtrīcis, f., *nurse, especially a wet-nurse*

nympha, -ae, f., *nymph,* semi-divine female spirit of nature

O

ō, interj., *O* (with voc.)

obeō, obīre, obiī, obitum, *go to, meet, die*

obligō, obligāre, obligāvī, obligātum, *tie up, pledge, dedicate*

oblīquus, -a, -um, adj., *slanting, zigzag*

oblīviōsus, -a, -um, adj., *producing forgetfulness, forgetful*

obsolētus, -a, -um, adj., *worn out, shabby, ordinary*

obstrepō, obstrepere, obstrepuī, obstrepitum, *make a loud, noise, roar, drown by louder noise*

obvius, -a, -um, adj. (with dat.), *in the way, placed so as to meet, situated so as to confront*

occidō, occidere, occidī, occāsum, *fall, die*

occupō, occupāre, occupāvī, occupātum, *seize, forestall, take the lead over*

occurrō, occurrere, occurrī/ occucurrī, occursum, *meet, hurry to meet, arrive, turn up*

ōcius, adv., *sooner, quicker*

oculus, -ī, m., *eye*

ōdī, ōdisse, ōsum (perfect with present sense), *have an aversion to, hate*

odor, odōris, m., *smell, odor, perfume*

officiō, officere, offēcī, offectum, *impede, interfere with* (with dat.)

ōlim, adv., *formerly, once, on an occasion, at some future date*

Olympicus, -a, -um, adj., *Olympic, Olympian*

omnis, -e, adj., *all, every*

onus, oneris, n., *burden*

operōsus, -a, -um, adj., *toilsome, laborious, painstaking, industrious*

oppēdō, oppēdere, *fart in the face of* (with dat.)

oppidum, -ī, n., *town*

oppōnō, oppōnere, opposuī, oppositum, *place against, place in front*, especially *put before someone for acceptance, proffer*

oppositus, -a, -um, *placed against, hostile*

opus, operis, n., *work, business, task, genre;* with esse, *be necessary, be needed* (with abl. of thing needed and dat. of person with the need)

ōra, -ae, f., *shore*

Orcus, Orcī, m., *Orcus, the god of the lower world, the lower world, death*

ordinō, ordināre, ordināvī, ordinātum, *set in order, arrange*

orior, orīrī, ortus sum, *rise, be born*

ornō, ornāre, ornāvī, ornātum, *prepare, decorate, adorn, honor* (with abl.)

ornus, -ī, f., *flowering ash tree*

Ornytus, -ī, m., *Ornytus,* man's name

Orpheus, -ī, m., *Orpheus;* he was able to charm animals and nature with his music

osculum, -ī, n., *kiss, mouth, lips* (as used in kissing)

ōtium, ōtiī, n., *free time, leisure, peace*

P

palma, -ae, f., *palm tree, palm branch, palm wreath, token of victory*

pār, paris, adj., *equal*

parcē, adv., *sparingly*

parcō, parcere, pepercī, parsum, *spare* (with dat.)

pariēs, parietis, m., *wall*

parmula, -ae, f., *little shield*

parō, parāre, parāvī, parātum, *prepare*

pars, partis, f., *part, party; stage role* (usually in pl.)

pateō, patēre, patuī, *be open*

pater, patris, m., *father*

patientia, -ae, f., *patience*

patior, patī, passus sum, *suffer, undergo, experience, endure, allow*

patrius, -a, -um, adj., *of a father, ancestral, native, inherited, belonging to one's country*

paucus, -a, -um, adj., in pl., *few*

paulum, adv., *for a short while*

paulum, -ī, n., *a little*

pauper, pauperis, adj., *poor* (with gen.)

pauperiēs, pauperiēī, f., *poverty*

paveō, pavēre, *be frightened, be terrified*

pavidus, -a, -um, adj., *frightened, terrified, trembling, fearful*

pavīmentum, -ī, n., *pavement, floor*

pectus, pectoris, n., *breast, chest*

pecus, pecoris, n., *farm animal;* sing. as collective, *farm animals, livestock,* especially *sheep and cattle*

pendeō, pendēre, pependī, *hang, hover, hang down, be suspended*

penitus, adv., *deeply*

per, prep. with acc., *through*

perdō, perdere, perdidī, perditum, *destroy, lose*

perennis, -e, adj., *lasting throughout the year, lasting for many years, enduring*

pereō, perīre, periī, peritum, *perish, die*

perfundō, perfundere, perfūdī, perfūsum, *pour over, fill with*

permisceō, permiscēre, permiscuī, permixtum, *mix together, confuse*

permittō, permittere, permīsī, permissum, *let go, allow, entrust*

permūtō, permūtāre, permūtāvī, permūtātum, *exchange, receive in exchange for* (with acc. of thing received and abl. of thing given up)

perpetuus, -a, -um, adj., *continuing, permanent, connected*

Persae, Persārum, m. pl., *Persians*

persequor, persequī, persecūtus sum, *pursue, chase*

Persicus, -a, -um, adj., *Persian*
pertinax, pertinācis, adj., *very tenacious, holding fast, persisting*
pēs, pedis, m., *foot, metrical foot*
petītor, petītōris, m., *seeker, candidate*
pharetra, -ae, f., *quiver*
Philippī, -ōrum, m. pl., *Philippi,* town in eastern Macedonia where Brutus and Cassius were defeated
philyra, -ae, f., *fibrous membrane under the bark of the linden or lime tree, bast;* used to bind together elaborate garlands of flowers
Phrygius, -a, -um, adj., *Phrygian*
pietās, pietātis, f., *duty, devotion*
piger, pigra, pigrum, adj., *inactive, lazy*
pignus, pigneris/pignoris, n., *pledge, token, symbol*
pīnus, -ūs, f., *pine*
Pīrithous, -ī, m., *Pirithous,* a king of the Lapiths who fights with the Centaurs; son by Dia of Zeus or Ixion
piscis, piscis, m., *fish*
pius, -a, -um, adj., *dutiful, devoted*
placeō, placēre, placuī, placitum, *please*
plācō, plācāre, plācāvī, plācātum, *appease, calm*
plaga, -ae, f., *hunting net, trap*
plūs, plūris, n., *more;* **plūrēs, plūra,** pl. adj., *more*
Plūtō, Plūtōnis, m., *Pluto,* king of the underworld
pōculum, -ī, n., *cup, drink*
podagra, -ae, f., *gout*
Polyhymnia, -ae, f., *Polyhymnia,* one of the Muses
pōmifer, pōmifera, pōmiferum, adj., *fruit-bearing, fruitful*
Pompēius, Pompēiī, m., *Pompeius;* identity unknown
pōnō, pōnere, posuī, positum, *put, place*

pontifex, pontificis, m., *high priest, pontiff*
pōpulus, -ī, f., *poplar tree*
populus, -ī, m., *people, public, multitude*
portentum, -ī, n., *portent, abnormal phenomenon*
poscō, poscere, poposcī, *demand*
possum, posse, potuī, *be able, can*
post, prep. with acc., *behind, after*
posterus, -a, -um, adj., *next, following, future, later*
postis, postis, m., *door-post, door*
Postumus, -ī, m., *Postumus;* this name was often given to boys who were born after the death of their fathers
potens, potentis, adj., *able, powerful, potent*
potior, potīrī, potītus sum, *get possession of, obtain, possess*
potior, potius, adj., *more able, more powerful, preferable*
praebeō, praebēre, praebuī, praebitum, *give, supply, provide*
praecēdō, praecēdere, praecessī, praecessum, *go in front, go on ahead*
praecipiō, praecipere, praecēpī, praeceptum, *take beforehand, teach*
praemium, praemiī, n., *prize, reward*
praeparō, praeparāre, praeparāvī, praeparātum, *prepare*
praesidium, praesidiī, n., *protection, defense*
praeter, prep. with acc., *except, beyond*
praetereō, praeterīre, praeteriī, praeteritum, *go by, go past, pass by, go beyond, omit*
premō, premere, pressī, pressum, *press, follow closely*
pressō, pressāre, pressāvī, pressātum, *press*
prex, precis, f., *prayer*
prīmus, -a, -um, adj., *first*
princeps, principis, adj., *first in time, leading, first*

priscus, -a, -um, adj., *ancient, former*
prius, adv., *previously, before*
prīvātus, -a, -um, adj., *private, not in public life*
prō, prep. with abl., *for, on behalf of, in front of*
procella, -ae, f., *storm, trouble*
prōditor, prōditōris, m., *betrayer, traitor*
proelium, proeliī, n., *battle*
profānus, -a, -um, adj., *profane, secular, impious, uninitiated*
prope, prep. with acc., *near*
properō, properāre, properāvī, properātum, *hurry, hasten*
propinquus, -a, -um, adj., *near, neighboring*
proprius, -a, -um, adj., *one's own, personal*
prōterō, prōterere, prōtrīvī, prōtrītum, *trample down, crush*
protervus, -am, -um, adj., *bold, violent*
proxumus, -a, -um, adj., *nearest, next*
pūbēs, pūbis, f., *adult population, age of puberty, the pubic region*
pudīcus, -a, -um, adj., *having a sense of modesty or shame, modest, honorable, chaste*
pudor, pudōris, m., *restraint, feeling of shame*
puella, -ae, f., *girl, young woman, girlfriend*
puer, puerī, m., *boy, non-adult male, male beloved, (young) male slave*
pulcher, pulchra, pulchrum, adj., *beautiful*
pullus, -a, -um, adj., *gray, somber*
pulsō, pulsāre, pulsāvī, pulsātum, *beat, strike repeatedly*
pulvīnar, pulvīnāris, n., *sacred couch on which the image of a god was placed*
pulvis, pulveris, m., *dust*
pūmex, pūmicis, m., *pumice-stone*

purpura, -ae, f., *shellfish yielding a purple dye, the purple dye from the shellfish, purple-dyed cloth, purple*
pūrus, -a, -um, adj., *pure, innocent*
pȳramis, pȳramidis, f., *pyramid*
Pyrrha, -ae, f., *Pyrrha,* woman's name

Q

quā, adv., *where*
quadrīmus, -a, -um, adj., *four-year-old*
quaerō, quaerere, quaesīvī, quaesītum, *look for, seek, ask, acquire, earn*
quālis, -e, rel. adj., *of which sort*
quam, interr. and rel. adv., *how;* with the superlative, *as...as possible;* after a comparative, *than*
quamquam, conj., *although*
quandō, interr. adv., *when*
quandōcumque, adv., *at some time or other*
quārē, interr. and rel. adv., *in what way, how, why, because, therefore*
quartus, -a, -um, adj., *fourth*
quatiō, quatere, quassum, *shake, beat upon*
-que, enclitic conj., *and*
querimōnia, -ae, f., *complaint*
questus, -ūs, m., *complaint, lament*
quī, quae, quod, rel. pron., *who, which, that;* interr. adj. *what, which*
quia, conj., *because*
quīcumque, quaecumque, quodcumque, indef. pron., *whoever, whichever, whatever*
quid, adv., *why*
quīdam, quaedam, quiddam, pron., *a certain person, a certain thing*
quīlibet, quaelibet, quidlibet, pron., *anyone or anything whatever, whoever or whatever you please*
Quintilius, -Quintiliī, m., *Quintilius Varus,* friend of Horace and Vergil

quintus, -a, -um, adj., *fifth*
Quirīs, Quirītis, m., *Roman citizen*
quis, quid, interr. pron., *who, what;*
  indef. pron., *anyone, anything*
quisquam, quicquam, pron.,
  anyone, anything
quisque, quaeque, quidque, pron.,
  each one
quisquis, quidquid (or quicquid),
  pron. and adj., *whoever, whatever*
quō, adv., *where, for what purpose*
quod, conj., *because*
quodsī, conj., *but if*
quōmodo, interr., rel. adv., *how, in
  the manner in which*
quondam, adv., *once, formerly,
  sometimes, in the future*
quoque, adv., *also, too*
quotiens, adv., *how often*
quotquot, indecl. adj., *however many*

R

rāmus, -ī, m., *branch*
rapiō, rapere, rapuī, raptum, *seize,
  snatch away*
ratis, ratis, f., *raft, boat, ship*
raucus, -a, -um, adj., *hoarse, noisy,
  raucous*
recens, recentis, adj., *fresh, recent,
  modern*
recipiō, recipere, recēpī, receptum,
  take back, accept, regain
reclīnō, reclīnāre, reclīnāvī,
  reclīnātum, *cause to lean back*
reclūdō, reclūdere, reclūsī,
  reclūsum, *open up, undo*
recreō, recreāre, recreāvī,
  recreātum, *recreate, restore, revive*
rectus, -a, -um, adj., *straight, right,
  correct, proper*
recurrō, recurrere, recurrī,
  recursum, *run back, return*
reddō, reddere, reddidī, redditum,
  give back, deliver

redemptor, redemptōris, m.,
  contractor
redeō, redīre, rediī, reditum, *go
  back, come back, return*
redigō, redigere, redēgī, redactum,
  drive back, reduce
redōnō, redōnāre, redōnāvī,
  redōnātum, *give back*
redūcō, redūcere, reduxī,
  reductum, *bring back*
reficiō, reficere, refēcī, refectum,
  make again, repair
refugiō, refugere, refūgī, *run away,
  avoid*
rēgālis, -e, adj., *royal, regal*
rēgia, -ae, f., *palace*
rēgīna, -ae, f., *queen*
regnō, regnāre, regnāvī, regnātum,
  rule, rule over
regō, regere, rexī, rectum, *guide,
  direct, rule*
rēiciō, rēicere, rēiēcī, rēiectum,
  throw back, drive back, reject
religiō, religiōnis, f., *religious awe or
  conscience, religious practice,
  particular set of religious obser-
  vances, cult, religious feeling,
  superstition*
religō, religāre, religāvī, religātum, *tie,
  fasten behind; untie* (occasionally)
relinquō, relinquere, relīquī,
  relictum, *leave, leave behind,
  abandon*
removeō, removēre, remōvī,
  remōtum, *move back*
rēmus, -ī, m., *oar*
reor, rērī, ratus sum, *think*
reparō, reparāre, reparāvī, reparātum,
  obtain in exchange for, recover
repetō, repetere, repetīvī, repetītum,
  seek again, recall, resume
repōnō, repōnere, reposuī,
  repositum, *put down, place*
rēs, reī, f., *wealth, thing, circum-
  stance, affair, legal matter*

resecō, resecāre, resecuī, resectum,
cut back, prune, restrain

resorbeō, resorbēre, suck back,
swallow again

respondeō, respondēre, respondī,
responsum, answer, reply;
technical sense, appear in court

restituō, restituere, restituī,
restitūtum, restore, revive

restō, restāre, restitī, remain,
remain to be dealt with

rex, rēgis, m., king

rīdeō, rīdēre, rīsī, rīsum, laugh

rīpa, -ae, f., bank of a river, shore

rīsus, -ūs, m., laughter

rītus, -ūs, m., ritual, custom, manner,
style

rīvus, -ī, m., stream

rixa, -ae, f., fight

rogō, rogāre, rogāvī, rogātum, ask,
ask for

Rōmānus, -a, -um, adj., Roman

rosa, -ae, f., rose

roseus, -a, -um, adj., rosy

rota, -ae, f., wheel

ruber, rubra, rubrum, adj., red

rubus, -ī, m., bramble, prickly bush

rūga, -ae, f., wrinkle

ruīna, -ae, f., collapse, ruin

rumpō, rumpere, rūpī, ruptum,
break, shatter, destroy

rursus, adv., back, again

rūs, rūris, n., the country (as opposed
to the town), farm, estate

S

sabbata, sabbatōrum, n. pl., the
Jewish sabbath

Sabellus, -a, -um, adj., Sabine; the
Sabines were a people of central
Italy.

Sabīnus, -a, -um, adj., Sabine; the
Sabines were a people of central
Italy.

sacer, sacra, sacrum, adj., sacred,
holy

sacerdōs, sacerdōtis, c., priest or
priestess

saepe, adv., often

saeviō, saevīre, saeviī, saevītum,
rage, rave

saevus, -a, -um, adj., cruel, savage

sagitta, -ae, f., arrow

Saliāris, -e, adj., of the Salii, who
were a group of priests (at Rome
usually associated with Mars),
who performed ritual dances on
certain occasions.

salsus, -a, -um, adj., salted, witty,
funny

saltus, -ūs, m., forest or mountain
pasture, forest or mountain pass

salvus, -a, -um, adj., safe, alive, well

sanguis, sanguinis, m., blood

sānus, -a, -um, adj., healthy, sane

sapienter, adv., wisely

sapiō, sapere, sapīvī, have taste, be wise

sapor, sapōris, m., taste, flavor

sarculum, -ī, n., hoe

satis, adv., enough, sufficiently;
indecl. noun, enough

Satyrus, -ī, m., satyr; demi-god of
wild places, especially forests,
having the form of a man with
some animal characteristics

saxum, -ī, n., rock

scandō, scandere, climb, ascend, mount

scelus, sceleris, n., wrongdoing,
crime, affliction

scīlicet, adv., evidently, of course,
surely

sciō, scīre, scīvī, scītum, know

scrībō, scrībere, scripsī, scriptum,
write

sēcernō, sēcernere, sēcrēvī,
sēcrētum, separate, distinguish

secō, secāre, secuī, sectum, cut,
divide, traverse

sēcrētō, adv., secretly

sector, sectārī, sectātus sum, *pursue, chase*

secundus, -a, -um, adj., *following, second, favorable*

secus, adv., *otherwise, not so*

sed, conj., *but*

sedeō, sedēre, sēdī, sessum, *sit*

sēdēs, sēdis, f., *seat, site, home*

sēdulus, -a, -um, adj., *attentive, diligent*

semel, adv., *once, once and for all*

semper, adv., *always*

senecta, -ae, f., *old age*

sentiō, sentīre, sensī, sensum, *feel, sense, perceive, think, understand*

sequor, sequī, secūtus sum, *follow*

serēnus, -a, -um, adj., *calm*

seriēs (-ēī), f., *series, sequence, succession*

sērius, adv., *later*

serpens, serpentis, m., f., *snake, serpent*

sērus, -a, -um, adj., *late, blossoming after the normal time*

servō, servāre, servāvī, servātum, *keep, protect, save*

servus, -ī, m., *slave*

seu, conj., *or if*, **seu...seu,** *whether...or*

sī, conj., *if*

sīc, adv., *so, thus, in this way*

Siculus, -a, -um, adj., *Sicilian*

sīcut, adv., *just as, as*

sīdus, sīderis, n., *star; sky* (pl.)

silva, -ae, f., *forest*

similis, -e, adj., *similar, like*

simplex, simplicis, adj., *simple, artless, plain*

simul, conj., *as soon as* (also with **atque**); adv., *at the same time, together*

sine, prep. with abl., *without*

Sīsyphus, -ī, m., *Sisyphus; son of Aeolus, committed various crimes and is punished in the underworld by forever having to roll a rock up* a steep hill only to have it roll down again

situs, -ūs, m., *site*

situs, -ūs, m., *deterioration, neglect*

sīve, conj., *or if,* **sīve...sīve,** *whether...or*

sōbrius, -a, -um, adj., *sober, moderate, sensible*

sodālis, sodālis, m., *companion*

sōl, sōlis, m., *sun, a day* (as determined by the rising of the sun)

soleō, solēre, solitus sum, *be accustomed*

solidus, -a, -um, adj., *solid, complete, entire*

sollicitō, sollicitāre, sollicitāvī, sollicitātum, *rouse, excite, shake up, disturb with repeated attacks*

solum, -ī, n., *ground, floor, land*

sōlus, -a, -um, adj., *alone, lonely, deserted*

solvō, solvere, solvī, solūtum, *loosen, break up*

somnus, -ī, m., *sleep*

sonitus, -ūs, m., *sound*

sopor, sopōris, m., *sleep*

Sōracte, Sōractis, n., *Soracte, mountain in the south of Etruria*

sordēs, sordis, f., often used in pl., *dirt, squalor, baseness*

soror, sorōris, f., *sister*

sors, sortis, f., *lot, share*

sortior, sortīrī, sortītus sum, *cast lots over, choose*

sospes, sospitis, adj., *safe and sound, unhurt*

spatium, spatiī, n., *space, period of time*

spernō, spernere, sprēvī, sprētum, *remove, reject, scorn*

spērō, spērāre, spērāvī, spērātum, *hope, hope for, expect*

spēs, speī, f., *hope*

splendidus, -a, -um, adj., *bright, brilliant, glittering, illustrious*

sternō, sternere, strāvī, strātum, *stretch out, spread out, level, overthrow*

stō, stāre, stetī, statum, *stand*

suāviter, adv., *pleasantly, delightfully, nicely*

sub, prep. with acc. or abl., *under, below*

subeō, subīre, subiī, subitum, *go under, undergo*

sublīmis, -e, adj., *high, raised, elevated, sublime, lofty*

submoveō, submovēre, submōvī, submōtum, *move away, remove, ward off, banish*

subolēs, subolis, f., *offspring*

sūdor, sūdōris, m., *sweat*

sulcus, -ī, m., *a furrow, trench, track*

sum, esse, fuī, futūrus, *be*

summa, -ae, f., *sum, the whole*

summoveō = submoveō

summus, -a, -um, adj., *highest, topmost*

sūmō, sūmere, sumpsī, sumptum, *take, take on*

super, prep. with abl., *above*

superbia, -ae, f., *pride, arrogance*

superbus, -a, -um, adj., *proud, arrogant*

supercilium, supercilii, n., *eyebrow, nod*

superstes, superstitis, adj., *standing over, surviving*

superus, -a, -um, adj., *upper, higher*

suprēmus, -a, -um, adj., *last, final*

surgō, surgere, surrexī, surrectum, *get up, rise* (of heavenly bodies)

suscitō, suscitāre, suscitāvī, suscitātum, *rouse, awaken*

suspendō, suspendere, suspendī, suspensum, *hang up*

sustineō, sustinēre, sustinuī, sustentum, *hold up, support, withstand*

susurrus, -ī, m., *whispering*

suus, -a, -um, third person reflex. adj., *his, her, its, their* (own)

Syrius, -a, -um, adj., *Syrian*

Syrtis, Syrtis, f., *Syrtis* (especially pl.), name of two areas of sandy flats on the coast between Carthage and Cyrene; whole desert region next to this coast.

T

tabula, -ae, f., *board, plank, writing tablet,* (votive) *tablet*

taceō, tacēre, tacuī, tacitum, *be silent*

tacitus, -a, -um, adj., *silent*

tālus, -ī, m., *ankle bone, ankle, knuckle bone used in games*

tam, adv., *so*

tamen, adv., *nevertheless*

tandem, *at last, finally*

tangō, tangere, tetigī, tactum, *touch*

tantum, adv., *so much, only*

tantummodo, adv., *only*

tardus, -a, -um, adj., *slow, late, moving slowly, dull*

taurus, -ī, m., *bull*

tectum, -ī, n., *roof, house*

tēcum = cum tē

Tēlephus, -ī, m., *Telephus,* man's name

tellūs, tellūris, f., *land, earth, country, ground*

Tempē, n. pl. *Tempe,* valley of the Peneus river between Ossa and Olympus in Thessaly noted for its beauty; *any beautiful valley*

temperō, temperāre, temperāvī, temperātum, *moderate, hold back*

tempestīvus, -a, -um, adj., *timely, seasonable, ripe*

temptō, temptāre, temptāvī, temptātum, *try, attempt*

tempus, temporis, n., *time, occasion, proper time, an age or particular period in history, danger*

**tendō, tendere, tetendī, tentum/
tensum,** *stretch out, extend,
proceed, direct one's course*
tenebrae, -ārum, f. pl., *darkness*
teneō, tenēre, tenuī, tentum, *hold,
persist*
tener, tenera, tenerum, adj., *tender,
delicate, soft, young*
ter, adv., *three times*
teres, teretis, adj., *rounded, smooth,
polished*
tergeminus, -a, -um, adj., *triple*
terminus, -ī, m., *boundary line, limit*
terra, -ae, f., *land, ground, country*
Thaliarchus, -ī, m., *Thaliarchus,
Greek man's name*
Thēseus, Thēseī/Thēseos, m.,
*Theseus, son of Aegeus or
Poseidon; national hero of Athens*
Thrācius, -a, -um, adj., *Thracian*
Thrēicius, -a, -um, adj., *Thracian*
Thressa, -ae, f., *a Thracian woman;
as fem. adj., Thracian*
Thūrīnus, -a, -um, adj., *pertaining to
the town of Thurii in southern Italy*
Tiberis, Tiberis, m., *the river Tiber*
tībia, -ae, f., *shin bone, tibia, pipe, flute*
tigris, tigris/tigridis, f., *tiger*
timeō, timēre, timuī, *fear, be afraid,
be afraid of*
timor, timōris, m., *fear*
tinguō, tinguere, tinxī, tinctum, *wet,
stain*
Tityos, -ī, m., *Tityus;* giant primarily
known for attempting to rape Latona,
mother of Apollo and Diana; punished
in the underworld by being stretched
over nine acres while two vultures or
snakes ate his heart or liver
tollō, tollere, sustulī, sublātum, *lift,
raise, extol, take away, destroy*
Torquātus, -ī, m., *Torquatus;* identity
uncertain; a Torqutus, an orator,
also appears as addressee of
Horace Epistle 1.5; an orator; may

be a son of Lucius Manlius
Torquatus, consul in 65 B.C.E., the
year in which Horace was born
torreō, torrēre, torruī, tostum,
burn, parch
tōtus, -a, -um, adj., *the whole of, all*
trabs, trabis, f., *beam of wood, trunk
of tree, ship*
tractō, tractāre, tractāvī, tractātum,
handle
trādō, trādere, trādidī, trāditum,
hand over, deliver, introduce
trans, prep. with acc., *across*
trecēnī, trecēnae, trecēna, pl. adj.,
*three hundred each, three hundred
at a time*
tremō, tremere, tremuī, *tremble, quiver*
**trepidō, trepidāre, trepidāvī,
trepidātum,** *be agitated, hurry*
trēs, tria, adj., *three*
tribuō, tribuere, tribuī, tribūtum,
allot, assign
trīcēsimus, -a, -um, adj., *thirtieth*
trirēmis, trirēmis, f., *ship having
three banks of oars; trireme*
tristis, -e, adj., *sad*
triumphus, -ī, m., *triumph, triumphal
procession*
trivium, triviī, n., *meeting place of
three roads, crossroads*
tū, tuī, tibi, tē, tē, pron., *you* (sing.)
tuba, -ae, f., *straight war trumpet*
Tullus, -ī, m., *Tullus Hostilius,* third
king of Rome
tum, adv., *then*
tumeō, tumēre, tumuī, *swell*
tumultuōsus, -a, -um, adj., *full of
commotion, turbulent*
tunc, adv., *then*
turba, -ae, f., *crowd*
turgidus, -a, -um, adj., *swollen, turgid*
turpis, -e, adj., *ugly, shameful, disgraceful*
turpō, turpāre, turpāvī, turpātum,
make ugly
turris, -is, f., *tower*

tussis, tussis, f., *cough*
tūtus, -a, -um, adj., *safe, secure*
tuus, -a, -um, adj., *your* (sing.)
Tyrrhēnus, -a, -um, adj., *Tyrrhenian, Etruscan*

U

ubi, rel. adv., *where, when;* interr. adv., *where*
ūdus, -a, -um, adj., *wet, pliant*
ulcerōsus, -a, -um, adj., *full of ulcers or sores*
ullus, -a, -um, adj., *any*
ultimus, -a, -um, adj., *last, farthest, extreme*
ultrā, prep. with acc., *beyond*
umbra, -ae, f., *shade, shadow, ghost*
umbrōsus, -a, -um, adj., *shady*
umerus, -ī, m., *shoulder*
ūmor, ūmōris, m., *moisture, liquid*
unda, -ae, f., *wave, water*
unde, interr. and rel. adv., *from where, from whom, from which*
undique, adv., *on all sides, everywhere*
unguentum, -ī, n., *ointment, perfume*
ūnus, -a, -um, adj., *one, sole*
urbs, urbis, f., *city; the city of Rome*
urgeō, urgēre, ursī, *push, press upon*
urna, -ae, f., *urn*
ūrō, ūrere, ussī, ustum, *burn;* in pass., *be on fire*
usque, adv., *continuously, continually, all the way*
ūsus, -ūs, m., *use, enjoyment*
ut, conj. with indic., *as, like, when, considering how;* with subj., *so that, that, to;* interr. adv., *how*
ūtor, ūtī, ūsus sum (with abl.), *use, enjoy*
utrimque, adv., *on both sides*
ūvidus, -a, -um, *wet*
uxor, uxōris, f., *wife*

V

vacuus, -a, -um, adj., *empty, free, available*
vador, vadārī, vadātus sum, (of a plaintiff) *to accept a guarantee from the other party that the party will appear or reappear in court at an appointed date*
vae, interj., *alas, woe*
vagor, vagārī, vagātus sum, *wander*
vagus, -a, -um, adj., *roaming, wandering*
valeō, valēre, valuī, valitum, *be powerful, be strong enough to, be well*
vallēs, vallis, f., *valley*
vānus, -a, -um, adj., *empty, groundless, imaginary*
Varius, Variī, m., *L.Varius Rufus, writer of epic and tragedy, important literary friend of Horace*
vātēs, vātis, c., *prophet, singer, poet*
-ve, conj., *or*
vel, conj., *or*
vellō, vellere, vellī, vulsum, *pull, tug at*
vēlum, -ī, n., *sail*
velut, adv., *as, just as*
vēnātor, vēnātōris, m., *hunter*
venēnātus, -a, -um, adj., *poisonous*
venēnum, -ī, n., *poison, magical or medicinal potion*
veniō, venīre, vēnī, ventum, *come*
ventus, -ī, m., *wind*
venus, veneris, f., *Venus,* Roman goddess of love; *love, charm, sexual activity; best throw at dice*
vēr, vēris, n., *spring*
verberō, verberāre, verberāvī, verberātum, *beat, lash*
Vergilius, Vergiliī, m., *Publius Vergilius Maro* (70–19 B.C.E.)
vēritās, vēritātis, f., *truth*
vērō, adv., *in fact, indeed, certainly, truly*

verrō, verrere, versum, *sweep together, collect*

versō, versāre, versāvī, versātum, *keep turning, stir*

versus, -ūs, m., *line of verse*

vertex, verticis, m., *head, summit*

vērus, -a, -um, adj., *true, real*

vescor, vescī, *enjoy, feed on, eat* (with abl.)

Vesta, -ae, f., *Vesta,* Roman goddess of the domestic hearth; *temple or shrine of Vesta*

vestīmentum, -ī, n., *clothes, garments*

vetus, veteris, adj., *old*

via, -ae, f., *road, street, way*

vicis (gen.), f., *turn, succession, alternation*

victima, -ae, f., *victim, sacrifice*

victor, victōris, m., *victor, winner, conqueror*

vīcus, -ī, m., *group of dwellings, village; block of houses, street, group of streets,* often forming a social or administrative unit (used of specific districts in Rome)

videō, vidēre, vīdī, vīsum, *see*

vigeō, vigēre, viguī, *flourish, thrive*

villa, -ae, f., *country-house, estate, farm*

vincō, vincere, vīcī, victum, *conquer, defeat*

vinculum, -ī, n., *chain, bond*

vīnea, -ae, f., *vineyard*

vīnum, -ī, n., *wine*

violens, violentis, adj., *violent, vehement*

vir, -ī, m., *man, husband*

vireō, virēre, viruī, *be green, youthful, fresh*

virga, -ae, f., *staff, wand*

virgō, virginis, f., *girl of marriageable age, young woman, virgin*

viridis, -e, adj., *green, fresh, young*

virtūs, virtūtis, f., *manhood, courage, valor, virtue*

Viscus, -ī, m., *Viscus;* there were two brothers with this name; both were literary figures and friends of Horace and Maecenas

vīsō, vīsere, vīsī, *look at, go and see*

vīta, -ae, f., *life*

vītis, vītis, f., *vine*

vītō, vītāre, vītāvī, vītātum, *avoid, shun*

vitrum, -ī, n., *glass*

vīvō, vīvere, vixī, victum, *live*

vix, adv., *hardly, scarcely*

volens, volentis, adj., *willing*

volgus, -ī, n., *the common people, the general public, crowd*

volō, velle, voluī, *wish, want, be willing*

volō, volāre, volāvī, volātum, *fly, speed*

voltus, -ūs, m., *face, expression*

vōmer, vōmeris, m., *plowshare;* by metonymy, *the plow*

vōtīva, -a, -um, *votive, relating to a vow*

vox, vōcis, f., *voice*

Z

zephyrus, -ī, m., *west wind, zephyr*

Ovid: Amores, Metamorphoses Selections
Charbra Adams Jestin & Phyllis B. Katz
Latin text based on Loeb text by Goold: *Met.* I.452–567, IV.55–166, viii.183–235, VIII.616–724, X.238–297, and Oxford text by Kenney: *Amores* I.1, I.3, I.9, I.11, I.12, III.15.

Illus., xx + 196 pp. (1999), Paperback, ISBN 0-86516-414-2

Horace *Satire* 1.9: The Boor
Margaret A. Brucia & Madeleine M. Henry
The complete Latin text based on Oxford Wickham-Garrod edition.

Illus., 45 pp. (1998), Paperback, ISBN 0-86516-413-4

Vergil's *Aeneid,* 10 & 12: Pallas & Turnus
Barbara Weiden Boyd
Latin text for 10.420–509 and 12.791–842, 887–952.

xii + 44 pp. (1998), Paperback, ISBN 0-86516-415-0

Vergil's *Aeneid,* Books I–VI
Clyde Pharr

xvii + 518 pp. (1964, Reprint 1998 with bibliography)
Paperback, ISBN 0-86516-264-6

Cicero's *Pro Caelio,* AP Edition
Steve Ciraolo

xxxii + 192 pp. (1997), Paperback, ISBN 0-86516-264-6

Catullus, AP Edition
Henry V. Bender, Ph.D.
Phyllis Young Forsyth, Ph.D.

Student: 105 pp., 8½ x 11 (1996), ISBN 0-86516-275-1

Reference

Why Horace? A Collection of Interpretations
William S. Anderson, ed.

xvi + 264 pp. (1998), Paperback, ISBN 0-86516-417-7
xvi + 264 pp. (1998), Hardbound, ISBN 0-86516-434-7

Why Vergil? A Collection of Interpretations
Stephanie Quinn, ed.

(1999), Paperback, ISBN 0-86516-418-5
(1999) Hardbound ISBN 0-86516-435-5

BOLCHAZY-CARDUCCI Publishers, Inc.
orders@bolchazy.com ✦ http://www.bolchazy.com